Jung's Ethics

This volume presents the first organized study of Jung's ethics. Drawing on direct quotes from all of his collected works, interviews, and seminars, psychoanalyst and religious scholar Dan Merkur provides a compendium of Jung's thoughts on various topics and themes that comprise his theoretical corpus—from the personal unconscious, repression, dreams, good and evil, and the shadow, to collective phenomena such as the archetypes, synchronicity, the psychoid, the paranormal, God, and the Self, as well as his contributions to clinical method and technique including active imagination, inner dialogue, and the process of individuation and consciousness expansion. The interconnecting thread in Merkur's approach to the subject matter is to read Jung's work through an ethical lens.

What comes to light is how Merkur systematically portrays Jung as a moralist, but also as a complex thinker who situates the human being as an instinctual animal struggling with internal conflict and naturalized sin. Merkur exposes the tension and development in Jung's thinking by exploring his innovative clinical-technical methods and experimentation, such as through active imagination, inner dialogue, and expressive therapies, hence underscoring unconscious creativity in dreaming, symbol formation, engaging the paranormal, and artistic productions leading to expansions of consciousness, which becomes a necessary part of individuation or the working through process in pursuit of self-actualization and wholeness. In the end, we are offered a unique presentation of Jung's core theoretical and clinical ideas centering on an ethical fulcrum, whereby his moral psychology leads to a cure of souls.

Jung's Ethics will be of interest to academics, scholars, researchers, and practitioners in the fields of Jungian studies and analytical psychology, ethics, moral psychology, philosophy, religious studies, and mental health professionals focusing on the integration of humanities and psychoanalysis.

Dan Merkur, PhD, was a psychoanalyst and religious studies scholar in private practice and a faculty member at the Toronto Institute for Contemporary Psychoanalysis and the Living Institute. He was also a visiting scholar in the Department for the Study of Religion at the University of Toronto and had taught religious studies at five universities in the United States and Canada prior to his clinical training. His principle publications are in various areas of psychoanalysis, the psychology of religion, and the history of religion. This is his fifteenth and final book.

Jon Mills, PsyD, PhD, ABPP, is a philosopher, psychoanalyst, and clinical psychologist. He is Professor of Psychology and Psychoanalysis at the Adler Graduate Professional School in Toronto and is the author of many works in philosophy, psychoanalysis, psychology, and religion, including seventeen books. He runs a mental health corporation in Ontario, Canada.

'A strong, determined, sensitive exploration of Jung's writings on ethics and the role it plays in the quality and work of consciousness. Merkur's final book gives detailed exegeses of Jung's texts with extended suggestions of the importance of God and ethics in human experience and nature of the self. In so doing, he furthers the Freud–Jung dialectic, opening rich perspectives for reflection. Thanks to Jon Mills for completing the edit of this volume after Merkur passed away, receiving the manuscript on the latter's deathbed. A compendium of rich and committed thought profoundly affirming the human spirit.'

– Michael Eigen, author of *The Psychoanalytic Mystic and Faith*

'Dan Merkur was a scholar of religious studies who knew Freud better than almost anyone else in the discipline. In mid-career he left the discipline to become a professional psychoanalyst. In his final years he turned to Jung. In *Jung's Ethics*, Merkur ties ethics to the whole of Jung's psychology. Where most writers on Jung are in no position to match up Jung with Freud, Merkur does so handily. Jung's ethics prove to be another effort at achieving individuation. An exhilarating book.'

– Robert A. Segal, Sixth Century Chair in Religious Studies, University of Aberdeen; editor of *Jung on Mythology* and *The Gnostic Jung*

'It is sadly perplexing how the late Dan Merkur's extensive and ingenious contributions to both religious studies and psychoanalysis have not received the attention they most certainly deserve. In his final book on Jung's ethics, Merkur explores the clinical significance of Jung's shadow work and forges an original rapprochement with Freudian and ego psychological approaches. True to style, the work is insightful, erudite, and far reaching.'

– Keith Haartman, author of *Watching and Praying*

Philosophy & Psychoanalysis Book Series
Series Editor: Jon Mills

Philosophy & Psychoanalysis is dedicated to current developments and cutting edge research in the philosophical sciences, phenomenology, hermeneutics, existentialism, logic, semiotics, cultural studies, social criticism, and the humanities that engage and enrich psychoanalytic thought through philosophical rigor. With the philosophical turn in psychoanalysis comes a new era of theoretical research that revisits past paradigms while invigorating new approaches to theoretical, historical, contemporary, and applied psychoanalysis. No subject or discipline is immune from psychoanalytic reflection within a philosophical context including psychology, sociology, anthropology, politics, the arts, religion, science, culture, physics, and the nature of morality. Philosophical approaches to psychoanalysis may stimulate new areas of knowledge that have conceptual and applied value beyond the consulting room reflective of greater society at large. In the spirit of pluralism, *Philosophy & Psychoanalysis* is open to any theoretical school in philosophy and psychoanalysis that offers novel, scholarly, and important insights in the way we come to understand our world.

Titles in this series

Humanizing Evil
Psychoanalytic, Philosophical and Clinical Perspectives
Edited by Ronald C. Naso and Jon Mills

Inventing God
Psychology of Belief and the Rise of Secular Spirituality
Jon Mills

Jung's Ethics
Moral Psychology and his Cure of Souls
Dan Merkur, edited by Jon Mills

Jung's Ethics

Moral Psychology and his Cure of Souls

Dan Merkur

Edited by Jon Mills

LONDON AND NEW YORK

First published 2017
by Routledge
2 Park Square, Milton Park, Abingdon, Oxon OX14 4RN

and by Routledge
711 Third Avenue, New York, NY 10017

Routledge is an imprint of the Taylor & Francis Group, an informa business

© 2017 Jon Mills

The right of Dan Merkur to be identified as author of this work
has been asserted by him in accordance with sections 77 and 78
of the Copyright, Designs and Patents Act 1988.

All rights reserved. No part of this book may be reprinted or
reproduced or utilized in any form or by any electronic,
mechanical, or other means, now known or hereafter invented,
including photocopying and recording, or in any information
storage or retrieval system, without permission in writing from
the publishers.

Trademark notice: Product or corporate names may be trademarks
or registered trademarks, and are used only for identification and
explanation without intent to infringe.

British Library Cataloguing in Publication Data
A catalogue record for this book is available from the British Library

Library of Congress Cataloging in Publication Data
Names: Merkur, Daniel, author. | Mills, Jon, 1964– editor.
Title: Jung's ethics : moral psychology and his cure of souls / Dan
Merkur; edited by Jon Mills.Description: Abingdon, Oxon ; New
York, NY : Routledge, 2017. | Series: Philosophy and
psychoanalysis ; 3 | Includes bibliographical references and index.
Identifiers: LCCN 2016054855| ISBN 9781138731745 (hardback :
alk. paper) | ISBN 9781138731752 (pbk. : alk. paper) |
ISBN 9781315188539 (e-book)
Subjects: LCSH: Jung, C. G. (Carl Gustav), 1875–1961. | Ethics. |
Psychology–Moral and ethical aspects.
Classification: LCC BF173.J85 M475 2017 | DDC
150.19/54092–dc23
LC record available at https://lccn.loc.gov/2016054855

ISBN: 978-1-138-73174-5 (hbk)
ISBN: 978-1-138-73175-2 (pbk)
ISBN: 978-1-315-18853-9 (ebk)

Typeset in Times New Roman
by Wearset Ltd, Boldon, Tyne and Wear

Contents

Editor's introduction   xi

1 Jung's moral psychology   1

The original theory of repression 1
Jung's moral discourse 7
Will, the raison d'être *of consciousness 9*
The goal of subjective moral integrity 13
The psychological complexity of morality 16
Neurotic denial of guilt 22
Treatment 26
Owning projections 29
Risks of depression and inflation 35
Concluding reflections 36

2 Cure of souls   38

Psychotherapy as a non-ecclesiastic cure of souls 41
Numinous experiences in analytical psychology 43
Archetypes and the individuation process 52
Resolution of the transference 61
Religion in relation to numinous experience 66
The nature of religion 68
Synchronicity 73
Jung's client population 83
Apologies for irrationalism 88
Jung's limited therapeutic ambitions 91
Concluding reflections 98

x Contents

3 The creativity of dreams 102

Wilhelm Stekel 106
Alfred Adler 109
Alphonse Maeder 114
Freud's "An Evidential Dream" 117
Jung on dreams 120
Signs and symbols 123

4 Having it out with the unconscious 135

The transcendent function and symbol-formation 141
Amplification 144
Active imagination 146
Inner dialogues 155

5 Jung's individuation process 160

The depersonification of archetypes 161
The discovery of the self 163
The ego's surrender to the self 165
Individuation and numinosity 169
The wholeness archetype 170
Individuation includes integration 173
Revelation, vocation, and conscience 174
Symbols of individuation 178
Concluding reflections 180

6 Consciousness and its expansion 182

The development of consciousness 187
Consciousness expansion 190
Philosophical assumptions about consciousness 195
Concluding reflections 199

References	203
Index	219

Editor's introduction

Dan Merkur was a psychoanalyst and religious scholar who died on January 20, 2016 of pancreatic cancer at the age of sixty-four. Before he died, he delivered his final book manuscript to me on his deathbed. He had been working with Jung's texts for a couple of years before he became terminally ill, which was, as he told me, his morning reading, hoping that it would bring him "inspiration." Merkur is known in the literature for bringing a psychoanalytic focus to bear on many topics over his career, including Gnosticism, mysticism, myth, shamanism, psychedelics, the psychology and phenomenology of religious experience, Judaic medieval theology, Eastern philosophy, and the study of God. In many ways, these similarities to Jung's life project are self-evident. First and foremost, Merkur was concerned with the interface between morality and spirituality, both from a religious perspective as well as personally, and so it is fitting that his last contribution is on Jung's ethics.

In my interviews with Merkur in his final days, he was resigned to his fate yet averred his belief in God. A rather serious and intellectual person by nature, he maintained a stoicism and detached reserve before the advance of his illness, but was emotionally vibrant when discussing his scholarly passions and his personal path toward comprehending God. In this way he was very much like Jung, where cultivating an ethical life as the "formation of a spiritual character" was important to him as well as his apprehension of the numinous. In his words, "for me the ultimate item is always the ethics, and in this way a part of me is profoundly and typically Jewish. The ethics are primary." Merkur ultimately believed that all human beings are mystical and seek out unitive experiences, which he equated with higher levels of integration. Here we may be reminded of Jung's transcendent function and the notion of individuation. When asked if his views on spirituality or religiosity have changed given his impending death, he replied: "I am at peace with God. And I remain convinced that good comes from it. Dying is part of the unfolding of good." In the end, he accepted his mortality with bravery, grace, dignity, and wisdom.

Editing this volume did pose some challenges given Merkur's untimely demise, and having to make decisions about its organization and structure without his consult. Most of the manuscript was complete; however there were various sections that were in draft preparation and needed to be repositioned and/or cut while staying faithful to his original layout. He would have surely spent more time polishing the final project had he more time and energy to do so. Some ghostwriting was required to bridge transitions between topics in the last two chapters, but I have not altered the substance of the text from its original form.

Merkur's style of writing follows a methodological approach to exegetical scholarship, whereby he carefully focuses on topical themes, relying on heavy quotation, and builds his arguments based on a close reading of Jung's original texts, albeit in English translation, that are more reflective of the actual data rather than offering liberal interpretation. I assume his method of exegesis was developed during his training days as a religious scholar, but he also employs a stylized strategy of drawing on Jung's direct quotes from all of his collected works, interviews, and seminars in such a way that the reader is presented with a compendium of Jung's thoughts on various topics and themes that comprise his theoretical corpus—from the personal unconscious, repression, dreams, good and evil, and the shadow, to collective phenomena such as the archetypes, synchronicity, the psychoid, the paranormal, God, the Self, as well as his contributions to clinical method and technique including active imagination, inner dialogue, and the process of individuation and consciousness expansion. The interconnecting thread in his approach to the subject matter is to read Jung's work through an ethical lens.

Nowhere does Merkur engage the secondary literature on Jung, rather he relies on analyzing what Jung actually says in his collected body of works. When he does engage secondary sources, it is almost exclusively centered on classical psychoanalytic authors, paying very little attention to new lines of thought since the early key players in the psychoanalytic movement. In this way, he brings about a vibrant dialogue between the two theoretical frameworks of traditional psychoanalysis and analytical psychology. In his predilection for juxtaposing Jung to Freud as he compares and contrasts the two schools of psychoanalysis, he wanted to give Jung due diligence through a sympathetic reading of his theoretical and clinical contributions, despite the fact that Merkur was a contemporary Freudian. Although Merkur is no apologist, he is very much aligned with Jung's moral discourse and his spiritual quest for the numinous.

What comes to light is how Merkur systematically portrays Jung as a moralist, but also as a complex thinker who situates the human being as an instinctual animal struggling with internal conflict and naturalized sin. A chief preoccupation for Merkur, through the persona of Jung, is to articulate and come to terms with the shadow forces of the psyche and give validity to the creative urges within us all as an innate need for self-expression.

Nowhere does Merkur address the aporia of what constitutes the nature of archetypes, which is left to Jungian lore. He does, however, underscore their autonomous and objective presences and how they influence a person's complexes, and how people become possessed by these inner phenomena, which he apparently concurred with. Yet this conversation takes place against a moral backdrop that suffuses the very engagement of his approach to reading Jung. This reading is likely due to Merkur's own contributions to advancing superego theory, which he is known for in the literature, hence influencing his exegesis of Jung. He also offers some critique of Jungian technique and its ethical implications, which he ultimately believed was connected to how a person comes to terms with their own shadow or destructive forces, and working through the moral and practical consequences of such a confrontation.

Merkur exposes the tension and development in Jung's thinking by exploring his innovative clinical-technical methods and experimentation, such as through active imagination, inner dialogue, and expressive therapies, hence underscoring unconscious creativity in dreaming, symbol formation, engaging the paranormal, and artistic productions leading to expansions of consciousness, which becomes a necessary part of individuation or the working through process in pursuit of self-actualization and wholeness. In the end, we are offered a unique presentation of Jung's core theoretical and clinical ideas centering on an ethical fulcrum, whereby his moral psychology leads to a cure of souls.

Chapter 1

Jung's moral psychology

What psychoanalysts call the "dynamic unconscious repressed," C. G. Jung termed both the "personal unconscious" and "the shadow." The first term flowed from his belief that the unconscious is not limited to the repressed, but also contains inborn materials that he termed the "collective unconscious." On several occasions, Jung identified the collective unconscious with the superego of Freud (Jung, 1951b, p. 120; 1958a, p. 348; 1958d, pp. 39–40; 1970, p. 473). The metaphor of shadow expressed Jung's appreciation that consciousness determines what in the psyche is in light and in shadow. In one of his seminars, but in none of his scientific publications, Jung (1997) made a "hairsplitting" distinction between the personal unconscious and the shadow, calling the shadow "a normal and natural fact," but the Freudian or personal unconscious was "to a certain extent a cultural fact" (p. 567). However, distinctions among inborn and acquired contents of the repressed need not here detain us. In this chapter, I shall review Jung's discussions of his clinical work with the shadow, which is to say, the portion of analytical psychology that corresponds to psychoanalysis.

The original theory of repression

Jung introduced the term "shadow" in 1917. "Indeed it is a frightening thought that man also has a shadow-side to him, consisting not just of little weaknesses and foibles, but of a positively demonic dynamism" (Jung, 1943c, p. 30). Elsewhere he states: "The shadow personifies everything that the subject refuses to acknowledge about himself and yet is always thrusting itself upon him directly or indirectly—for instance, inferior traits of character and other incompatible tendencies" (Jung, 1939a, p. 284).

2 Jung's moral psychology

Jung's concept of the shadow had its basis in Freud's theory of repression, which Jung characterized as follows:

> The theory of repression forms the core of Freud's teaching. According to this theory, the unconscious is essentially a phenomenon of repression, and its contents are elements of the personal psyche that although once conscious are now lost to consciousness. The unconscious would thus owe its existence to a moral conflict.
>
> (Jung, 1951a, p. 478)

Because most psychoanalysts today entertain a rather different understanding of repression, it will immediately be appropriate to establish that Jung accurately summarized what he regarded as the salient components of Freud's theory. Jung's account of the role of consciousness in neurosis agreed with the position that Freud had taken from the 1890s onward. Freud wrote:

> The actual traumatic moment, then, is the one at which the incompatibility forces itself upon the ego and at which the latter decides on the repudiation of the incompatible idea.... The splitting of consciousness in these cases of acquired hysteria is accordingly a deliberate and intentional one. At least it is often *introduced* by an act of volition; for the actual outcome is something different from what the subject intended. What he wanted was to do away with an idea, as though it had never appeared, but all he succeeds in doing is to isolate it psychically.
>
> (Breuer and Freud, 1895, p. 123; see also p. 167)

Summarizing the case materials that he presented in *Studies on Hysteria*, Freud asserted that the traumatic moment regularly involved either sense perception of a traumatic event, or mental perception of a traumatic idea, which the person found abhorrent and deliberately pushed out of mind. This choice, to not know, to become unconscious, was subsequently perpetuated—Freud did not explain why or how—leading to symptom formation. But, Freud insisted, there must always be a moment of consciousness, of recognizing unpleasure, experiencing conflict, and pushing the unpleasure away (Merkur, 2011a).

Bakan *et al.* (2009) suggested that Freud took over his position from Moses Maimonides, a twelfth-century rabbi, who had contended that the voluntary commission of sin has, among its causes, the imagination that vice is virtuous and has, as its side-effects, unconsciousness of virtue and pathological symptom formation (for example, blindness, paralysis). Freud shifted the discussion from evil, whose definition rabbinical tradition treated as God-given, to a neurotic's own sense of morality; but he otherwise retained Maimonides' understanding of the intricate relations among fantasy, willful choice, disavowal, amnesia, and symptom formation.

From the 1890s onward, Freud had maintained that conventional morality was pathogenic, because it demanded the repression of healthy sexuality (Breuer and Freud, 1895, pp. 165, 167; Freud, 1908a; Freud, 1916, p. 316). Freud's position allowed Burrow (1914) to infer that neurosis is, at bottom, a moral reaction. Jung agreed, as did a few early ego psychologists such as Fenichel (1928) and Alexander (1929, pp. 7–8). Freud objected to the formulations, but validated the underlying phenomenology. He qualified but never abandoned the association of psychopathology with immorality when he introduced his tripartite model of the id, ego, and superego. When he differentiated the superego as a discrete moral agency, Freud (1923a, p. 17) allocated repression to the ego, distancing it slightly from morality. However, Freud (1923b) soon reduced the separation by identifying the superego with the "dream censorship" that he had been discussing from 1900 onward. Freud slightly increased the separation of neurosis from morality when he redefined trauma in 1926. Where he had formerly argued that what is unpleasurable (to consciousness) is repressed, he now suggested that repression ends the paralysis or psychic helplessness that the ego suffers during trauma (Freud, 1926). The possibility that mental paralysis might occur for non-moral or amoral reasons was subsequently assumed by classical psychoanalysis, but Freud never proposed the idea. In *New Introductory Lectures on Psycho-Analysis*, Freud (1933) maintained that "repression is the work of the super-ego—either ... it does its work on its own account or else ... the ego does it in obedience to its orders" (p. 98).

Jung (1914) agreed emphatically with Freud's assessment of conventional morality, as an unwholesome standard that imposed conflict and neurosis on many individuals.

In certain cases it is a recognized fact that "immoral" tendencies are not got rid of by analysis, but appear more and more clearly until it becomes evident that they belong to the biological duties of the individual. This is particularly true of certain sexual demands aiming at an individual evaluation of sexuality. This is not a question for pathology, it is a social question of today which imperatively demands an ethical solution. We are not yet far enough advanced to distinguish between moral and immoral behaviour in the realm of free sexual activity. This is clearly expressed in the customary treatment, or rather ill-treatment, of unmarried mothers. All the repulsive hypocrisy, the high tide of prostitution and of venereal diseases, we owe to the barbarous, wholesale legal condemnation of certain kinds of sexual behaviour, and to our inability to develop a finer moral sense for the enormous psychological differences that exist in the domain of free sexual activity.

(Jung, 1914, p. 288)

Because Jung habitually used the term "trauma" in its original medical sense as a physical effect of physical violence, he routinely referred to Freud's theory that neurosis originates through sexual abuse in childhood, not as Freud's "seduction theory," as it is known among psychoanalysts, but as Freud's "trauma theory." Freud's abandonment of the theory in 1897 is reflected in the many passages where Jung downplayed the role of trauma in psychopathology. At no time, however, did Jung deny the role of *psychical* trauma in the genesis of psychopathology. He was nevertheless more concerned with the content of the conflictual materials that became pathogenic when the ego was unable to integrate them. His attention to morality then followed.

Today we can take it as moderately certain that complexes are in fact "splinter psyches." The aetiology of their origin is frequently a so-called trauma, an emotional shock or some such thing, that splits off a bit of the psyche. Certainly one of the commonest causes is a moral conflict, which ultimately derives from the apparent impossibility of affirming the whole of one's nature.

(Jung, 1948f, p. 98)

Jung's clinical views on symptom formation were in close agreement with both Freud's original formulation and the position that Freud took in the *New Introductory Lectures*. Jung (1939b) wrote:

The symptoms were substitutes for impulses, wishes, and fantasies which, because of their moral or aesthetic painfulness, were subjected to a "censorship" that exercised ethical conventions. In other words, they were pushed out of the conscious mind by a certain kind of moral attitude, and a specific inhibition prevented them from being remembered. The "theory of repression," as Freud aptly called it, became the centre-piece of his psychology.

(p. 44; see also 1964, p. 199; 1977, p. 320)

Freud regarded pathological symptoms as the "return of the repressed" to consciousness in disguised fashions. Concerned as Freud was with clinical facts and therapeutic interventions, he never considered why the repressed returns.[1] He claimed that drives, never previously conscious, make use of the repressed as vehicles for their own manifestations; but the question of *how* the repressed returns is not the same as the question of *why*. Freud did not formulate the answer that is implicit in his work after 1920, namely, that Eros, the life drive that always seeks to make two into one, is a continuous psychic pressure toward integration. An entirely more speculative person, Jung did ask the question *why*; but the question that he asked was *why does the unconscious seek to manifest?* Because he postulated both a personal and a collective unconscious, he wanted a general concept that would include both the return of the repressed and a parallel or corresponding process that was appropriate to the collective unconscious. The concept on which he drew was Eugen Bleuler's "ambivalence or *ambitendency*, which formulates the psychological fact that every tendency is balanced by a contrary one" (Jung, 1911, p. 197). Jung developed Bleuler's appreciation of compromise formations into a general theory of compensation throughout the psyche.

How does a symbol originate? This question brings us to the most important function of the unconscious: the *symbol-creating function*. There is something very remarkable about this function, because it has only a relative existence. The compensatory function, on the other hand, is the natural, automatic function of the unconscious and

---

1 Editor's note: We may generally say that, following Freud's early theory of economics, the repressed is under the influence of the pleasure/pain principle as compromise formations operative within a homeostatic model of the psyche.

is constantly present. It owes its existence to the simple fact that all the impulses, thoughts, wishes, and tendencies which run counter to the rational orientation of daily life are denied expression, thrust into the background, and finally fall into the unconscious. There all the things which we have repressed and suppressed, which we have deliberately ignored and devalued, gradually accumulate and, in time, acquire such force that they begin to influence consciousness. This influence would be in direct opposition to our conscious orientation if the unconscious consisted only of repressed and suppressed material. But this, as we have seen, is not the case. The unconscious also contains the dark springs of instinct and intuition, it contains all those forces which mere reasonableness, propriety, and the orderly course of bourgeois existence could never call awake, all those creative forces which lead man onwards to new developments, new forms, and new goals. I therefore call the influence of the unconscious not merely complementary but compensatory, because it adds to consciousness everything that has been excluded by the drying up of the springs of intuition and by the fixed pursuit of a single goal.

(Jung, 1918, pp. 18–19)

Jung's theory of compensation had, as its corollary, a restatement of Freud's concept of psychic conflict. Once again, Jung aimed at a generalization that he could apply to both the personal and the collective unconscious.

The qualities of the main conscious function, i.e., of the conscious attitude as a whole, are in strict contrast to those of the unconscious attitude. In other words, we can say that between the conscious and the unconscious there is normally an opposition.

(Jung, 1923, p. 522)

For Freud, neuroses arose from conflicts between consciousness and the unconscious, but otherwise the two systems might function harmoniously in an integrated manner. For Jung, however, consciousness and the unconscious were intrinsically opposed. They were categorical opposites. Once again, Jung's view was not acceptable among psychoanalysts until it was independently proposed by an orthodox analyst, in this case, by Anna Freud. In *The Ego and the Mechanisms of Defense* (1966), first published in 1936, Anna Freud (1966) postulated "the ego's primary antagonism to instinct—its dread of the strength of the instincts" (p. 157). She maintained her position throughout her life. "Many disputed it when I said it, and I still say that the ego as such is hostile rather than friendly and helpful to the instincts, because it's against its nature to be friendly" (Sandler with Freud, 1985, p. 494).

Jung's moral discourse

Apart from the changes in nomenclature, Jung conceptualized symptom formation in orthodox Freudian terms.

> The symptom is therefore, in Freud's view, the fulfillment of unrecognized desires which, when conscious, come into violent conflict with our moral convictions. As already observed, this shadow-side of the psyche, being withdrawn from conscious scrutiny, cannot be dealt with by the patient. He cannot correct it, cannot come to terms with it, nor yet disregard it; for in reality he does not "possess" the unconscious impulses at all. Thrust out from the hierarchy of the conscious psyche, they have become autonomous complexes which it is the task of analysis, not without great resistances, to bring under control again.
>
> (Jung, 1943, p. 25)

Jung's formulations departed significantly from those of Freud in their respective choices of discourse. Freud wished to position psychoanalysis within the world of nineteenth-century science, with its aspirations to objectivity, universality, and materialism. Jung prided himself, by contrast, in his empiricism. As a result, he avoided experience-distant theoretical formulations, in order to stay closer to the observable data. Where Freud eliminated the moral language of his patients when writing up his scientific ideas, Jung expressed what often amounted to the same theories in language that patients would find meaningful. Jung (1930) explained: "I appeal to his sense of values deliberately, because I have to make the man well and therefore I must use all available means to achieve the therapeutic aim" (p. 33). In a similarly pragmatic manner, Jung (1932) deliberately blurred the differences between theological and psychotherapeutic concepts in an article that he penned for clergy: "The conflict

8　Jung's moral psychology

may be between the sensual and the spiritual man, or between the ego and the shadow.... A neurosis is a splitting of personality" (p. 341).

The equation of the unconscious with evil, which led to its designation as the shadow, flowed from Jung's empiricism. Consider, for example, the following phrasing of the theory of repression. Speaking of the child's maturational attainment that Freud described variously as the dissolution of the Oedipus complex, the origin of the superego, and the transition between the pleasure ego and the reality ego, Jung (1966b) wrote:

> When the personal development of the mind begins, ... reason discovers the irreconcilable nature of the opposites. The consequence of this discovery is the conflict of repression. We want to be good, and therefore must repress evil; and with that the paradise of the collective psyche comes to an end.
>
> (p. 277)

In place of Freud's language of libidinal energy and its counter-cathexis, Jung wrote directly and empathically of the repression of evil by the desire to be good. Freud speculated about unconscious drive energies; Jung phrased the same clinical observations with experience-near references to human evil.

Jung's choice of discourse led him to an original understanding of the depth psychology of morality.

> The ... theories [of depth psychology] ... pitilessly unveil everything that belongs to man's shadow-side. They are theories or, more correctly, hypotheses which explain in what the pathogenic factor consists. They are accordingly concerned not with a man's positive values, but with his negative values which make themselves so disturbingly conspicuous.
>
> (Jung, 1943, p. 47)

Having retained the patient's moral discourse, Jung arrived at the novel formulation that people unconsciously have "negative values," of whose existence they are unaware. The negative values of the shadow invariably become known when and because they manifest in the form of neurotic symptoms. "The values which the individual lacks are to be found in the neurosis itself" (Jung, 1943, p. 61).

Will, the *raison d'être* of consciousness

Freud's early writings made frequent and occasionally important references to will. Around 1911, when he introduced the reality principle and began to ponder the ego's involuntary or automatic features, he avoided further discussions of will—except to assert, from time to time, that will is not free. However, he never stopped making passing references to will. Neither did he renounce the place of will in his original theory of repression (Merkur, 2011a).

In "The Transcendent Function," a paper that Jung wrote in 1916 but did not publish until 1958, he expressed the theory of repression with reference to the directive functions of consciousness. "Consciousness, because of its directive functions, exercises an inhibition (which Freud calls censorship) on all incompatible material, with the result that it sinks into the unconscious" (Jung, 1958c, p. 69). Where Freud had argued that inhibition conforms to the pleasure principle, Jung stressed that inhibition is an inevitable and often inadvertent by-product of the conscious direction of attention.

> Directedness is absolutely necessary for the conscious process, but … it entails an unavoidable one-sidedness. Since the psyche is a self-regulating system, just as the body is, the regulating counteraction will always develop in the unconscious. Were it not for the directedness of the conscious function, the counteracting influences of the unconscious could set in unhindered. It is just this directedness that excludes them. This, of course, does not inhibit the counteraction, which goes on in spite of everything. Its regulating influence, however, is eliminated by critical attention and the directed will, because the counteraction as such seems incompatible with the conscious direction. To this extent the psyche of civilized man is no longer a self-regulating system but could rather be compared to a machine whose speed-regulation is so insensitive that it can continue to function to the point of self-injury, while on the other hand it is subject to the arbitrary manipulations of the one-sided will.
>
> (Jung, 1958c, p. 79)

Like Freud, Jung denied the existence of *free* will. "I do not mean anything philosophical, only the well-known psychological fact of 'free choice,' or rather the subjective feeling of freedom" (Jung, 1969a, p. 5).

Not only is "freedom of the will" an incalculable problem philosophically, it is also a misnomer in the practical sense, for we seldom find anybody who is not influenced and indeed dominated by desires, habits, impulses, prejudices, resentments, and by every conceivable kind of complex.

(Jung, 1938b, p. 86)

At the same time, Jung affirmed the factual existence of a phenomenon that is fairly to be called will. "As a matter of fact, there do exist psychic contents which are produced or caused by an antecedent act of the will, and which must therefore be regarded as products of some intentional, purposive, and conscious activity" (Jung, 1926a, p. 91). Jung regularly associated will with consciousness. "Free will only exists within the limits of consciousness. Beyond these limits there is mere compulsion" (Jung, 1973a, p. 227).

The advantage of "free" will is indeed so obvious that civilized man is easily persuaded to leave his whole life to the guidance of consciousness, and to fight against the unconscious as something hostile, or else dismiss it as a negligible factor.

(Jung, 1980, p. 658)

In several passages, Jung discussed will in terms of psychic energy. "I regard the will as the amount of psychic energy at the disposal of consciousness. Volition would, accordingly, be an energic process that is released by conscious motivation" (Jung, 1921, p. 486; see also 1954a, pp. 182–3; 1989, p. 70). These remarks on will and psychic energy built on Freud's (1914) ideas of neutralized energies available to the ego; but Jung developed Freud's ideas in a direction that psychoanalysts embraced only in 1939 when they were presented by Heinz Hartmann (1958) under the name of "ego autonomy."

Philosophers have traditionally discussed two phenomena under the single term *will*. In the Middle Ages, theological discussions of will referred to the capacity to make moral choices as the outcome of intellectual reflection. In the seventeenth century, Hobbes introduced the usage that subsequently became popular, which pertains to the voluntary component of motor control (Pink, 2004, pp. 62–5). Freud regularly kept to Hobbes' use of the term; Jung (as also Wälder, 1936) instead kept to the medieval concept.

Jung affirmed a limited but crucial sense in which will was free. He argued that will was free of instinct and archetype and that this freedom was the very *raison d'être* of consciousness. "The development of consciousness and of free will naturally brings with it the possibility of deviating from the archetype and hence from instinct" (Jung, 1931e, p. 374; see also 1984, p. 605; 1988, p. 10).

> The will, volition, is a moral action, and naturally it has a direct connection with repression and inhibition. You can repress instincts by your will, easily or, it may be, with great difficulty. You cannot bring about so-called sublimation by means of instinct; that will not happen. But you can bring it about by volition.
>
> (Jung, 1977, p. 104)

Psychology must reckon with the fact that despite the causal nexus, man does enjoy a feeling of freedom, which is identical with autonomy of consciousness. However much the ego can be proved to be dependent and preconditioned, it cannot be convinced that it has no freedom. An absolutely preformed consciousness and a totally dependent ego would be a pointless farce, since everything would proceed just as well or even better unconsciously. The existence of ego consciousness has meaning only if it is free and autonomous (Jung, 1954e, p. 259).

Having linked will to consciousness, Jung went on to identify consciousness-will with the ego, by which term he apparently meant what is currently being called subjectivity.

> Since it is the point of reference for the field of consciousness, the ego is the subject of all successful attempts at adaptation so far as these are achieved by the will. The ego therefore has a significant part to play in the psychic economy.
>
> (Jung, 1969a, p. 6)

Jung most definitely did not use the term *ego* in the conventional psychoanalytic manner, which refers to an elaborate system or structure, complete with subsidiary features such as perception apparatuses, stimulus barriers, defenses, linguistic functions, and so forth.

Jung's views on will, consciousness, and the ego allowed him to return to Freud's theory of repression, only to appreciate how very one-sided consciousness must inevitably be. "Our actual willful consciousness, which claims to have free will, is a very disturbing factor; it can choose, it can build up what it finds useful" (Jung, 1997, p. 31).

> As soon as there is consciousness there is the possibility of choice, and that is the beginning of differentiation with the resultant one-sidedness. Once such one-sidedness of development reaches a certain culmination, however, there comes a break; then comes a sort of collapse, what you call in America a breakdown. The differentiated function collapses because the opposite function was wanted and could not be produced.
>
> (Jung, 1997, p. 31)

A further problem of the one-sidedness of ego-consciousness was its capacity to induce psychosomatic illness.

> Our consciousness having a certain amount of real freedom of will can deviate from the inexorable laws of nature which govern man, from our own laws which are organically formed in the surface of the lower brain surface. Inasmuch as we have ethical freedom we can deviate but we do it with fear; we have a certain idea that something untoward will happen to us because we are instinctively aware of the power of those lower centers. Since they are connected with the sympathetic nervous system which rules all the important centers of our bodies—digestion, in their secretions, the functioning of the liver and kidneys and so on—a serious deviation means upsetting the functioning of those nervous systems and we eventually risk a great disturbance in our glandular organs or in our blood circulation ... this lower nervous system is a constant threat, a sort of Damocles, and we are—and we ought to be—instinctively careful, always a bit afraid lest we might deviate too far.
>
> (Jung, 1988, pp. 749–50)

Because consciousness creates the shadow through the one-sidedness of its willfulness, only to lose its autonomy to the symptoms produced by the shadow, the "assimilation of the shadow"—that is, making the personal unconscious conscious—has the function of restoring freedom of will.

First, you must gain a certain amount of freedom, and you only gain that by the assimilation of the shadow. You must learn to deal with the shadow to a certain extent at least, and then proportionately you acquire free will. One has no free will in a state of complete dilemma, of complete dissociation or disintegration; that is obvious.

(Jung, 1988, p. 124)

The goal of subjective moral integrity

Like Freud, Jung aimed in his clinical work to make the unconscious conscious. Because the personal unconscious was a correlate of the shadow, the first phase in a Jungian treatment (Jung, 1948d, pp. 197–8; 1954f, p. 271; 1969a, pp. 22, 266; 1970, p. 365) consisted of "moral unmasking," the encounter with the negative values of the shadow. Its goal was the patient's honesty. "The best result for a person who undergoes an analysis is that he shall become in the end what he really is, in harmony with himself, neither good nor bad, just as he is in his natural state" (Jung, 1913b, p. 196; see also 1934a, p. 174; 1936a, p. 126; 1938a, p. 54).

Man is, on the whole, less good than he imagines himself or wants to be. Everyone carries a shadow, and the less it is embodied in the individual's conscious life, the blacker and denser it is. If an inferiority is conscious, one always has a chance to correct it. Furthermore, it is constantly in contact with other interests, so that it is continually subjected to modifications. But if it is repressed and isolated from consciousness, it never gets corrected, and is liable to burst forth suddenly in a moment of unawareness. At all events, it forms an unconscious snag, thwarting our most well-meant intentions.

(Jung, 1938b, p. 76)

If asked, a person might list a conventional group of items as evil, while neglecting to mention most of the negative values in his shadow. However, the contents of the shadow, as they may be discovered analytically, disclose what the person considers acceptable and unacceptable. In most cases, the shadow has less to do with major crimes than with misdemeanors. "The shadow is merely somewhat inferior, primitive, unadapted, and awkward; not wholly bad. It even contains inferior, childish or primitive qualities which would in a way vitalize and embellish human existence, but—convention forbids!" (Jung, 1938b, p. 78).

> This "inferior" personality is made up of everything that will not fit in with, and adapt to, the laws and regulations of conscious life. It is compounded of "disobedience" and is therefore rejected not on moral grounds only, but also for reasons of expediency.
>
> (Jung, 1948d, p. 198; see also 1989, p. 255)

Negative values are complex. Because everyone aspires to virtues beyond their own achievement, people are invariably moral underachievers who consistently sabotage themselves.

> A man who is possessed by his shadow is always standing in his own lights and falling into his own traps. Whenever possible, he prefers to make an unfavourable impression on others. In the long run luck is always against him, because he is living below his own level and at best only attains what does not suit him. And if there is no doorstep for him to stumble over, he manufactures one for himself and then fondly believes he has done something useful.
>
> (Jung, 1950b, p. 123; see also 1977, p. 320; 1997, p. 568)

In some cases, a person's knowledge of underachievement is conscious and results in feelings of shame and/or guilt. In other cases, however, the knowledge is denied. The denial may take form as hypocrisy. It may instead result in a shamelessness that performs negative values as though they were virtues. In still other cases, however, the denial is automatic or involuntary, in which event the knowledge of underachievement may be said to be repressed. The processes of ambivalence—splitting, doubling, dissociation, and so forth—add further complexities. Many people, for example, see their way clear to doing what they feel ashamed or guilty over, while nevertheless secretly believing, with some indignation, that circumstances entitle them to behave as they have done. Again, people often maintain two or more sets of values; for example, people are often more kind and generous in their family lives than in their work lives, where they instead feel obligated to be more ruthless, self-seeking, and so forth (Merkur, 2011b).

In all cases of conscious ignorance of moral underachievement, whether through hypocrisy or through repression, the knowledge that has been excluded from consciousness persists unconsciously as the shadow. The shadow contains what people are unaware or unconscious of, that gives the lie to their ignorance, their rationalizations, and to their concessions to a public, societal moral standard to which they do not truly subscribe. The therapeutic goal, in making the shadow conscious, is accordingly to make the patient aware of the actual contents of the shadow, so that conscious choices may proceed in accurate self-knowledge. Because everyone has a shadow, Jung's procedures for working with the shadow are effective with wholesome as well as with morbid personalities. "If it comes to a neurosis, we invariably have to deal with a considerably intensified shadow" (Jung, 1938a, pp. 76–7); but the same procedures may be used to promote moral integrity quite generally. Many people seek psychotherapy, Jung wrote in 1938, out of a sense of "moral inferiority." The existentialists have since taught us to describe the same complaint as ennui, malaise, meaninglessness, or lack of purpose.

> [Repressed materials] are the integral components of the personality, they belong to its inventory, and their loss to consciousness produces an inferiority in one respect or another—an inferiority, moreover, that has the psychological character not so much of an organic lesion or an inborn defect as of a lack which gives rise to a feeling of moral resentment. The sense of moral inferiority always indicates that the missing element is something which, to judge by this feeling about it, really ought not be missing, or which could be made conscious if only one took sufficient trouble. The moral inferiority does not come from a collision with the generally accepted and, in a sense, arbitrary moral law, but from the conflict with one's own self which, for reasons of psychic equilibrium, demands that the deficit be redressed. Whenever a sense of moral inferiority appears, it indicates not only a need to assimilate an unconscious component, but also the possibility of such assimilation. In the last resort it is a man's moral qualities which force him, either through direct recognition of the need or indirectly through a painful neurosis, to assimilate his unconscious self and to keep himself fully conscious.
>
> (Jung, 1938c, p. 136)

At the same time, because integrity always conforms to a person's subjective standards, psychic integration was not always the appropriate choice. When psychotherapy can do no more than make people aware of suffering that, due to external life circumstances, cannot be ameliorated, therapy is contraindicated. Increasing suffering by increasing consciousness of it is no gain, whether through psychoanalysis or through analytical psychology. In some cases, Jung suggested, becoming conscious of one's shadow may discover only that it is best, for interpersonal or objective reasons, to leave at least part of the shadow unintegrated. Jung (1928a) wrote:

> I do not at all subscribe to the view that fundamentally man is always good, and that his evil qualities are merely misunderstood good. On the contrary, I hold that there are very many persons who represent such an inferior combination of inherited characteristics that it would be far better both for society and for themselves if they refrain from expressing their individual idiosyncrasies. We can therefore claim with a clear conscience that collective education is, at bottom, of undoubted value.
>
> (p. 151; see also 1997, p. 569)

The psychological complexity of morality

Jung opposed Freud's (1913b, 1927, 1930, 1933, 1939) thesis that morality is an imposition of culture, mediated by the parents, that consciousness—later, the superego—internalizes at the inevitable cost of conflict with inborn, unconscious motivations. Jung asserted that morality is not reducible to the moral code. The psyche has an inborn need for self-control; and societal institutions that facilitate this goal, such as religion and the legal system, are created not to oppose instinct but in fact to express it.

> Moral law is not just an evil that has to be resisted, but a necessity born from the innermost needs of man. Moral law is nothing other than an outward manifestation of man's innate urge to dominate and control himself. This impulse to domestication and civilization ... can never be conceived as the consequence of laws imposed from without. Man himself, obeying his instincts, created his laws. We

shall never understand the reasons for the fear and suppression of the sexual problem in a child if we take into account only the moral influences of education.

(Jung, 1913b, p. 213; see also 1921, p. 212)

Jung's thesis that morality has an inborn foundation was not accepted by classical psychoanalysis. At the very end of Jung's life, the view was asserted by D. W. Winnicott, a member of the British Middle School whose writings have enjoyed increased acceptance since the 1980s. Winnicott wrote:

Those who hold the view that morality needs to be inculcated teach small children accordingly, and they forgo the pleasure of watching morality develop naturally in their children, who are thriving in a good setting that is provided in a personal and individual way.

(1958, p. 15; see also 1963, p. 94)

Jung seems not to have appreciated that he had conclusively falsified Freud's theory of morality in the course of his scattered discussions of the problematics of moral thinking. Rejecting theological and philosophical perspectives, Jung defined good and evil in psychological terms that made the moral categories do the work of Freud's contrast of pleasure and unpleasure. "Psychology does not know what good and evil are in themselves; it knows them only as judgments about relationships. 'Good' is what seems suitable, acceptable, or valuable from a certain point of view; evil is its opposite" (Jung, 1969a, p. 53). The functional equivalence of evil with unpleasure allowed Jung to assert the reality of evil. "There are things which from a certain point of view are extremely evil, that is to say dangerous" (Jung, 1969a, p. 53). Immediately that Jung defined good and evil from a subjective, psychological perspective, the inconsistency of moral judgment with the moral code became undeniable.

In practical terms, this means that good and evil are no longer so self-evident. We have to realize that each represents a *judgment* ... moral evaluation is always founded upon the apparent certitudes of a moral code which pretends to know precisely what is good and what evil. But once we know how uncertain the foundation is, ethical decision becomes a subjective, creative act.... Nothing can spare us the torment of ethical decision.

(Jung, 1973b, pp. 329–30)

In some situations, Jung noted, it was plainly wrong to do the right thing. What was good according to the code could be evil according to moral judgment, or vice versa. "Harsh as it may sound, we must have the freedom in some circumstances to avoid the known moral good and do what is considered to be evil, if our ethical decision so requires" (Jung, 1973b, p. 330).

> Let us take as an example the universally valid commandment: Thou shalt not lie. What is one to do if, as frequently happens to a doctor, one finds oneself in a situation where it would be a catastrophe to tell the truth or to suppress it? If one does not want to precipitate the catastrophe directly, one cannot avoid telling a convincing lie, prompted by psychological common sense, readiness to help, Christian charity, consideration for the fate of the other people concerned—in short, by ethical motives just as strong as if not stronger than those which compel one to tell the truth. One comforts oneself with the excuse that it was done in a good cause and was therefore moral. But anyone who has insight will know that on the one hand he was too cowardly to precipitate a catastrophe, and on the other hand that he has lied shamelessly. He has done evil but at the same time good.
>
> (Jung, 1969c, p. 620; see also 1997, p. 137)

Jung offered a second example where medical ethics confronted a physician with circumstances in which moral judgment opposed the moral code. In these cases, a physician's best intervention was to withhold treatment and allow individuals to come to grief. He was writing of the many people who either avoid therapy entirely or are in treatment but not cooperating with it, and will continue to do so until they meet catastrophe. Alcoholics and other addicts, for example, often must "hit bottom" before they will abandon their addictions and turn their lives around.

> It is presumptuous to think we can always say what is good or bad for the patient. Perhaps he knows something is really bad and does it

anyway and then gets a bad conscience. From the therapeutic, that is to say the empirical, point of view this may be very good indeed for him. Perhaps he *has* to experience the power of evil and suffer accordingly, because only in that way can he give up his Pharisaic attitude to other people. Perhaps fate or the unconscious or God—call it what you will—had to give him a hard knock and roll him in the dirt, because only such a drastic experience could strike home, pull him out of his infantilism, and make him more mature. How can anyone find out how much he needs to be saved if he is quite sure that there is nothing he needs saving from?

(Jung, 1958d, pp. 459–60)

In his concern to explain the complexity of the decisions that medical ethics demand, Jung overlooked the fact that his examples conclusively refuted Freud's theory of morality. Like Freud, Jung rejected conventional European moral codes; but where Freud followed Nietzsche in claiming natural, scientific amorality, Jung advocated morality. He maintained, however, that moral codes are always inevitably inadequate, because no single action is always good. "There is absolutely no truth that does not spell salvation to one person and damnation to another ... there is no good that cannot produce evil and no evil that cannot produce good" (Jung, 1952d, pp. 30–1). Moral conflicts are inevitable because some moral standards are intrinsically inconsistent with each other.

Virtues, like all things which are named and specified, easily get into a quarrel; a virtue which is named has the disagreeable quality of being very imperious. Justice, being named, wants to be nothing but justice, and of course it gets into conflict right away with compassion; one cannot be just and compassionate at the same time because justice must be hard and cruel, otherwise it is not justice.... And true and essential compassion, compassion as it should be, from the standpoint of man cannot be just. And so on.

(Jung, 1988, p. 434)

The divergence of Freud and Jung on the question of morality was not a mere difference of opinion. Because Freud traced morality to the inculcation of the moral code in childhood, Freud's theory has no room for moral decision making to proceed on criteria independent of the moral code. If morality were nothing more than an internalization of the moral code, it would be impossible for morality ever to be inconsistent with the moral code. Garbage in, garbage out, with no *moral* criteria for calling garbage garbage. It is nevertheless the case that not only amorality, but morality itself can and often does differ from the moral code. People implicitly make moral judgments or decisions on the basis of moral criteria that are independent of the moral code. The independent criteria must logically be attributed to moral sensibilities that are not learned, but are either inborn or independently invented (in the sense that walking is not inborn, but invented).[2]

In most cases, Jung estimated, people who behave in conformance to the moral code nevertheless suffer a sense of moral inauthenticity.

> Nor is it a matter of living in accordance with accepted moral values, for the observance of customs and laws can very easily be a cloak for a lie so subtle that our fellow human beings are unable to detect it. It may help us to escape all criticism, we may even be able to deceive ourselves in the belief of our obvious righteousness. But deep down, below the surface of the average man's conscience, he hears a voice whispering, "There is something not right," no matter how much his rightness is supported by public opinion or by the moral code ... there exists a terrible law which stands beyond man's morality and his ideas of rightness—a law which cannot be cheated.
>
> (Jung, 1931d, p. 40)

In contrast with the position taken by Jung, classical psychoanalysis held to the view, accurately reported by Jung, that morality is always a reaction-formation against unconscious immorality. Jung remonstrated, however, that in his clinical experience this unearned assumption was provably incorrect. Moral reaction-formations are never pure or categorical; they are always manifestly contaminated by their latent trend.

---

2 Editor's note: Here Merkur is intimating the domain of moral realism, which is the metaphysical postulate that moral criteria and ethical properties exist as objective facts outside of the human mind or consciousness versus the position from ethical constructivism, which is the view that moral facts and truths are constituted and dependent upon human subjectivity.

In a way one can create the appearance of having created a virtue out of a devil—humility out of vanity, for instance, and generosity out of miserliness; but if one has really created generosity out of miserliness, then it will be a miserly generosity. One's cleanliness will be an impurity at the same time, and one's frankness will be a lie in a miraculous way, because one forgets that the shadow is still there.

(Jung, 1988, pp. 433–4)

The claim that morality rests on a foundation of unconscious amorality is further falsified by the clinical experience that no one, no matter how seemingly amoral or immoral, lacks an unconscious moral sense.

The Freudian theory of repression certainly does seem to say that there are, as it were, only hypermoral people who repress their unmoral, instinctive natures. Accordingly the unmoral man, who lives a life of unrestrained instinct, should be immune to neurosis. This is obviously not the case, as experience shows. Such a man can be just as neurotic as any other. If we analyse him, we simply find that his morality is repressed.

(Jung, 1943c, p. 26)

Jung concluded that Freud's moral theory was a systematic, methodological error. It is incorrect to reduce all that is good, by means of the theory of reaction-formation, to its instinct-driven opposite.

Our mistake lies in supposing that the radiant things are done away with by being explained from the shadow-side. This is a regrettable error into which Freud himself has fallen. Shadow pertains to light as evil to good, and vice versa.

(Jung, 1931c, p. 64)

At the same time, Jung was no more able than Freud had been to bring his several observations on morality together into a coherent whole. Consider, for example, the following passage, written during wartime, where Jung began by asserting the biological basis of morality, only to extend his discussion to include evidence of its educative, cultural dimensions.

It should never be forgotten—and of this the Freudian school must be reminded—that morality was not brought down on tables of stone from Sinai and imposed on the people, but is a function of the human soul, as old as humanity itself. Morality is not imposed from outside; we have it in ourselves from the start—not the law, but our moral nature without which the collective life of human society would be impossible. That is why morality is found at all levels of society. It is the instinctive regulator of action which also governs the collective life of the herd. But moral laws are valid only within a compact human group. Beyond that, they cease. There the old truth runs: *Homo homini lupus.* With the growth of civilization we have succeeded in subjecting ever larger human groups to the rule of the same morality, without, however, having yet brought the moral code to prevail beyond the social frontiers, that is, in the free space between mutually independent societies. There, as of old, reign lawlessness and license and mad immorality—though of course it is only the enemy who dare say it out loud.

(Jung, 1943c, p. 27)

Neurotic denial of guilt

Because the directing will casts a shadow, excluding materials from consciousness through inattention, as well as through denial and repression, it was inevitable, in Jung's view, that conscious good and unconscious evil vary in parallel. As consciousness pursues the good, the good becomes better, but the unconscious evil becomes worse.

When one tries desperately to be good and wonderful and perfect, then all the more the shadow develops a definite will to be black and evil and destructive. People cannot see that; they are always striving to be marvellous, and then they discover that terrible destructive things happen which they cannot understand, and they either deny that such facts have anything to do with them, or if they admit them, they take them for natural afflictions, or they try to minimize them and to shift the responsibility elsewhere. The fact is that if one tries beyond one's capacity to be perfect, the shadow descends into hell and becomes the devil.

(Jung, 1997, p. 569)

Jung offered his theory of compensation in explanation of clinical findings, for some of which Freud offered his theory of reaction-formation. To Freud's way of thinking, it is because unconscious amorality becomes more energetic that the conscious portion of the reaction-formation is driven to ever increasing perfection; but Freud's formulation does not account for as much of the data as Jung's theory does. Freud made no reference to the will, as though the conscious experience ceased to be important once its freedom was recognized as an illusion. Jung too rejected the idea that will was free; but because he allowed that conscious decision making has its own sources of energy and is, accordingly, independent of unconscious sources of energy, he counted will as an independent variable. It is tenable that both Freud and Jung were correct, Freud in cases of unconscious motivation and Jung in cases of conscious motivation; but it was Freud, and not Jung only, who theorized that all neuroses trace to conscious decisions to repress unpleasure.

Jung's theory of neurosis flowed from his way of formulating Freud's theory of repression. Because the psyche unconsciously compensates for repression, the repression of evil serves only to produce further evil, which is to say, neurosis. Jung (1969c) claimed that "the chief causes of a neurosis are conflicts of conscience and difficult moral problems that require an answer" (p. 616).

> Nature is not at all lenient with unconscious sinners. She punishes them just as severely as if they had committed a conscious offence. Thus we find, as the pious Henry Drummond once observed, that it is highly moral people, unaware of their other side, who develop particularly hellish moods which make them insupportable to their relatives.
>
> (Jung, 1938b, p. 76)

Jung expressed his concept of unconscious self-punishment for sin the same year that Wilhelm Stekel (1950) proposed the concept of "diseases of the conscience" (p. 320). "The patient suppresses remorse, tries to drown the voice of conscience, and feigns immunity. Nature takes vengeance" (p. 327). Similar views were later expressed with reference to the unconscious superego by an impressive roster of psychoanalysts (Fenichel, 1945, p. 132; Flugel, 1945, pp. 149–50; Alexander, 1952, p. 15; Bibring, 1953, p. 45; Glover, 1960, p. 302; Hartmann, 1960, pp. 42–3;

Hartmann and Loewenstein, 1962, pp. 169–70; Grinberg, 1964, p. 366; Brenner, 1976, pp. 79–83; Rangell, 1974; 1976; 1980; Blum, 1985, p. 890). In these cases, pathology is due not to an inordinately demanding conscience, but to the neglect of the demands of an entirely reasonable conscience (see also Merkur, 2009).

Although Jung published the generalization in 1938, he was working clinically with the concept by the mid-1920s. Jung only very rarely provided clinical case material that illustrates his theories. One notable instance concerned an initial assessment session, where he lost a patient by raising the issue of the man's unconscious guilt. The man came for treatment of a neurosis that included psychosomatic features. He was unemployed, had no intention of seeking employment, and lived through the financial support of a lover whom he treated condescendingly. Jung felt obliged to raise the issue immediately, that would have to come up sooner or later if the man were to be cured.

> "Don't you think," I asked, "that the fact that you are financially supported by this poor woman might be one of the chief reasons why you are not yet cured?" But he laughed at me when he called my absurd moral innuendo, which according to him had nothing to do with the scientific structure of his neurosis. "Moreover," he said, "I have discussed this point with her, and we have both agreed that it is of no importance." "So you think that by the mere fact of having discussed this situation you have talked the other fact—the fact of your being supported by a poor woman—out of existence? Do you imagine you have any lawful right to the money tingling in your pocket?" Whereupon he rose and indignantly left the room, muttering something about moral prejudices. He was one of the many who believe that morals have nothing to do with neurosis and that sinning on purpose is not sinning at all, because it can be intellectualized out of existence.
>
> Obviously I had to tell this young gentleman what I thought of him. If we could have reached agreement on this point, treatment would have been possible. But if we had begun our work by ignoring the impossible basis of his life, it would have been useless.
>
> (Jung, 1926a, p. 99; see also 1931g, p. 356)

In another case, Jung's interpretation of unconscious guilt led to a successful recovery from psychosis.

Another patient of mine dreamt she had a child just five years ago who gave her terrible trouble and might have a bad effect on her mind. I asked: "In the same month just five years ago, what happened?" The woman could not think at first and then she became very much embarrassed: she had fallen in love with a man and had declared her feeling non-existent. She had had a hell of a life in her marriage to another man, and was now devil-haunted for fear she would go crazy. Women who have kept that fact secret have really gone crazy! Because she was of a simple family, and he of a more aristocratic one, she felt her love was hopeless, never assuming that he could love her; so she married another man and had two children. Then three years ago she met a friend of the first man who told her that he had loved her and had therefore never married. "Your marriage stabbed him to the heart." Soon after this, while bathing her older child, a little girl of three or four, with the eyes of her first lover—she liked to think of her as the child of her lover—she noticed the little girl drinking the water from the bathtub, very infectious, unfiltered water. She knew this but let it happen, and even let her boy drink the same water. Both children were taken ill with typhoid, and the older child died. The woman went into a deep depression, like dementia praecox, and was sent to a lunatic asylum where I treated her. I soon found out the whole story and felt that the only hope for her was to tell her the brutal truth: "You have killed your child in order to kill your marriage." Of course she didn't know what she was doing; because she denied her former love, declared it non-existent, she fed her devils and they suggested killing the daughter of her husband. In this case the awful thing in her dream was born of the bogie of three years ago at the moment when she heard that her first lover was deeply grieved that she had married another man. She had "fed her devils," the animus, and they had killed her child. The woman recovered.

(Jung, 1989, p. 54)

Logically, one must postulate a biological basis to morality, as Jung and Winnicott did, before one may conceptualize particular pathological syndromes as symptoms of repressed morality—as distinct from repressed instinctual amorality. Jung consequently was positioned to notice, and to level the charge, that classical psychoanalysts, obliged to conform to

Freud's exclusively sexual theory of neurosis, routinely misrepresented moral neuroses, such as the example above, as though the conflicts were primarily sexual.

> The theory of repressed infantile sexuality or of infantile traumata has served in innumerable times in practice to divert one's attention from the actual reasons for the neurosis, that is to say, from all the slacknesses, carelessnesses, callousnesses, greedinesses, spitefulnesses, and sundry other selfishnesses for whose explanation no complicated theories of sexual repression are needed.
>
> (Jung, 1926a, p. 111)

Treatment

Jung regarded Freud's clinical procedure as an enormous advance in the field of psychotherapy. The several elements—dream interpretation, free association, analytic listening, and the construction of the patient's biography—together constituted what Jung called a "method of elucidation" that was unprecedented in human history. Among its excellences was its capacity for bringing the shadow to light.

> Naturally the investigation revealed not merely incestuous material in the stricter sense of the word, but every conceivable kind of filth of which human nature is capable—and it is notorious that a lifetime would be required to make even a rough inventory of it.
>
>   The results of the Freudian method of elucidation is a minute elaboration of man's shadow-side unexampled in any previous age.
>
> (Jung, 1931c, p. 63)

Referring to the role of elucidation in analytical psychology, Jung outlined the expectable initial phases of the treatment.

> I should now like to deal with the effects of elucidation. The fixation having been traced back to its dark origins, the patient's position becomes untenable; he cannot avoid seeing how inept and childish his demands are. He will either climb down from his exalted position of despotic authority to a more modest level and except any insecurity which may prove very wholesome, or he will realize the inescapable

truth that to make claims on others is a childish self-indulgence which must be replaced by a greater sense of responsibility.

The man of insights will draw his own moral conclusions. Armed with the knowledge of his deficiencies, he will plunge into the struggle for existence and consume in progressive work and experience all those forces and longings which previously caused him to cling obstinately to a child's paradise, or at least to look back at it over his shoulder. Normal adaptation and forbearance with his own shortcomings: these will be his guiding moral principles, together with freedom from sentimentality and illusion. The inevitable result is a turning away from the unconscious as from a source of weakness and temptation—the field of moral and social defeat.

(Jung, 1931c, p. 65)

Jung here discussed, in the moral discourse that he favored, therapeutic processes that were closely comparable to ego psychologists' practices of "defense analysis." By bringing patients' attention to their defenses, ego psychologists optimally bring their patient to monitor their defenses, to recognize them as counter-productive or "ego dystonic," and to abandon them.

In the following passage, Jung drew attention to a by-product of the method of elucidation: "moments of overwhelming affectivity" that disclose unconscious materials.

As a result of the repressive attitude of the conscious mind, the other side is driven into indirect and purely symptomatic manifestations, mostly of an emotional kind, and only in moments of overwhelming affectivity can fragments of the unconscious come to the surface in the form of thoughts or images. The inevitable accompanying symptom is that the ego momentarily identifies with these utterances, only to revoke them in the same breath. And, indeed, the things one says when in the grip of an affect sometimes seem very strange and daring. But they are easily forgotten, or wholly denied. This mechanism of deprecation and denial naturally has to be reckoned with.

(Jung, 1938c, p. 202)

The potential of the method of elucidation to produce disclosures during moments of overwhelming affectivity, that are subsequently forgotten or denied, made Jung critical of Freud's therapeutic procedure. The value of psychoanalysis was limited, Jung suggested, to the small part of the patient population that is able to benefit from insight, that is, to apply insight by "working through" its implications in their daily lives.

> For many morally sensitive natures, mere insight into themselves has sufficient motive force to drive them forward, but it is not enough for people with little moral imagination. For them—to say nothing of those who may have been struck by the analyst's interpretation but still doubt it in their heart of hearts—self-knowledge without the spur of external necessity is ineffective even when they are deeply convinced of its truth. Then again it is just the intellectually differentiated people who grasp the truth of the reductive explanation but cannot tolerate mere deflation of their hopes and ideals. In these cases, too, the power of insight will be of no avail ... in many cases the most thorough elucidation leaves the patient an intelligent but still incapable child.
>
> (Jung, 1931c, pp. 65–6)

Classical psychoanalysts expressed similar concerns when they limited analysis to "classically analyzable patients," that is, to higher functioning neurotics who possessed sufficient ego-strength to benefit from psychoanalysis. The "widening scope" of psychoanalysis in the early 1950s (Stone, 1954) proceeded along markedly different lines, however, than Jung had elected in response to the same clinical problem over a quarter-century earlier.

Freud's "method of elucidation" sufficed Jung only for the initial phases of his work with patients' shadows.

> The encounter with the dark half of the personality, or "shadow," comes about of its own accord in any moderately thorough treatment.... The open conflict is unavoidable and painful. I have often been asked, "And what do you *do* about it?" I do nothing; there is nothing I can do except wait, with a certain trust in God, until, out of the conflict borne with patience and fortitude, there emerges the solution destined—although I cannot foresee it—for that particular person. Not that I am passive or inactive meanwhile: I help the patient to understand all the things that the unconscious produces during the conflict. The reader may believe me that these are no

ordinary products. On the contrary, they are among the most significant things that have ever engaged my attention. Nor is the patient inactive; he must do the right thing, and do it with all his might, in order to prevent the pressure of evil from becoming too powerful in him. He needs "justification by works," for "justification by faith" alone has remained an empty sound for him.... In these cases what is needed is real work.

(Jung, 1952d, pp. 31–2)

Jung referred here to the same phenomenon that is called "backsliding" in the literature on Christian revivalism (Haartman, 2004). It is also well known in the context of recovery from addictions. The newly converted may not only falter in their resolve, but may sin with a vengeance, as their resistance attempts to thwart their newly attained, and not yet habitual, better inclinations.

The shadow is a moral problem that challenges the whole ego-personality, for no one can become conscious of the shadow without considerable moral effort. To become conscious of it involves recognizing the dark aspects of the personality as present and real. This act is the essential condition for any kind of self-knowledge, and it therefore, as a rule, meets with considerable resistance. Indeed, self-knowledge as a psychotherapeutic measure frequently requires much painstaking work extending over a long period.

(Jung, 1969a, p. 8)

The "moral effort" that Jung described is a variant of "working through." A repression that is initiated voluntarily and consciously becomes preconscious through the automatization (Hartmann, 1958) of the will to repress. Retraining the preconscious, automatized ego cannot be achieved by insight alone. The preconscious habit of will must additionally be repented and the procedural memory must be reversed through the cultivation of a replacement habit.

Owning projections

By the late 1930s, Jung had recognized that the mutative interpretations in his procedure pertained to projections of the shadow.

> All gaps in our actual knowledge are still filled out with projections. We are still so sure we know what other people think or what their true character is. We are convinced that certain people have all the bad qualities we do not know in ourselves or that they practise all those vices which could, of course, never be our own. We must still be exceedingly careful not to project our shadows too shamelessly; we are still swamped with projected illusions. If you imagine someone who is brave enough to withdraw all these projections, then you get an individual who is conscious of a pretty thick shadow. Such a man has saddled himself with new problems and conflicts. He has become a serious problem to himself, as he is now unable to say that *they* do this or that, *they* are wrong, and *they* must be fought against.... Such a man knows that whatever is wrong in the world is in himself, and if he only learns to deal with his own shadow he has done something real for the world. He has succeeded in shouldering at least an infinitesimal part of the gigantic, unsolved social problems of our day. These problems are mostly so difficult because they are poisoned by mutual projections. How can anyone see straight when he does not even see himself and the darkness he unconsciously carries with him into all his dealings?
>
> (Jung, 1938b, p. 83)

This formulation represented an advance over Jung's understanding in 1931, when he had thought "man had an inalienable right to behold all that is dark, imperfect, stupid, and guilty in his fellow man" and that pathology arose only from reserving one's opinions to oneself. "To cherish secrets and hold back emotion is a psychic misdemeanour for which nature finally visits us with sickness" (Jung, 1931c, p. 58). By 1938, Jung had instead recognized that the opinions were not valid, but were instead projections. For clinical purposes, they were the most difficult contents of the shadow to treat.

> One has, of course, to overcome certain moral obstacles, such as vanity, ambition, conceit, resentment, etc., but in the case of projections all sorts of purely intellectual difficulties are added, quite apart from the contents of the projection which one simply doesn't know how to cope with.
>
> (Jung, 1969a, p. 17)

Jung's innovations in clinical procedure may have been preconditions of his advance in theory. Certainly he addressed the issue of projection not through Freud's classical method of elucidation, but rather through the more actively dialogical and mutual candid approach that he termed *dialectical discussion.* "During the process of treatment the dialectical discussion leads logically to a meeting between the patient and his shadow, that dark half of the psyche which we invariably get rid of by means of projection" (Jung, 1952d, p. 29). Although relational psychoanalysts have traced our contemporary dialogical approach to Sandor Ferenczi's innovations in the late 1920s, Jung experimented with mutual analysis with Otto Gross in 1907 (Bair, 2003, pp. 140, 142) and mentioned his own dialogical procedure in print (Jung, 1913a, p. 233) shortly prior to leaving the psychoanalytic movement. Ferenczi cannot have been innocent of Jung's innovations.

Jung's accounts of how he brought patients to own their shadows often summarized or abbreviated the information that a clinician needs.

> Although, with insight and goodwill, the shadow can to some extent be assimilated into the conscious personality, experience shows that there are certain features which offer the most obstinate resistance to moral control and prove almost impossible to influence. These resistances are usually bound up with *projections*, which are not recognized as such, and their recognition is a moral achievement beyond the ordinary. While some traits peculiar to the shadow can be recognized without too much difficulty as one's own personal qualities, in this case both insight and goodwill are unavailing because the cause of the emotion appears to lie, beyond all possibility of doubt, in the *other person*. No matter how obvious it may be to the neutral observer that it is a matter of projections, there is little hope that the subject will perceive this himself. He must be convinced that he throws a very long shadow before he is willing to withdraw his emotionally-toned projections from their object.
>
> (Jung, 1969a, p. 9)

How precisely did Jung persuade his patients to own their shadows? What did he say? In owning projections, a Freudian patient is asked to recognize the error, the failure, for example, of the employer actually to be the parent, and the patient is expected to repent of the error. Jung asserted that Freud's procedure did not go far enough.

> Freud halted the process at the reduction to the inferior half of the personality and tended to overlook the daemonic dangerousness of the dark side, which by no means consists only of relatively harmless infantilisms. Man is neither so reasonable nor so good that he can cope *eo ipso* with evil. That darkness can quite well engulf him, especially when he finds himself with those of like mind.
>
> (Jung, 1970, p. 256)

Jung asked his patients not only to recognize the error of projections, but also to own the evil that they projected onto others as their own shadows, as evil within themselves. The patient must "accept ... the 'dark' as his own darkness, to the extent of producing a real 'shadow' belonging to him personally" (Jung, 1952d, p. 177).

> When he projects negative qualities and therefore hates and loathes the object, he has to discover that he is projecting his own inferior side, his shadow, as it were, because he prefers to have an optimistic and one-sided image of himself. Freud, as you know, deals only with the objective side. But you cannot really help a patient to assimilate the contents of his neurosis by indulgence in a childish lack of responsibility, or by resignation to a blind faith of which he is the victim. His neurosis means him to become a total personality, and that includes recognition of and responsibility for his whole being, his good and his bad sides, his superior as well as his inferior functions.
>
> (Jung, 1936a, p. 160)

Freud asked people to become aware of their unconscious neuroticism, to understand it as something that happened to them, for which they were not responsible, and for which they need feel no further guilt, so that they could develop or construct a more positive and optimistic view of themselves than they had ever previously had. Jung instead asked people to become responsible for their neuroses, by understanding their shadow as part of themselves, as an unconscious negativity that corresponded to an equally one-sided positive self-regard that they maintained in consciousness.

Freud sought for people to forgive themselves of their neuroses. Jung, by comparison, wished his patients to recognize that the evil that they feared was an evil that they also projected and might enact, hence doing harm to others. Jung wanted his patients to arrive at the emotional position that a Freudian patient might reach if the projection were interpreted as an "identification with the aggressor" (Ferenczi, 1932, p. 162). Not only was the other person (for example, the employer, the spouse, the analyst) not the patient's parent, but the patient was not the victim in the situation.

> The whole meaning of sin is that you carry it. What is the use of the sin if you can throw it away? If you are thoroughly aware of your sin, you must carry it, live with it, it is your self. Otherwise you deny your brother, your shadow, the imperfect being in you that follows after and does everything which you are loath to do, all the things you are too cowardly or too decent to do. He commits the sin, and if that fellow is denied, he is pressed towards the collective unconscious and causes disturbances there. For it is against nature, you should be in contact with your shadow, you should say: "Yes, you are my brother, I must accept you."
>
> (Jung, 1989, p. 76)

What Ferenczi called identification with the aggressor describes a particular instance, in one-person psychological terms, of the more general process that Jessica Benjamin (1998) has conceptualized in a two-person psychology as complementarity: "Subject and object, active and passive, observer and participant, knower and known—these [are] reversible complementarities" (p. xiv). Benjamin (2004) adds that the "push-me/pull-you, doer/done-to dynamics that we find in most impasses … generally appear to be one-way—that is, each person feels *done to* and not like an agent helping to shape a cocreated reality" (p. 9). The therapeutic movement from projecting the shadow to realizing and owning it, involves, among other matters, disavowed or repressed materials becoming conscious, resulting in a conscious experience of one-sidedness giving way to a consciousness of complementarity. As I have put the issue elsewhere, the victim is inevitably also a victimizer who must, if therapy is to succeed, integrate the two self-perceptions and modify both behaviors (Merkur, 2009).

Jung relied on theological discourse, presumably because he did not develop a psychological formulation by which to express his clinical understanding and experience, that speaking of projection as the patient's own shadow invites the patient not only to admit to the error of the projection, but also to admit to the wickedness that was being projected. Imagining others as victimizers, by projecting evil-doing onto them, is itself an act of victimization. It falsely accuses others of the patient's own wickedness—wicked fantasies, if not also wicked behavior. Accordingly, a therapeutic interpretation that does not stop halfway, as one-person interpretations do, but instead makes the full relational connection, in a two-person perspective, can bring about the clinical results that Jung reported as the consequence of interpreting a shadow. The difference between interpreting a projection and interpreting a shadow is a difference between allaying a patient's fear, and precipitating the same patient's awareness of secret sins.

In Jung's view, owning the shadow was an indispensable moral element in every psychotherapeutic treatment.

> It is indeed no small matter to know of one's own guilt and one's own evil, and there is certainly nothing to be gained by losing sight of one's shadow. When we are conscious of our guilt we are in a more favourable position—we can at least hope to change and improve ourselves. As we know, anything that remains in the unconscious is incorrigible; psychological corrections can be made only in consciousness. Consciousness of guilt can therefore act as a powerful moral stimulus. In every treatment of neurosis the discovery of the shadow is indispensable, otherwise nothing changes.
>
> (Jung, 1945c, pp. 215–16)

The knowledge of one's capacity for doing evil is "a powerful moral stimulus" when it is followed by renunciation of the evil. The successful realization of the shadow accordingly referred to much the same therapeutic attainment that Melanie Klein named the depressive position, with its motivation of reparation, and Winnicott called the achievement of a capacity for concern. Klein and Winnicott expressed themselves in two-person terms—reparation and concern imply loved objects—where Jung conceptualized the psychotherapeutic process in the solitary soul categories of Christian sin and redemption; but all three formulations

Jung's moral psychology   35

pertained to the psychotherapeutic production of moral transformations. Jung's priority deserves to be acknowledged.

Risks of depression and inflation

Jung cautioned that making the shadow conscious provokes depression in some patients. In these cases, the newly conscious materials cannot, or cannot as yet, be assimilated and integrated within the ego.

Since human nature is not compounded wholly of light, but also abounds in shadows, the insight gained in practical analysis is often somewhat painful, the more so if, as is generally the case, one has previously neglected the other side. Hence there are people who take their newly won insight very much to heart, far too much in fact, quite forgetting that they are not unique in having a shadow-side. They allow themselves to get unduly depressed and are then inclined to doubt everything, finding nothing right anywhere (Jung, 1938c, pp. 141–2).

In my own clinical experience, people suffer a depressive reaction of this kind when they are unable to forgive themselves for having been flawed. Only when they cease to demand superhuman performance of themselves retroactively and limit their ambitions to improved performance in the future, on a going-forward basis, can they find it within themselves to integrate their shame and move beyond depression.

Jung also noted a second prominent adverse reaction to the emergence of the shadow. He termed it "inflation" and explained it as an identification with the emergent archetype (Jung, 1938c, pp. 143, 169). The process might be termed narcissistic or grandiose, but is better comprehended, I suggest, with reference to Melanie Klein's concept of the manic defense (Winnicott, 1935). Owing to their intensely shameful character, the newly emergent unconscious materials have the potential of precipitating depression. When the ego defends against the potential depression, it produces elation through its exercise of denial and reaction-formation.

The analysis and conscious realization of unconscious contents engender a certain superior tolerance, thanks to which even relatively indigestible portions of one's unconscious characterology can be accepted. This tolerance may look very wise and superior, but often it is no more than a grand gesture that brings all sorts of consequences in its train. Two spheres have been brought together which before were kept anxiously apart. After considerable resistances have been overcome, the union of opposites is successfully achieved, at least to all appearances. The deeper understanding thus gained, the juxtaposition of what was before separated, and hence the apparent overcoming of the moral conflict, give rise to a feeling of superiority that may well be expressed by the term "godlikeness."

(Jung, 1938c, pp. 140–1)

A manic defense is often regarded as a means of warding off depression. Whether the concept of "warding off" is precisely correct, the manic defense is a reaction-formation whose conscious elation masks an underlying depression.

Concluding reflections

In Jung's view, the successful realization of the shadow invited "a complete spiritual renewal."

> The question remains: How am I to live with this shadow? What attitude is required if I am to be able to live in spite of evil? In order to find valid answers to these questions a complete spiritual renewal is needed. And this cannot be given gratis, each man must strive to achieve it for himself. Neither can old formulas which once had a value be brought into force again. The eternal truths cannot be transmitted mechanically; in every epoch they must be born anew from the human psyche.

(Jung, 1945c, p. 217)

Jung's work with the personal unconscious was based in the work of Freud and repeatedly innovated in manners that psychoanalysts introduced, allegedly independently, only at later dates. Jung was doing what amounted to defense analysis a year or two in advance of the foundational books by Wilhelm Reich and Anna Freud. He considered consciousness and the unconscious as categorical opposites in advance of Anna Freud. His concepts of will, psychic energy, and the freedom of ego-consciousness from instincts and archetypes, anticipated Hartmann's concept of ego autonomy by nearly two decades. He used the realization of the shadow to precipitate moral transformations, several years in advance of the equivalent achievement by Melanie Klein. He advocated the inborn capacity of morality in the child, half a lifetime before D. W. Winnicott advanced the idea. He traced some pathologies to repressions of morality, rather than sexuality, over a decade before Stekel and two decades before ego psychologists followed suit. Jung likely influenced Ferenczi's final adoption of relational clinical procedures. The crucial, mutative element in his interpretation of the shadow was an understanding of the process that Ferenczi called "identification with the aggressor." Jung was doing effective interpretations in advance of Ferenczi's 1932 paper, but worked out a formulation that he found satisfactory only afterward.

What in Jung's shadow work is not psychoanalytic?

One may grant that Jung's therapy of the shadow was a valuable addition to depth psychology, appropriate to pathological syndromes that involved repressions of the superego, which Rangell (1974, 1976, 1980) called "the syndrome of the compromise of integrity," while leaving future research to determine whether every psychopathology involves repressions of both morality and sexuality, the superego and the id, as I think often to be the case, or whether some pathologies involve repressions exclusively of the one or the other.

Chapter 2

Cure of souls

Jung pioneered the integration of psychoanalysis with spirituality, and the current *Zeitgeist* has much to learn from both his successes and his failures. Jung was a psychiatrist, expert in the treatment of psychotics, whereas Freud was a neurologist, who treated neuroses. The distinction was an important one in Europe at the time. Jung had the ambition from his student days onward "to work out the unconscious phenomena of the psychoses" (Jung, 1989, pp. 7–8). He contacted Freud in 1906 because he "found that Freud's technique of dream analysis and dream interpretation cast a valuable light upon schizophrenic forms of expression" (Jung, 1973b, p. 146). Freud's "Delusion and Dreams in Jensen's *Gradiva*" (1907) both encouraged and appropriated Jung's ambition. In analyzing a fictional character who was undergoing a psychotic break, Freud created parameters for the psychoanalysis of psychosis. Freud made his intentions for Jung explicit the next year. In a letter dated August 13, 1908, Freud proposed a "mission" for Jung: "My selfish purpose, which I frankly confess, is to persuade you to continue and complete my work by applying to psychoses what I have begun with neuroses" (Freud and Jung, 1974, p. 168).

In 1909, immediately following his visit to America to lecture with Freud at Clark University, Jung took up an interest in mythology. He did so because he believed that the symbolism of myths recurred spontaneously in latent psychoses (Jung, 1973b, pp. 131, 162; 1989, p. 23), and he hoped that study of myths would advance his work with psychosis. Almost a half century later, Jung evaluated the success of his venture:

> When I was working in 1906 on my book *The Psychology of Dementia Praecox* (as schizophrenia was then called), I never dreamt that in the succeeding half-century psychological investigation of

the psychoses and their contents would make virtually no progress whatever.

(Jung, 1952b, p. 349)

In the meantime, Jung found a research topic for himself. For Jung, mythology was integral to religion. "In my psychology the 'mythological' aspect means 'religious attitude'" (Jung, 1976, p. 468). "Religion means, if anything at all, precisely that function which brings us back to the eternal myth" (Jung, 1952a, p. 409). What began as an indirect attack on the problem of psychosis developed into a modern, non-ecclesiastical cure of souls.

In later years, Jung frequently remarked that Freud focused psychoanalysis exclusively on medical concerns, which is to say, on the theory and technique of what today is called symptom analysis. Jung, by contrast, insisted that Freud's account of dreams was itself a contribution to the general psychology of normality.

In so far as psychoanalysis is a branch of medical psychology, it concerns itself solely with abnormal cases and should therefore be reserved for the physician; but dream psychology, studied for the light it throws up on normal human behaviour, will be of ever-increasing interest to thoughtful people generally, and especially to those with educational inclinations.

(Jung, 1926a, p. 68; see also Jung, 1922, pp. 68–9; 1928b, p. 50; 1930a, p. 31; 1935a, pp. 773–4; 1939b, p. 45; 1951a, pp. 478–9)

Freud's (1901, 1905) contributions on slips of the tongue and jokes were further studies of normal psychology; but after 1906, when Freud was first importantly endorsed in the international medical community (by Eugen Bleuler and Jung), Freud prioritized the creation of the psychoanalytic movement and restricted his research to topics of clinical interest. Whatever he addressed for the remainder of his life he viewed through the medical lens of morbid psychology.

In Jung's view, the general field of normal psychology included ethics, aesthetics and, of keenest interest to himself, spirituality. "Long years of experience have shown me over and over again that a therapy along purely biological lines does not suffice, but requires a spiritual complement" (Jung, 1952c, p. 300). The inventor of the word association test, Jung knew that analysis was not the only method of accessing the unconscious that had therapeutic value. "It would be a dangerous prejudice to imagine that analysis of the unconscious is the one and only panacea which should therefore be employed in every case" (Jung, 1946b, p. 186).

> Fidelity to the law of one's own being is ... a loyal perseverance and confident hope; in short, an attitude such as a religious man should have towards God ... personality can never develop unless the individual chooses his own way, consciously and with moral deliberation. Not only the causal motive—necessity—but conscious moral decision must lend its strength to the process of building the personality ... But a man can make a moral decision to go his own way only if he holds that way to be the best. If any other way were held to be better, then he would live and develop that other personality instead of his own. The other ways are conventionalities of a moral, social, political, philosophical, or religious nature.
>
> (Jung, 1934a, p. 174)

Following the introduction of character analysis by psychoanalytic ego psychologists in the late 1920s and early 1930s, Jung (1938c, p. 221) emphasized that his therapy addressed personality development; but the term re-branded clinical procedures over which he had broken with Freud in 1912. To the analytic component of his therapeutic work, Jung "add[ed] a synthesis which emphasizes the purposiveness of unconscious tendencies with respect to personality development" (Jung, 1936b, p. 537). In an interview that Jung gave in 1928, he made clear that he employed the term "development" not, as Freudians do, in a biological sense that has to do with growth, but in reference to the continuation, elaboration, or enhancement of existing interests.

> The repressed tendencies that are made conscious should not be destroyed but, on the contrary, should be developed further. An example will make this clear. Among savage peoples this is evident from the fact that the warrior decks his spear with feathers or paints his shield. In our mechanized world this urge for artistic creation is repressed by the one-sided work of the day and is very often the cause of psychic disturbances. The forgotten artist must be fetched

up again from the darkness of the subconscious and the path cleared for the urge for artistic expression—no matter how worthless the paintings and poems may be that are produced in this way.

(Jung, 1977, p. 42)

Jung employed the term development in contexts where psychoanalysts use the term "sublimation," presumably because he objected to Freud's concept, with its unearned assumptions about hypothetical transformations of unconscious psychosexuality (Jung, 1932a, p. 37). Freud, who considered any teaching activity to be a departure from the task of analysis, insisted that the task of sublimation be left to patients' discretion. Jung disagreed. He felt that the manifest contents of dreams provided sufficient indication of the "synthetic" direction in which patients were developing on their own that therapists might give them assistance without infringing on their autonomy.

Psychotherapy as a non-ecclesiastic cure of souls

Presumably in response to Freud's *Future of an Illusion* (1927), Jung published an article entitled "Psychoanalysis and the Cure of Souls" in 1928. In it, he asserted the value of psychoanalysis for the Protestant cure of souls. Jung began by stating clearly the categorical difference of the two procedures.

Psychoanalysis and the pastoral cure of souls … are concerned with essentially different things. The cure of souls as practised by the clergyman or priest is a religious influence based on a Christian confession of faith. Psychoanalysis, on the other hand, is a medical intervention, a psychological technique … [that] seeks to lead the contents of the unconscious over into the conscious mind, thereby destroying the roots of the disturbances or symptoms. Freud seeks, therefore, to remove the disturbance of adaptation by an undermining of the symptoms, and not through treatment of the conscious mind.

(Jung, 1928b, p. 348)

Having distinguished the religious goal of the soul's salvation from the therapeutic ambitions of psychoanalysis, Jung went on to defend psychoanalysis as an adjunct to the cure of souls. Psychoanalysis was invaluable

42   Cure of souls

for religious purposes, owing to its ability to remove impediments to the attainment of intimacy with God.

> The cure of souls can only be practised in the stillness of a colloquy, carried on in the healthful atmosphere of unreserved confidence. Soul must work on soul, and many doors be unlocked that bar the way to the innermost sanctuary. Psychoanalysis possesses the means of opening doors otherwise tightly closed.
>
> (Jung, 1928b, p. 351)

Although Jung shared the conventional verbal distinction between psychoanalysis and the cure of souls, he collapsed the categories on other occasions. In Jung's view, his own therapy, analytical psychology, was both a depth psychology and a cure of souls.

> The main interest of my work is not concerned with the treatment of neurosis, but rather with the approach to the numinous. But the fact is that the approach to the numinous is the real therapy, and inasmuch as you attain to the numinous experiences, you are released from the curse of pathology. Even the very disease takes on a numinous character.
>
> (Jung, 1973a, p. 377)

Jung sometimes conceptualized his procedure in secular terms. "It is the kind of training that enables a young person to adapt ... to the self, to the powers of the psyche, which are far mightier than all the Great Powers of the earth" (Jung, 1934b, p. 153). "He needs to return, not to Nature in the manner of Rousseau, but to his own nature. His task is to find the natural man again" (Jung, 1936b, p. 534). "Analytical treatment could be described as a readjustment of psychological attitude achieved with the help of the doctor ... this newly won attitude ... is better suited to the inner and outer conditions" (Jung, 1958c, p. 72).

Jung was equally comfortable expressing himself in religious terms. He treated "spiritual" as a synonym of "psychical" (Jung, 1931b, p. 69; 1970, p. 113) and maintained that a single unconscious process might be experienced either as the self or as God. "Symbols of the self cannot be distinguished empirically from a God-image" (Jung, 1948d, p. 194). "The self ... is a God-image, or at least cannot be distinguished from one" (Jung, 1969a, p. 22). By the self, Jung conceptualized a center of the unconscious that was simultaneously the supraordinate whole of both consciousness and the unconscious. Jung (1958a) denied that the equivalence of the self with God had metaphysical implications. "The symbols of divinity coincide with those of the self.... This is not to assert a metaphysical identity of the two, but merely the empirical identity of the images representing them, which all originate in the human psyche" (p. 339).

Numinous experiences in analytical psychology

Jung's treatment of secular and religious discourses as alternate ways to discuss single psychological phenomena was consistent with his overall program, which deployed religious experiences for therapeutic purposes. Discussing his technique with an alcoholic patient, Jung explained:

> Here and there, once in a while, alcoholics have had what are called vital spiritual experiences. To me these occurrences are phenomena. They appear to be in the nature of huge emotional displacements and rearrangements. Ideas, emotions, and attitudes which were once the guiding forces of the lives of these men are suddenly cast to one side, and a completely new set of conceptions and motives begin to dominate them. In fact, I have been trying to produce some such emotional rearrangement within you. With many individuals the methods which I employed are successful.
>
> (Anon., 2001, p. 27)

Neither in Freud's time nor since have analysts ever claimed psychoanalysis to cure alcoholism or drug addiction. The clinical wisdom is first to get the addict to stop using the addictive substance and only start psychoanalysis after sobriety has been achieved. In advocating spiritual experience, Jung was talking of a non-analytic but nonetheless psychotherapeutic intervention that could do what psychoanalysis cannot. Spiritual experiences uniquely had the potential power to motivate addicts to stop using the addictive substance.

Jung was well aware that religious experiences cannot be produced on demand, but he also recognized that appropriate means can favor their occurrence.

44 Cure of souls

> Gifts of grace ... are neither to be taught nor learned, neither given nor taken, neither withheld nor earned, since they come through experience, which is an irrational datum not subject to human will and caprice. Experiences cannot be *made*. They happen—yet fortunately their independence of man's activity is not absolute but relative. We can draw closer to them—that much lies within our human reach.
>
> (Jung, 1932b, p. 331)

For his clinical purposes, Jung regarded spiritual experiences agnostically as psychological phenomena. His cure of souls did not aim at the salvation of his patients' souls. He psychologized the Christian procedure by replacing its traditional theological goal with his own psychotherapeutic one. Whether spiritual experiences are veridical or only apparent, they have unparalleled clinical use.

> These situations are intense inner experiences which can lead to lasting psychic growth and a ripening and deepening of the personality, if the individual affected by them has the moral capacity for ... loyal trust and confidence. They are the age-old psychic experiences that underlie "faith" and ought to be its unshakable foundation—and not of faith alone, but also of knowledge.
>
> (Jung, 1950, p. 350)

> What modern man needs and what would afford the only possibility of a religious attitude is precisely *not* an effort of the will and *not* moral compulsion, but rather the experience that his view of the world, which reflects his hubris of consciousness, is really and truly inadequate. This experience is possible only when something happens to him personally which is not of his conscious doing. It is only the experience of the spontaneous activity of the psyche, independent of his will and consciousness, that has this power of conviction. It seems to me that the most important task of the educator of the soul would be to show people the way to the primordial experience which most clearly befell St. Paul, for example, on the road to Damascus. In my experience this way opens up only during the psychic development of the individual.
>
> (Jung, 1973a, pp. 216–17)

Jung claimed that numinous experiences were effective therapeutically not only for the conscious syndromes that were traditional concerns of the cure of souls, but also for neuroses.

> The well-meaning rationalist will point out that I am casting out the devil with Beelzebub and replacing an honest neurosis by the swindle of a religious belief. As to the former charge, I have nothing to say in reply, being no metaphysical expert. But as to the latter one, I beg leave to point out that it is not a question of belief but of experience. ... No matter what the world thinks about religious experience, the one who has it possesses a great treasure, a thing that has become for him a source of life, meaning, and beauty, and that has given a new splendour to the world and to mankind. He has *pistis* and peace. Where is the criterion by which you could say that such a life is not legitimate, that such an experience is not valid, and that such *pistis* is mere illusion? Is there, as a matter of fact, any better truth about the ultimate things than the one that helps you to live? ... The thing that cures a neurosis must be as convincing as the neurosis, and since the latter is only too real, the helpful experience must be equally real. It must be a very real illusion, if you want to put it pessimistically. But what is the difference between a real illusion and a healing religious experience? It is merely a difference of words.
>
> (Jung, 1938b, pp. 104–5)

By the early 1930s, Jung (1938b, p. 7; 1977, p. 230; 1997, p. 846) had read and adopted the terminology of Rudolf Otto's *Das Heilige* (1917), which introduced the neologism "numinous" in order to refer to a category of values that distinguish different kinds of religious experience. The numinous includes both the holy and the demonic. Both phenomena are characterized by their capacities to arouse wonderment and awe, urgency, fascination, and mystery at the august and tremendous. Otto denied that he was making supernatural, theological, or metaphysical assertions. He instead listed the numinous together with the ethical and the aesthetic as discrete categories of value. He also subdivided the *numinosum* into two major subcategories, the *tremendum* and the *fascinosum*, corresponding respectively to the Apolline and Dionysian drives of Nietzsche. Otto's terms, which belonged to the academic study of religion, permitted Jung to express himself in a secular manner. At the same time, Jung was conversant with theological discourse. In his Terry Lectures at Yale University, for example, he paraphrased Paul Tillich's definition of religion as whatever cross-culturally may be an individual's ultimate concern. Jung (1938b) wrote:

> Religion is a relationship to the highest or most powerful value, be it positive or negative. The relationship is voluntary as well as involuntary, that is to say you can accept, consciously, the value by which you are possessed unconsciously. That psychological fact which wields the greatest power in your system functions as a god, since it is always the overwhelming psychic factor which is called "God." As soon as a god ceases to be an overwhelming factor he dwindles to a mere name.
>
> (p. 81)

The varieties of numinous experience that Jung made available to his patients were five. Listed in the order of their additions to Jung's clinical procedures, they were: (1) dreams, (2) archetypes, (3) active imagination, and two experiential milestones of personality development, (4) "becoming conscious" and the (5) "coming-to-be of the self (individuation)" (Jung, 1954b, p. 226).

Many dreams are manifestly numinous. "Often it is simply the deep impression made on the patient by the independent way the dreams deal with his problem" (Jung, 1932b, p. 346). Again, "the unconscious is capable at times of manifesting an intelligence and purposiveness superior to the actual conscious insight. There can be no doubt that this is a basic religious phenomenon" (Jung, 1938b, p. 39). "As a rule, when 'archetypal' contents spontaneously appear in dreams, etc., numinous and healing effects emanate from them. They are *primordial psychic experiences* which very often give patients access again to blocked religious truths" (Jung, 1976, pp. 56–7).

In other cases, dreams are found to be numinous only after they have been interpreted. "Interpretation is the crux of the whole matter" (Jung, 1930a, p. 32). By 1911, Jung had added a "synthetic" approach to Freud's "analytic" method of dream interpretation. The synthetic approach to dream interpretation can be crucial to dreams' appreciation as numinous. So too is Jung's further technique of "amplification."

In order to interpret the products of the unconscious, I also found it necessary to give a quite different reading to dreams and fantasies. I did not reduce them to personal factors, as Freud does, but—and this seemed indicated by their very nature—I compared them with the symbols from mythology and the history of religion, in order to discover the meaning they were trying to express. This method did in fact yield extremely interesting results, not least because it permitted an entirely new reading of dreams and fantasies, thus making it possible to unite the otherwise incompatible and archaic tendencies of the unconscious with the conscious personality.

(Jung, 1930b, p. 330)

Jung's work with dreams had led him "about 1912" (Jung, 1948a, p. 472) to his theory of the collective unconscious, whose component archetypes he postulated on the basis of imagery that dreams had in common with the world's mythologies and religions. "Since every archetype is psychologically a *fascinosum*, i.e., exerts an influence that excites and grips the imagination, it is liable to clothe itself in religious ideas (which are themselves of an archetypal nature)" (Jung, 1942a, p. 168).

The archetypal contents of the collective unconscious can often assume grotesque and horrible forms in dreams and fantasies, so that even the most hard-boiled rationalist is not immune from shattering nightmares and haunting fears. The psychological elucidation of these images, which cannot be passed over in silence or blindly ignored, leads logically into the depths of religious phenomenology.

(Jung, 1952d, pp. 32–3)

The archetypes have, when they appear, a distinctly numinous character which can only be described as "spiritual," if "magical" is too strong a word. Consequently this phenomenon is of the utmost significance for the psychology of religion. In its effects it is anything but unambiguous. It can be healing or disruptive, but never indifferent, provided of course that it has attained a certain degree of clarity. This aspect deserves the epithet "spiritual" above all else. It not infrequently happens that the archetype appears in the form of a spirit in dreams or fantasy-products, or even comports itself like a ghost. There is a mystical aura about its numinosity, and it has a corresponding effect upon the emotions. It mobilizes philosophical and religious convictions in the very people who deem themselves miles above any such fits of weakness. Often it drives with unexampled passion and remorseless logic towards its goal and draws the subject under its spell, from which despite the most desperate resistance he is unable, and finally no longer even willing, to break free, because the experience brings with it a depth and fulness of meaning that was unthinkable before.

(Jung, 1954b, pp. 205–6)

The archetype appears as a numinous factor, as an experience of fundamental significance. Whenever it clothes itself in suitable symbols (which is not always the case), it seizes hold of the individual in a startling way, creating a condition amounting almost to possession, the consequences of which may be incalculable.... All religious and metaphysical concepts rest upon archetypal foundations.

(Jung, 1949, pp. 518–19)

In December 1913, Jung began to experiment with a procedure for visualizing mental imagery, by which he could produce waking dream states on demand. In 1916, Jung wrote an article, "The Transcendent Function," explaining his method of interpreting the mental imagery that he produced, but he withheld the article from publication until 1957. In public, he often referred to "fantasy" without explaining that the fantasies were products of formal procedures for visualizing mental images that he taught to a very few selected patients. Jung's mental imagery procedure received its first public mention, together with its name "active imagination," in Jung's Tavistock Lectures of 1936; but he explained its details only in unpublished seminars that he gave to students in Zurich (Jung, 1997; for a summary of the procedures, see Merkur, 1993, pp. 40–9). Some twenty years later he acknowledged:

I myself have said little about it and have contented myself with hints.... I tried it out on myself and others thirty years ago and must admit that although it is feasible and leads to satisfactory results it is also very difficult.

(Jung, 1970, p. 530)

For present purposes, it suffices to note that he considered the visual experiences both numinous and therapeutic. "Like the instincts, these images have a relatively autonomous character; that is to say, they are 'numinous' and can be found above all in the realm of numinous or religious ideas" (Jung, 1957a, p. 533).

> In most cases it is contents of an archetypal nature, or the connections between them, that exert a strong influence of their own whether or not they are understood by the conscious mind. This spontaneous activity of the psyche often becomes so intense that visionary pictures are seen or inner voices heard—a true, primordial experience of the spirit.
> Such experiences reward the sufferer for the pains of the labyrinthine way. From now on a light shines through the confusion; more, he can accept the conflict within him and so come to resolve the morbid split in his nature on a higher level.
>
> (Jung, 1932b, p. 346)

Not only were the images numinous that Jung's patients produced through active imagination, but Jung's interpretations of the images were calculated to bring their unconsciously conflictual or oppositional content to consciousness, precisely in order to provoke the unconscious to generate an original compromise formation or symbol. In some patients, the union of opposites in a transcendent, compromising third constituted a spiritual awakening or religious conversion experience.

> It is not in the least astonishing that numinous experiences should occur in the course of psychological treatments and that they may even be expected with some regularity, for they also occur very frequently in exceptional psychic states that are not treated and may even cause them.
>
> (Jung, 1970, p. 547)

The only certain thing is that both parties will be changed; but what the product of the union will be it is impossible to imagine. The empirical material shows that it usually takes the form of a subjective experience which, according to the unanimous testimony of history, is always of a religious order. If, therefore, the conflict is consciously endured and the analyst follows its course without prejudice, he will

50   Cure of souls

unfailingly observe compensations from the unconscious which aim at producing a unity. He will come across numerous symbols similar to those found in alchemy—often, indeed, the very same. He will also discover that not a few of the spontaneous formations have a numinous quality in harmony with the mysticism of the historical testimonies. It may happen, besides, that the patient, who until then had shut his eyes to religious questions, will develop an unexpected interest in these matters.

(Jung, 1970, p. 366)

Because Jung employed mental imagery or visions in order to precipitate symbols of unity, he considered it appropriate to define mysticism in terms of visionary experiences. "Mystics are people who have a particularly vivid experience of the processes of the collective unconscious. Mystical experience is experience of archetypes" (Jung, 1936a, p. 98).

In contrast with dreams, archetypes, and active imagination, which were numinous means of attaining personality development, the fourth and fifth varieties of numinous experience that Jung made available to his patients were themselves therapeutic attainments. In his article "A Psychological Approach to the Dogma of the Trinity," Jung interpreted the three persons of the Christian Trinity as personifications of three stages of personal development. God the Father personified the personality in need of development. The Son correlated with the therapeutic attainment of widened or heightened consciousness, which is a development of the ego; while the Holy Spirit symbolized individuation, the realization of the self (Jung, 1948d, pp. 181–2). Both therapeutic achievements generally had a numinous quality.

It is clear that these changes are not everyday occurrences, but are very fateful transformations indeed. Usually they have a numinous character, and can take the form of conversions, illuminations, emotional shocks, blows of fate, religious or mystical experiences, or their equivalents.

(Jung, 1948d, pp. 181–2)

The two therapeutic goals were independent variables. Individuation might be achieved, for example, in the absence of widened or heightened consciousness. Jung explained the issue to an interviewer in 1928.

I said it had always bothered me whether, say, a Hindu yogin or a primitive medicine man, a truly wise one, of course, could be considered to be individuated, since they were not "conscious" in our sense of what went on inside them. "Well, I don't know about that," he [Jung] said. "They may not be conscious but they hear the inner voice, they *act* on it, they do not go against it—that is what counts. The primitives may not *formulate* it in the way you mean, but he has a pretty clear idea what goes on; I understand his language. When I go to him, we speak the same language."

"You know, it is possible to have 'consciousness' *in globo*, so to speak, without its being differentiated."

(Jung, 1977, p. 211)

Jung's racial theories entailed a historical growth or expansion of consciousness from primitives to civilized men; but individuation was a constant of the enlightened few within each order of cultural advance. "The numinous experience of the individuation process is, on the archaic level, the prerogative of shamans and medicine man; later, of the physician, prophet, and priest; and finally, at the civilized stage, of philosophy and religion" (Jung, 1954e, p. 294).

What Jung meant by consciousness was, most generally, the psychological phenomenon that Freud (1914a, 1921, 1933) called "self-observation" and attributed to the agency that he variously called conscience, the ego ideal, and the superego. In some contexts, Jung discussed increased consciousness in educational terms, much as we today speak of raising consciousness by increasing available information. In the context of the therapeutic process, however, Jung's discussions of consciousness pertained to psychological mindedness. Jung nowhere discussed how analytic psychology expands consciousness; but it implicitly occurs as a by-product of self-reflection, precisely as it does in psychoanalysis (Sterba, 1934). It is impossible, I should think, to undergo the first phase of a Jungian treatment, the analysis of the personal unconscious or shadow, without attaining heightened consciousness or psychological mindedness along the way. The phenomenon is numinous in the Jungian procedure because it is attributed not to a secular process, the self-observation of the superego, but to the portion of the psyche that Jung termed the self and explained as the psychic image of God—the "God within."

Archetypes and the individuation process

Jung (1989, pp. 132–3) maintained that Freud and Adler had limited their discoveries to the personal unconscious, which was the concern of his own work with the shadow. His ideas of the collective unconscious were instead unparalleled. So too was "individuation or rebirth" (Jung, 1984, p. 301; 1997, p. 871), the portion of the therapeutic process that concerned itself with the collective unconscious. Jung claimed that when psychotherapeutic work with the personal unconscious reached an advanced stage, so that comparatively little of its contents remained unconscious, the unconscious began manifesting collective representations. Jung's clinical finding may be translated into Freudian terms as the observation that the therapeutic resolution of fixations causes dreams and fantasies to exhibit a decrease of fixated materials together with a corresponding increase of sublimations. Because the sublimations are frequently adopted from cultural sources, rather than invented *de novo*, they are often collective representations in the sense of the term that Jung took over from anthropology: he credited Lucien Lévy-Bruhl, having apparently been unaware that the notion of collective representations had been introduced by Emile Durkheim.

Jung claimed to discern a pattern in the manifestation of collective representations. "The chaotic assortment of images that at first confronted me reduced itself in the course of the work to certain well-defined themes and formal elements, which repeated themselves in identical or analogous form with the most varied individuals" (Jung, 1946a, p. 203). Reasoning that unknown psychological processes must cause the repetition of the collective representations, Jung introduced the terms "primordial image" and "archetype" to designate not the collective representations, but the unconscious psychological processes that caused them. The roster of archetypes that Jung recognized was modest: "I would mention in particular the shadow, the animal, the wise old man, the anima, the animus, the mother, the child, besides an indefinite number of archetypes representative of situations" (Jung, 1943c, pp. 109–10).

Jung appreciated that the pattern that he discerned in the manifestations of collective representations—the so-called individuation process—was an artefact of his clinical practices. What occurs naturally in the unconscious is an ebb and flow of ever-repeating individuation and de-individuation. "There is no linear evolution; there is only a circumambulation of the self" (Jung, 1973b, p. 196).

That psychological process ... in our unconscious ... is a process of continuous transformation with no end if we don't interfere. It needs our conscious interference to bring it to a goal—by our interference we make a goal. Otherwise, it is like the eternal change of the seasons in nature, a building up and a pulling down, integration and disintegration without end.

(Jung, 1988, pp. 236–7; see also p. 955)

The devotion of consciousness to the unconscious process, by investing attention in dreams and active imagination, gives the unconscious circumambulation of the self a different direction and purpose. "Individuation takes place when it is realized, when someone is there who notices it; otherwise it is like the eternal melody of the wind in the desert" (Jung, 1997, p. 1314).

The moment the conscious peeps into the unconscious and the line of communication is established the unconscious no longer moves in mere circles, but in a spiral. It moves in a circle to the moment when it would join the former tracks again, and then find itself a bit above ... consciousness looks into the process and so hinders it from being a mere circle. It is a spiral which is moving up to a certain goal.

(Jung, 1988, pp. 955–6; see also 1952d, p. 28; 1997, p. 267)

Because Jung had his patients construct a mythology only in order to deconstruct it during a later phase in the individuation process, his invention of a roster of archetypes need not here detain us. He knew and befriended the eminent anthropologist Leo Frobenius (Bair, 2003, p. 373), whose *Kulturkreislehre*, "culture circle doctrine," had been designed specifically to explain the empirical fact that myths and symbols are found cross-culturally, but never universally (Campbell, 1959). Jung was considerably closer to two members of the American school of cultural anthropology: Jaime de Angulo, a self-taught Jungian analyst, patient, and guide to the Pueblos during Jung's 1924 visit to Taos, New Mexico; and Paul Radin, who attended Jung's 1925 seminars and later collaborated on *The Trickster* (Radin *et al.*, 1956). (The culture-bound distributions of collective representations, which Frobenius amply mapped, might harmonize with ideas about inborn *racial* archetypes, which were an occasional element in Jung's theories; Jung nowhere

54 Cure of souls

advanced the logical alternative, that his ideas about inborn archetypes required the additional postulation of a secondary cause of the cultural-boundedness of the manifest symbols.) Jung's preposterous claims about the universality of the archetypes that he invented were made in knowing contempt of the ethnographic data. At the same time, for clinical purposes it scarcely matters what the archetypes are, or the pattern to which they conform in any individual. It would equally be a matter of clinical indifference if the motifs were conceptualized from a psychoanalytic perspective as sublimations and ego ideals. What is crucial for clinical purposes is the patient's growth in awareness that they conform to a pattern.

Jung maintained that people are ordinarily "possessed" by their archetypes. They identify with their archetypes, act them out, and project them onto other people. Jung appropriated Lévy-Bruhl's (1923) term *participation mystique* in order to describe people's embeddedness in the archetypes, but he explained the embeddedness without acknowledgment in terms that conformed to Freud's (1921) ideas about the regressive identifications in group psychology. The individuation process had the function of moving a person out of *participation mystique* into individuality; and the initial phase of the treatment depended on the personification of archetypes in dreams and active imagination. An example will illustrate. In the following passage, Jung addressed the circumstances of the anima and animus, but his remarks may be applied to further archetypes as well.

> The immediate goal of the analysis of the unconscious … is to reach a state where the unconscious contents no longer remain unconscious and no longer express themselves indirectly as animus and anima phenomena; that is to say, a state in which animus and anima become functions of relationship to the unconscious. So long as they are not this, they are autonomous complexes, disturbing factors that break through the conscious control and act like true "disturbers of the peace." … The more "complexes" a man has, the more he is possessed…. But if such a man makes himself conscious of his unconscious contents, as they appear firstly in the factual contents of his personal unconscious, and then in the fantasies of the collective unconscious, he will get to the roots of his complexes, and in this way rid himself of his possession.
>
> (Jung, 1938c, p. 232)

Jung's goal was not to resolve the complexes but to reclaim them for the ego. "Our task is not ... to deny the archetype, but to dissolve the projections, in order to restore their contents to the individual who has involuntarily lost them by projecting them outside himself" (Jung, 1954c, p. 84).

The simplest way to get archetypes to stop functioning as unconscious producers of acting-out and projections, was to bring them to consciousness by envisioning them in dreams and active imagination. The following comments on personifying the shadow may be treated as illustrative of Jung's procedure in personifying archetypes quite generally.

> As you know, I personify the shadow: it becomes "he" or "she" because it is a person. If you don't handle the shadow as a person in such a case, you are just making a technical mistake, for the shadow *ought* to be personified in order to be discriminated. As long as you feel it as having no form or particular personality, it is always partially identical with you; in other words, you are unable to make enough difference between that object and yourself. If you call the shadow a psychological aspect or quality of the collective unconscious, it then appears in you; but when you say, this is I and that is the shadow, you personify the shadow, and so you make a clean cut between the two, between yourself and that other, and inasmuch as you can do that, you have detached the shadow from the collective unconscious.
>
> (Jung, 1988, p. 1360)

Only after a personification has been consolidated, so that the unconscious complex and its symptoms have been conceptualized clearly, it is time to begin to de-personify the archetypal images that have been envisioned in dreams and active imagination.

> Whether an archetype is encountered in an inner dialogue or an active imagination, it manifests a personality. Its analytic understanding as an archetype, that is, as an unconscious function, strips it of its personification and makes it comprehensible as an impersonal defense mechanism.
>
> (Jung, 1932b, p. 345)

The consciousness of the archetype that depersonifies it ostensibly deprives it of its power to generate unconscious possessions and projections.

The immediate goal has been achieved, namely the conquest of the anima as an autonomous complex, and her transformation into a functional relationship between the conscious and the unconscious. With the attainment of this goal it becomes possible to disengage the ego from its entanglements with collectivity and the collective unconscious. Through this process the anima forfeits the daemonic power of an autonomous complex; she could no longer exercise the power of possession, since she is depotentiated.

(Jung, 1938c, p. 227)

Importantly, an archetype is not depersonified merely as an intellectual proposition. To be therapeutic, depersonification must proceed in an experiential manner, through the patient's active engagement of the personified archetype during active imagination. "To the degree that the patient takes an active part, the personified figure of anima or animus will disappear. It becomes the functional relationship between conscious and unconscious" (Jung, 1938c, p. 224). Watching a personified archetype in a vision or hearing a personified archetype speak in one's mind, allows the archetype to appear responsible for its activity. When, however, a person engages an interior image or voice with active responses, by speaking to it and demanding answers, the unconscious responses gradually make it apparent that the image or voice is not responsible for its activities, but is itself a sort of puppet or mask that is being animated by an unconscious agency that remains latent or unmanifest. When this process of "having it out with the unconscious" is repeated with a plurality of archetypes, two inferences become obvious. The unconscious complexes that manifest in possessions (acting out) and projections match up with the images and voices; but all of the complexes are animated, like so many puppets or masks, by a single ulterior agency.

In the following discussion of depersonifying the anima and animus, Jung touched on two further features that merit emphasis. Once an archetype is depersonified, it can be converted into a bridge to the unconscious, that is, it becomes a conduit through which communication with the ulterior agency can proceed. Second, the contents of each archetype or complex become fully known only after they have been depersonified. As long as they are confused with the ulterior agency, and mistakenly perceived as "relatively independent personalities," their actual contents cannot be discerned accurately.

The autonomous complex of anima and animus is essentially a psychological function that has usurped, or rather retained, a "personality" only because this function is itself autonomous and undeveloped. But already we can see how it is possible to break up the personification, since by making them conscious we convert them into bridges to the unconscious. It is because we are not using them purposefully as functions that they remain personified complexes. So long as they are in this state they must be accepted as relatively independent personalities. They cannot be integrated into consciousness while their contents remain unknown. The purpose of the dialectical process is to bring these contents into the light; and only when this task has been completed, and the conscious mind has become sufficiently familiar with the unconscious processes reflected in the anima, will the anima be felt simply as a function.

(Jung, 1938c, p. 210)

With the ego's growing ability to differentiate the unconscious agency from the archetypal images and voices that, together with the possessions and projections, constitute the complexes, the ego is able to recognize the complexes as split-off or dissociated portions of the psyche. The dissociated complexes can then be reclaimed and integrated within an enlarged ego-consciousness.

The patient has to undergo an important change through the reintegration of his hitherto split-off instinctuality, and is thus to be made over into a new man. The modern mind has forgotten these old truths that speak of the death of the old man and the making of a new one, of spiritual rebirth and such-like old-fashioned "mystical absurdities."

(Jung, 1954a, pp. 34–5)

At the same time, the enlarged ego-consciousness is increasingly able to recognize the unconscious agency in its own right, as it were, unmasked. What remains when an archetype is depersonified? The mental state, detached from the archetype, from which its depersonification proceeded. "All we can say rationally about this condition of detachment is to define it as a sort of centre within the psyche of the individual, but not within the ego. It is a non-ego centre" (Jung, 1936a, p. 167).

58 Cure of souls

In Jung's individuation process, the phases of personifying and depersonifying archetypes subserve the goal of isolating an active, latent agency, a supraordinate factor in the unconscious, that communicates with ego-consciousness by means of the archetypes.

> If the unconscious can be recognized as a co-determining factor along with consciousness, and if we can live in such a way that conscious and unconscious demands are taken into account as far as possible, then the centre of gravity of the total personality shifts its position. It is then no longer in the ego, which is merely the centre of consciousness, but in the hypothetical point between conscious and unconscious. This new centre might be called the self.
>
> (Jung, 1938a, pp. 45–6)

Jung (1921, p. 447) defined individuation as becoming an individual, differentiated from the collective. He also defined it as becoming whole, complete, or integrated.

> Individuation appears, on the one hand, as the synthesis of a new unity which previously consisted of scattered particles, and on the other hand, as the revelation of something which existed before the ego and is in fact its father or creator and also its totality.
>
> (Jung, 1954e, p. 263)

Because individuation presupposed the manifestation, realization, and integration of the self, Jung (1954c, p. 84) was able to write summarily of "the experience of individuation, the attainment of the self." "Insofar as 'individuality' embraces our innermost, last, and incomparable uniqueness, it also implies becoming one's own self. We could therefore translate individuation as 'coming to selfhood' or 'self-realization'" (Jung, 1938c, p. 173). When the self manifests, it displaces the ego as the center of the personality. "The centre of the personality is displaced from the limited ego into the more comprehensive self, into that centre which embraces both realms, the conscious and the unconscious, and unites them with each other" (Jung, 1943a, p. 819). The ego's awareness of its own limitation is intrinsically humbling. "Quite often these experiences are numinous" (Jung, 1970, p. 547).

Jung deployed the term *self* with the resonances of the Hindu concept of *atman*, the "self" that is all being (Jung, 1921, pp. 198–9; 1997, p. 1270; see also Coward, 1978, 1985). The self is the psychic representation of the all, the archetype of wholeness. "The collective unconscious is anything but an encapsulated personal system; it is sheer objectivity, as wide as the world and open to all the world ... this self is the world" (Jung, 1954a, p. 22). Its manifestation constitutes a spiritual awakening, an experience of becoming aware of and uniting with the divine. "The inner experience of individuation is what the mystics called 'the experience of God'" (Jung, 1984, p. 289).

> This inner unity, or experience of unity, is expressed most forcibly by the mystics in the idea of the *unio mystica*, and above all in the philosophies and religions of India, in Chinese Taoism, and in the Zen Buddhism of Japan. From the point of view of psychology, the names we give to the self are quite irrelevant.
>
> (Jung, 1946b, p. 314)

Jung was not here privileging unitive experiences. Rather, he was privileging dreams and visionary experiences, from whose patterns of imagery he deduced abstract ideas of unity. The philosophical or theological attainment of the ideas of unity constituted the apprehension of a self that in many ways remained so very abstract as to be an ineffable mystery.

> We can say nothing about the contents of the self. The ego is the only content of the self that we do know. The individuated ego senses itself as the object of an unknown and supraordinate subject. It seems to me that our psychological inquiry must come to a stop here, for the idea of a self is itself a transcendental postulate which, although justifiable psychologically, does not allow of scientific proof.
>
> (Jung, 1938c, p. 240)

The self "might equally well be called the 'God within us'" (Jung, 1938c, p. 238; see also 1948d, p. 194; 1969a, pp. 22, 40). Jung (1921) claimed that prior to its manifestation, the self pre-exists unconsciously as a potential.

> The psychological individual, or his *individuality* (q.v.), has an a priori unconscious existence, but exists consciously only so far as a

60 Cure of souls

consciousness of his particular nature is present, i.e., so far as there exists a conscious distinction from other individuals.

(p. 447)

He proposed that "man's striving for a spiritual goal is … a genuine instinct" (Jung, 1958a, p. 343) that is not to be reduced, by reference to the theory of sublimation, to a secondary manifestation of sexuality. His clinical findings remain unaffected, however, when one interprets unitive experiences, as I have done elsewhere (Merkur, 1999, 2010), in terms of Freud's (1900, 1913b, 1920) concepts of Eros, condensation, and the unconscious intellectual function that is most familiar in the systematizing of paranoia. Individuation may be an achievement that is constructed by means of condensation and unconscious logical thinking, rather than an inborn archetypal image that has merely to manifest. For clinical purposes, however, the upshot is much the same.

The de-centering of the ego, through its recognition of its position vis-à-vis the self or, in psychoanalytic terms, the unconscious superego, inevitably has a powerful impact on the ego and its willfulness. Jung was discussing ethics, but he might as easily have discussed artistic or other creativity, when he addressed the phenomenon of conflict between the self and the ego.

> The self, in its efforts at self-realization, reaches out beyond the ego-personality on all sides; because of its all-encompassing nature it is brighter and darker than the ego, and accordingly confronted with problems which you would like to avoid. Either one's moral courage fails, or one's insight, or both, until in the end fate decides. The ego never lacks moral and rational counter-arguments, which one cannot and should not set aside so long as it is possible to hold on to them. For you only feel your self on the right road when the conflicts of duty seem to have resolved themselves, and you have become the victim of a decision made over your head or in defiance of the heart. From this we can see the numinous power of the self, which can hardly be experienced in any other way. For this reason *the experience of the self is always a defeat for the ego.* The extraordinary difficulty in this experience is that the self can be distinguished only conceptually from what has always been referred to as "God," but not practically. Both concepts apparently rest on an identical

numinous factor which is a condition of reality. The ego enters into the picture only so far as it can offer resistance, defend itself, and in the event of defeat still affirm its existence.

(Jung, 1970, pp. 545–6)

When Jung described the collapse of the ego's resistance toward the self as the ego's defeat, he unwittingly disclosed his own emotional reaction. A person less invested in his narcissism might instead welcome the discovery of the self as an extension of the person's powers and abilities. The psychoanalyst Marion Milner, for example, discussed this type of access to the unconscious, in the context of creative artists, as a *creative surrender* (Field, 1957). Jung's term individuation pertained to the equivalent phenomenon of surrender to the unconscious, as it manifests in religious contexts as a surrender to guidance by a numinous will or power.

Resolution of the transference

In adding numinous experiences to the armamentum of psychotherapy, Jung devised a modern, would-be scientific cure of souls. Not only was it indicated for a variety of complaints that differed from the psychoneuroses, but it also filled an important gap in psychoanalysis, as Jung implied by giving a small book on individuation the title "The Psychology of the Transference" (1946b). Gathering together several of Jung's scattered remarks on the transference will clarify his concerns.

In agreement with the correspondence of Freud and Pfister, Jung recognized the value of religion in the clinical handling of the transference. Jung made the case that the cure of souls should not be conceptualized as it has traditionally been, as a matter of conscious psychology alone. Like psychoanalysis, the cure of souls provokes a transference relationship that can only be understood by reference to depth psychology. In Catholicism, the transference is displaced onto Mother Church, but in Protestantism it ordinarily remains devoted to the pastoral worker.

Owing to the absence of ritual forms, the Protestant (as opposed to the Catholic) cure of souls develops into a personal discussion in the sense of an "I–Thou" relationship. It cannot translate the fundamental problem of the transference into something impersonal, as the

Catholic can, but must handle it with confidence as a personal experience. Any contact with the unconscious that goes at all deep leads to transference phenomena. Whenever, therefore, the clergyman penetrates any distance into the psychic background, he will provoke a transference (with men as well as with women). This involves him personally, and on top of that he has no form which he could substitute for his own person, as the Catholic priest can, or rather must do. In this way he finds himself drawn into the most personal participation for the sake of his parishioner's spiritual welfare, more so even than the analyst, for whom the specific salvation of the patient's soul is not necessarily a matter of burning importance.

(Jung, 1928b, p. 353)

In agreement with Freud's suggestion to Pfister that he had the option of resolving the transference by shifting it onto God, Jung suggested that the transference might itself be a compromise formation that exploited the person of the doctor as an object through which the patient might become conscious of God.

Was it ... the case that the unconscious was trying to *create* a god out of the person of the doctor, as if it were to free a vision of God from the veils of the personal, so that the transfers to the person of the doctor was no more than a misunderstanding on the part of the conscious mind, a stupid trick played by "sound common sense"? Was the urge of the unconscious perhaps only apparently reaching out towards the person, but in a deeper sense towards a god? Could the longing for a god be a *passion* welling up from our darkest, instinctual nature, a passion unswayed by any outside influences, deeper and stronger perhaps than the love for a human person?

(Jung, 1938c, p. 133)

Jung appreciated and agreed with Freud's postulate that the transference displaced the patient's dependence on a parent. "The nature of the tie in question corresponds more or less to the relation between father and child. The patient falls into a sort of childish dependence from which he cannot defend himself even by rational insight" (Jung, 1931c, p. 61). Jung's clinical procedure was, in part, identical with a classical psychoanalytic approach.

I am *in loco parentis* and have a high authority. Naturally I am also persecuted by the corresponding resistances, by all the manifold emotional reactions they have had against their parents.

Now that is the structure you have to work through first in analysing the situation, because the patient in such a condition is not free, is a slave. He is utterly dependent on the analyst, like the patient with an open abdomen on the operating table. He is in the hands of the surgeon, for better or worse, and so the thing *must* he finished. This means we have to work through that condition in the hope of reaching a situation where the patient is able to see that I am not the father, not the mother, that I am an ordinary human being. Everybody would naturally suppose such a thing to be possible, that the patient could arrive at such an insight if he or she is not a complete idiot, that they could see I am just a doctor and not that emotional figure of their fantasies. But that is very often not the case.

(Jung, 1977, p. 345)

The failure of an apparently successful transference interpretation attracted Jung's attention. As a general rule, Jung postulated that in addition to the reductive, analytic meaning of any psychological event, the phenomenon had also a synthetic, developmental meaning, a telos that it served simultaneously. In the particular case of the transference, Jung noted that the clinical reality of the transference is not adequately explained by Freud's formulation. Something more is necessarily involved than Freud's formulation is able to explain. It often occurs, for example, that an apparently successful interpretation of the transference proves illusory when the analysis is terminated.

Let us suppose that in the given case the cathartic confession has occurred, the neurosis has vanished, or rather the symptoms are no longer visible. The patient could now be dismissed as cured—if it depended on the doctor alone. But he—or especially she—cannot get away. The patient seems bound to the doctor through the confession. If this seemingly senseless attachment is forcibly severed, there is a bad relapse.

(Jung, 1931c, p. 60)

This circumstance, which psychoanalysts term a "transference cure," is understood as a failure to internalize the transferential object. Having

64 Cure of souls

substituted the analyst for the parent, the patient is no longer dependent on the parent, but remains dependent on the analyst. Jung rightly asked: How is this possible? If the power of the parental imago has been broken, how can it continue to inform transferences?

Jung cited another vicissitude of the transference that points to the same problem with the conventional psychoanalytic theory.

> When, therefore, I am treating practising Catholics, and then faced with the transference problem, I can, by virtue of my office as a doctor, step aside and lead the problem over to the Church. But if I am treating a non-Catholic, that way out is debarred, and by virtue of my office as a doctor I cannot step aside, for there is as a rule nobody there, nothing towards which I could suitably lead the father-imago. I can, of course, get the patient to recognize with his reason that I am not the father. But by that very act I become the reasonable father and remain despite everything the father.
>
> (Jung, 1945b, p. 100)

Resolution of the negative father-transference does not simultaneously resolve the positive father-transference. According to Freud's theories, it ought to do so. Why does it not?

Jung also drew attention to a third vicissitude of the transference: patients who become dependent on the analytic process. They may be able to dispense with an analyst by substituting self-analysis for analysis by an analyst; but they are unable to dispense with preoccupation with themselves. They cannot get on with the normal business of living a life in the world.

> Significantly enough, and most curiously, there are cases where no attachment develops; the patient goes away apparently cured, but he is now so fascinated by the hinterland of his own mind that he continues to practice catharsis [i.e., self-analysis] on himself at the expense of his adaptation to life. He is bound to the unconscious, to himself, and not to the doctor.
>
> (Jung, 1931c, pp. 60–1)

Jung concluded that even after a successful analysis of the transference, its synthetic dimension remains to be addressed. Consider the following discussion from his last major work, *Mysterium Coniunctionis*:

The analyst has a right to shut his door when a neurosis no longer produces any clinical symptoms and has debouched into the sphere of general human problems. The less he knows about these the greater his chances are of coming across comparatively reasonable patients who can be weaned from the transference that regularly sets in. But if the patient has even the remotest suspicion that the analyst thinks rather more about these problems then he says, then he will not give up the transference all that quickly but will cling to it in defiance of all reason—which is not so unreasonable after all, indeed quite understandable. Even adult persons often have no idea how to cope with the problem of living, and on top of that are so unconscious in this regard that they succumb in the most uncritical way to the slightest possibility of finding some kind of answer or certainty. Were this not so, then numerous sects and -isms would long since have died out. But, thanks to unconscious, infantile attachments, boundless uncertainty and lack of self-reliance, they all flourish like weeds.

Even Freud regarded the transference as a neurosis at secondhand and treated it as such. He could not simply shut the door, but honestly tried to analyse the transference away. This is not so simple as it sounds when technically formulated. Practice often turns out to be rather different from theory. You want, of course, to put a whole man on his feet and not just a part of him. You soon discover that there is nothing for him to stand on and nothing for him to hold on to. Return to the parents has become impossible, so he hangs on to the analyst. He can go neither backwards nor forwards, for he sees nothing before him that could give him a hold.

(Jung, 1970, p. 527)

What was needed in such cases was not analysis of the transference but individuation. The patient needed to go forward, becoming dependent on neither parents nor analyst nor preoccupation with introversion. A transference onto God, such as Freud had approved in Pfister's practice, was, in Jung's terms, a transference onto the self, which was empirically indistinguishable from a transference onto the internal image of God. Jung's therapeutic strategy to displace the transference from the person of the psychotherapist, initially to one or another archetype of the unconscious—in Jones's 1914 report to Freud, onto a Platonic Idea—and later, to the self, was equivalent, for psychoanalytic purposes, to Pfister's procedure of displacing his patients' transferences from himself onto God. Jung's procedure was complicated and difficult to perform successfully, but it had two advantages. It psychologized the concept of God, by speaking of the God image that was indistinguishable from the self. A psychoanalyst could instead speak of the superego. Second, it arrived at its concept of God, not dogmatically through Christian teaching, but experientially through the interpretation of dreams, visions, and their archetypal contents.

Religion in relation to numinous experience

Jung (1938b) recognized that many religious rituals are intended precisely to produce numinous experiences.

> A great many ritualistic performances are carried out for the sole purpose of producing at will the effects of the *numinosum* by means of certain devices of a magical nature, such as invocation, incantation, sacrifice, meditation and other yoga practices, self-inflicted tortures of various descriptions, and so forth.
>
> (Jung, 1938b, p. 7)

For the most part, however, he placed numinous experiences and religion in opposition. "Since the dawn of humanity there has been a marked tendency to limit this unruly and arbitrary 'supernatural' influence by means of definite forms and laws," resulting in "a multiplication of rites, institutions, and beliefs" (Jung, 1938b, p. 19).

> The consolidation of consciousness ... was the purpose of rite and dogma; they were dams and walls to keep back the dangers of the unconscious, the "perils of the soul." Primitive rites consist accordingly in the exorcising of spirits, the lifting of spells, the averting of the evil omen, propitiation, purification, and the production by sympathetic magic of helpful occurrences.
>
> (Jung, 1954a, p. 22)

Further features of religions that resisted the occurrence of numinous experiences included magical rites. "There are any amount of magical rites that exist for the sole purpose of erecting a defense against the unexpected, dangerous tendencies of the unconscious" (Jung, 1938b, p. 18).

> What is ordinarily called "religion" is a substitute to such an amazing degree that I ask myself seriously whether this kind of "religion," which I prefer to call a creed, may not after all have an important function in human society. The substitute has the obvious purpose of replacing *immediate experience* by a choice of suitable symbols tricked out with an organized dogma and ritual.
>
> (Jung, 1938b, p. 43)

Jung regularly cautioned that numinous experiences manifest the same archetypal materials as psychosis, and that the attention that analysis pays to the archetypes invigorates them, placing patients at risk of psychosis.

> The danger inherent in analysis is that, in a psychopathically disposed patient, it will unleash a psychosis. This very unpleasant possibility generally presents itself at the beginning of the treatment, when, for instance, dream-analysis has activated the unconscious. But if it has got so far that the patient can do active imagination and shape out his fantasies, and there are no suspicious incidents, then there is as a rule no longer any danger.
>
> (Jung, 1970, p. 530)

The crucial variable, in Jung's view, was the capacity of consciousness to integrate the manifesting materials—a question, in psychoanalytic terms, of ego strength and mastery. In so far as the dogmas, rites, myths, and symbols of religion helped consciousness accomplish its work of integration, religion was a positive good, that aided consciousness to benefit from numinous experiences, rather than to be devastated by them. Referring to a variety of patients, he wrote:

> I had to go with them through the crises of passionate conflicts, through the panics of madness, through desperate confusions and depressions which were grotesque and terrible at the same time, so that I am fully aware of the extraordinary importance of dogma and ritual, at least as methods of mental hygiene.
>
> (Jung, 1938, pp. 43–4)

68 Cure of souls

Numinous manifestations of the unconscious could be pathological, making religion's opposition to them psychohygienic.

> My attitude to all religions is therefore a positive one. In their symbolism I recognize those figures which I have met with in the dreams and fantasies of my patients. In their moral teachings I see efforts that are the same as or similar to those made by my patients when, guided by their own insight or inspiration, they seek the right way to deal with the forces of psychic life. Ceremonial ritual, initiation rites, and ascetic practices, in all their forms and variations, interest me profoundly as so many techniques for bringing about a proper relation to these forces.
>
> (Jung, 1929b, p. 337)

At the same time, and on a more personal note, Jung's interest in producing and managing numinous experiences may be understood biographically in terms of his ambition to conquer psychosis. In leaving the psychoanalytic movement, he abandoned the administrative chores with which Freud had burdened him, and he resumed intensive work on his own psychiatric—as distinct from neurological—research agenda. Years before Freud likened religion to psychosis, Jung developed a program of research and treatment that proceeded on the same basis. If analysis, dream interpretation, and active imagination all ran the risk of precipitating psychoses by strengthening latent psychoses to the point of acute manifestation, then both analytical psychology and, more generally, the many religions of the world, warranted inclusion in the armamentum of psychiatry.

The nature of religion

In Freud's view, religion was a misunderstanding, a deification of a father figure. Psychoanalysis ought to dispel religion as an illusion, but is clinically unable to do so, because religion has an intransigence equivalent to the delusions of psychosis. The gap between Freud's theory of religion and his clinical impotence attested, however, to the existence of an unidentified deficiency in Freud's formulation. In Jung's view, religion was innate and inalienable. "Man has, always and everywhere, spontaneously developed a religious function, and ... the human psyche from time immemorial has been shot through with religious feeling" (Jung, 1929b, p. 339).

According to Jung, religion was not imposed from the outside, but experienced inwardly and devised in explanation of inalienable psychological experiences.

Neither the moral order, nor the idea of God, nor any religion has dropped into man's lap from outside, straight down from heaven, as it were, but ... he contains all this *in nuce* within himself, and for this reason can produce it all out of himself. It is therefore idle to think that nothing but enlightenment is needed to dispel these phantoms. The ideas of the moral order and of God belong to the ineradicable substrate of the human soul.

(Jung, 1948b, p. 278)

Experience shows that religions are in no sense conscious constructions, but that they arise from the natural life of the unconscious psyche and somehow give adequate expression to it. This explains their universal distribution and their enormous influence on humanity throughout history, which would be incomprehensible if religious symbols were not at the very least truths of man's psychological nature.

(Jung, 1934c, p. 409)

I know people for whom the encounter with the strange power within themselves was such an overwhelming experience that they called it "God." So experienced, "God" too is a "theory" in the most literal sense, a way of looking at the world, an image which the limited human mind creates in order to express an unfathomable and ineffable experience. The experience alone is real, not to be disputed.

(Jung, 1934b, p. 155)

Jung offered contradictory reasons for the existence of religion. One trend of argumentation, dating as early as 1917, made religion a mistaken evaluation of unconscious archetypes.

Here we see the characteristic effect of the archetype: it seizes hold of the psyche with that kind of primeval force and compels it to transgress the bounds of humanity. It causes exaggeration, a puffed-up attitude (inflation), loss of free will, delusion, and enthusiasm in good and evil alike. This is the reason why men have always needed

70   Cure of souls

demons and cannot live without gods, except for a few particularly clever specimens of *homo occidentalis* who lived yesterday or the day before, supermen for whom "God is dead" because they themselves have become gods—but tin-gods with thick skulls and cold hearts. The idea of God is an absolutely necessary psychological function of an irrational nature, which has nothing whatever to do with the question of God's existence.

(Jung, 1943c, pp. 70–1)

This trend in Jung's discussion of the archetypes agreed reasonably tidily with Freud's (1913b) account of evil spirits as projections. Jung made the sources of the projection inborn, where Freud assumed that they were memories; but they agreed on the empirical, clinical aspects of the phenomena. "Spirits, therefore, viewed from the psychological angle, are unconscious autonomous complexes which appear as projections because they have no direct association with the ego" (Jung, 1948e, p. 309).

If we deny the existence of the autonomous systems, imagining that we have got rid of them by a mere critique of the name, then the effect which they still continue to exert can no longer be understood, nor can they be assimilated to consciousness. They become an inexplicable source of disturbance which we finally assume must exist somewhere outside ourselves. The resultant projection creates a dangerous situation in that the disturbing effects are now attributed to a wicked will outside ourselves.

(Jung, 1938a, p. 36)

Consistent with Jung's treatment of psychical and spiritual as synonyms, the archetypes of the collective unconscious were neurotic symptoms.

We are still as much possessed by autonomous psychic contents as if they were Olympians. Today they are called phobias, obsessions, and so forth; in a word, neurotic symptoms. The gods have become diseases; Zeus no longer rules Olympus but rather the solar plexus, and produces curious specimens for the doctor's consulting room, or disorders the brains of politicians and journalists who unwittingly let loose psychic epidemics on the world.

(Jung, 1938a, p. 37)

Jung argued that for clinical purposes, religious discourse had significant advantages over secular language.

> It is not a matter of indifference whether one calls something a "mania" or a "god." To serve a mania is detestable and undignified, but to serve a God is full of meaning and promise because it is an act of submission to a higher, invisible, and spiritual being. The personification enables us to see the relative reality of the autonomous system, and not only makes its assimilation possible but also depotentiates the daemonic forces of life. When the god is not acknowledged, egomania develops, and out of this mania comes sickness.
>
> (Jung, 1938a, p. 38)

Where Freud had conceptualized religious phenomena as symptoms, ego psychology revalorized them, as we have seen, as defense mechanisms. Jung wrote of archetypes as symptoms, but he also anticipated the latter assessment. His reasoning was predicated on his general view of religion.

> The aim of the great religions is expressed in the injunction "not of this world," and this implies the inward movement of libido into the unconscious. Its withdrawal and introversion create in the unconscious a concentration of libido which is symbolized as the "treasure."
>
> (Jung, 1921, p. 250)

By their otherworldliness, religions direct psychic energy away from the external world and toward the unconscious, producing an introversion that made the energy available to the unconscious. The archetypes then put the energy to defensive use. Jung (1932b, p. 345) explained:

> To put it in scientific terms: instinctive defence-mechanisms have been built up which automatically intervene when the danger is greatest, and their coming into action during an emergency is represented in fantasy by helpful images which are ineradicably imprinted on the human psyche.

Because the archetypes functioned as defense mechanisms, they manifested consciously as provident beings—gods—whose "compensatory function" provided a corrective for inhibitions imposed by consciousness.

72 Cure of souls

Just as the products of personal complexes can be understood as compensations of onesided or faulty attitudes of consciousness, so myths of a religious nature can be interpreted as a sort of mental therapy for the sufferings of mankind, such as hunger, war, disease, old age, and death.

(Jung, 1964, p. 238)

It was in reference to religion's facilitation of the compensatory function of the unconscious that Jung named religions psychotherapeutic. "Religions are psychotherapeutic systems in the truest sense of the word, and on the grandest scale. They express the whole range of the psychic problem in mighty images" (Jung, 1934d, p. 172; see also Jung, 1930b, p. 327; 1936a, p. 162; 1946b, p. 193; 1951b, p. 121; 1970, p. 256; 1980, p. 658). Once Jung had conceptualized religion as defense mechanisms whose overall function was psychotherapeutic, he was able to entertain a series of subsidiary observations. When religions were not precisely therapeutic, they were nonetheless what might be called adaptive in ego psychology's sense of the term. Jung defended the speculative ideas of religion, for example, as hygienic.

As a doctor I am convinced that it is hygienic—if I may use the word—to discover in death a goal towards which one can strive, and that shrinking away from it is something unhealthy and abnormal which robs the second half of life of its purpose.

(Jung, 1934c, p. 402)

Other religious fantasies had equivalent merits.

The Christian doctrine of original sin on the one hand, and of the meaning and value of suffering on the other, is therefore of profound therapeutic significance.... Similarly the belief in immortality gives life that untroubled slope into the future so necessary if stoppages and regressions are to be avoided.

(Jung, 1943c, p. 81)

Jung similarly endorsed religious consolation and hope. "Sometimes spiritual consolation or psychological influence alone can cure, or at least will help to cure an illness" (Jung, 1936a, p. 103). Yet another formulation rephrased Freud's (1930, pp. 84–5) assessment that "by forcibly fixing them in a state of psychical infantilism and by drawing them into a mass-delusion, religion succeeds in sparing many people an individual neurosis. But hardly anything more." Once again, Jung agreed to the observation but evaluated it optimistically.

> In the East a great amount of practical therapy is built upon this principle of raising the mere personal ailments into a generally valid situation, and ancient Greek medicine also worked with the same method. Of course the collective image or its application has to be in accordance with the particular psychological condition of the patient. But if he is shown that his particular ailment is not his ailment only, but a general ailment—even a god's ailment—in the company of men and gods, this knowledge produces a healing effect. Modern spiritual therapy uses the same principle: pain or illness is compared with the sufferings of Christ, and this idea gives consolation. The individual is lifted out of his miserable loneliness and represented as undergoing a heroic meaningful fate which is ultimately good for the whole world, like the suffering and death of a god.
>
> (Jung, 1936a, pp. 103–4)

Where Freud had deplored religion for doing no more than sparing people the need to invent a personal neurosis, Jung praised religion for the reduction of suffering that was achieved by the process. Benefits that Freud scorned as "secondary gains" of illness, Jung valued as benefits.

Synchronicity

When Jung appropriated numinous experiences for psychotherapy, as a means to add a cure of souls to the procedures of Freud and Adler, he did so from his standpoint as a self-styled empiricist who habitually confined his remarks on religion to its phenomenology and depth psychology. He maintained the same methodological standards in his discussions of the paranormal. Jung introduced the term "synchronicity" in the late 1930s in brief remarks on the relation of body and mind (Jung, 1936a, p. 34) and matter and spirit (Jung, 1954c, p. 109). These passages were followed by major discussions of the paranormal, beginning with an article "On Synchronicity" in 1951 and the first edition of a small book, entitled

74 Cure of souls

Synchronicity, in 1952. In them, he refined his definition of synchronicity to pertain to the relation of internal, psychical events and external events in the physical world. "The synchronicity principle ... becomes the absolute rule in all cases where an inner event occurs simultaneously with an outside one" (Jung, 1969b, p. 500). Jung recognized the empirical fact of three categories of paranormal events:

1 The coincidence of a psychic state in the observer with a simultaneous, objective, external event that corresponds to the psychic state or content ... where there is no evidence of a causal connection between the psychic state and the external event, and where, considering the psychic relativity of space and time, such a connection is not even conceivable.
2 The coincidence of a psychic state with the corresponding (more or less simultaneous) external events taking place outside the observer's field of perception, i.e., at a distance, and only verifiable afterwards...
3 The coincidence of a psychic state with the corresponding, not yet existent future events that is distant in time and can likewise only be verified afterward.

(Jung, 1951c, p. 526)

Freud acknowledged the reality only of the second category, which he termed "thought-transference." Like Freud, Jung objected to the theoretical assumptions that were implicit in the term "telepathy." "A telepathically perceived event—a vision, let us say—is not the product of a telepathic faculty but rather ... the outer event *occurs simultaneously inside the psyche* and reaches consciousness by the usual pathways of the inner perception" (Jung, 1976, p. 539). Because every term carries historical baggage with it, I see no obstacle to the traditional term "clairvoyance," referring to truthful dreams, visions, and intuitions of objectively real events that are transpiring at a distance.

Freud had considered impossible what Jung (1951c, pp. 521–2; 1954d, p. 503; 1969b, pp. 447, 493, 503; 1973a) repeatedly affirmed as empirical facts: the occurrence of the third category of synchronous events.

I was able to predict the last war simply from analysing my patients' dreams, because Wotan always used to appear in them. I was not able to predict the first World War however, because even though I had premonitions myself, I was not analysing dreams in those days. Altogether, I have analysed forty-one dreams which forecast grave illness or death.

(Serrano, 1966, pp. 88–9)

These phenomena may be called "prophecy" in the language of the Bible, or "precognition" in the language of parapsychology. Both terms refer to truthful dreams, visions, and intuitions of objectively real events, outside the prophet's control, that will occur in the future.

Lastly, Freud did not so much as mention the first category that Jung listed, which may be termed a "miracle" in the language of the Bible. The same term has been adopted for cross-cultural use in the academic study of religion. Miracles are physical events whose time and place of occurrence are coincidental and, nevertheless, personally meaningful or coherent to their observer.

Jung attached no particular significance to the variable whether a synchronistic event occurred in the mind as a dream, a vision, or intuition, as clairvoyance and precognition do, or instead occurred in the physical world of sense perception, as do miracles. What was crucial for purposes of definition was the occurrence of a coincidence that was meaningful. From the fact of meaning or coherence, Jung inferred the existence of a psychic state that was unconsciously disposed to find meaning; and he built this concept of an unconscious psychic state into his description of the three categories of synchronistic phenomena.

Whichever its variety, a synchronistic experience is ordinarily numinous.

This run of events made a considerable impression on me. It seemed to me to have a certain numinous quality. In such circumstances we are inclined to say, "that cannot be mere chance," without knowing what exactly we are saying.

(Jung, 1969b, p. 426)

"The numinosity of a series of chance happenings grows in proportion to the number of its terms" (Jung, 1969b, p. 426, n. 10). "Synchronicity ... closely resembles numinous experiences where space, time, and causality are abolished" (Jung, 1977, p. 230).

Jung (1969b) referred to "meaningful coincidence" as "an acausal connection" (p. 426) because he was writing exclusively of material causality that is demonstrable by scientific means.

> It is impossible, with our present resources, to explain ESP, or the fact of meaningful coincidence, as a phenomenon of energy. This makes an end of the causal explanation as well, for "effect" cannot be understood as anything except a phenomenon of energy. Therefore it cannot be a question of cause and effect, but of a falling together in time, a kind of simultaneity. Because of this quality of simultaneity, I have picked on the term "synchronicity" to designate a hypothetical factor equal in rank to causality as a principal of explanation.
>
> (Jung, 1969b, p. 435)

Jung's conformance to the discourse of material science owed, I suggest, to his historical circumstance. Whether for reasons of his own assumptions, or those of his anticipated readers, it sufficed him to contrast causality with synchronicity. The neologism denoted the production of meaning through a coincidence in time.

> I chose this term because the simultaneous occurrence of two meaningfully but not causally connected events seem to me an essential criterion. I am therefore using the general concept of synchronicity in this special sense of a coincidence in time of two or more causally unrelated events which have the same or a similar meaning.
>
> (Jung, 1969b, p. 441)

The distinction between coincidences, which are ordinarily not meaningful, and synchronistic events, the subcategory of coincidences that are meaningful, enabled Jung to begin to move beyond the discourse of material science. "If—and it seems plausible—the meaningful coincidence or 'cross-connection' of events cannot be explained causally, then the connecting principle must lie in the equal significance of parallel events; in other words, their *tertium comparationis* is meaning" (Jung, 1969b, p. 482). "Synchronicity postulates a meaning which is a priori in relation to human consciousness and apparently exists outside of man" (Jung, 1969b, pp. 501–2; see also p. 512).

Jung recognized the difficulty of his conclusion for a conventional scientific worldview, but his commitment to empiricism left him no other option.

> We are so accustomed to regard meaning as a psychic process or content that it never enters our heads to suppose that it could also exist outside the psyche.... If, therefore, we entertain the hypothesis that one and the same (transcendental) meaning might manifest itself simultaneously in the human psyche and in the arrangement of an external and independent event, we at once come into conflict with the conventional scientific and epistemological views.
>
> (Jung, 1969b, p. 482)

Jung's commitment to empiricism may be credited with his foreclosure of the traditional theistic option. It was scientifically indemonstrable that a transcendental cause, such as God, causes synchronous events; and because the theory was indemonstrable, Jung had no use for it.

> For want of a demonstrable cause, we are all too likely to fall into the temptation of positing a transcendental one. But "cause" can only be a demonstrable quantity. A "transcendental cause" is a contradiction in terms, because anything transcendental cannot by definition be demonstrated.
>
> (Jung, 1969b, p. 446)

In his search for closure, Jung arrived at an original way of speaking of the noetic, intelligible, or thinkable realities that Freud (1927) had called *Geist*, "spirit," and "our God *Logos*." Jung spoke instead of "a general acausal orderedness" and urged that it not be confused with the archetypes; the latter are instead subject to it.

> I incline in fact to the view that synchronicity in the narrow sense is only a particular instance of general acausal orderedness—that, namely, of the equivalence of psychic and physical processes where the observer is in the fortunate position of being able to recognize the *tertium comparationis*. But as soon as he perceives the archetypal background he is tempted to trace the mutual assimilation of independent psychic and physical processes back to a (causal) effect of

78 Cure of souls

the archetype, and thus to overlook the fact that they are merely contingent. This danger is avoided if one regards synchronicity as a special instance of general acausal orderedness. In this way we also avoid multiplying our principles of explanation illegitimately, for the archetype *is* the introspectively recognizable form of a priori psychic orderedness. If an external synchronistic process now associates itself with it, it falls into the same basic pattern—in other words, it too is "ordered."

(Jung, 1969b, pp. 516–17)

Jung reverted to the topic of the general acausal orderedness in a later publication, where he introduced the puzzle of "natural or absolute knowledge."

There is also the possibility of a natural or absolute "knowledge" when the unconscious psyche coincides with objective facts. This is a problem that has been raised by the discoveries of parapsychology. "Absolute knowledge" occurs not only in telepathy and precognition, but also in biology, for instance in the attunement of the virus of hydrophobia to the anatomy of dog and man as described by Portmann, the wasp's apparent knowledge of where the motor ganglia are located in the caterpillar that is to nourish the wasp's progeny, the emission of light by certain fishes and instincts with almost 100 per cent efficiency, the directional sense of carrier pigeons, the warning of earthquakes by chickens and cats, and the amazing co-operation found in symbiotic relationships. We know, too, that the life process itself cannot be explained only by causality, but requires "intelligent" choice.

(Jung, 1958a, p. 336)

Jung, like Freud, was groping for language to express a paradigm shift. Freud (1900) had made bold to assert that dreams have meanings. His postulate necessitated the inference that unconscious meaning-making processes must exist. On its basis, he designed psychotherapy as a semiotic science (D'Andrade, 1986; Danesi, 2007) that differed from the materialistic model of the physical sciences. Where Freud composed his remarks on *Geist* and Logos in equivocal language, leaving his full meaning as esoteric subtexts for the knowledge of initiated readers, Jung expressed himself openly. He cited the empirical evidence of synchronicity as reason to place the general problem of semiotics before his readers. Why is anything meaningful? Why does the universe (apparently) conform to an orderliness that may be described (in part) by natural laws?

Because Jung rejected the concept of a "transcendental cause" as indemonstrable, we find two very different lines of thought in his further discussions. In his scientific publications and seminars, he adhered to a position that he considered empirical and scientific. He expressly rejected the traditional Tibetan Buddhist view, whose Aristotelian equivalent Freud had elected in his references to *Geist* and Logos.

> There is no evidence for, and no possibility of proving, the validity of a metaphysical postulate such as "Universal Mind." If the mind asserts the existence of a Universal Mind, we hold that it is merely making an assertion. We do not assume that by such an assertion the existence of a Universal Mind has been established. There is no argument against this reasoning, but no evidence, either, that our conclusion is ultimately right. In other words, it is just as possible that our mind is nothing but a perceptible manifestation of a Universal Mind. Yet we do not know, and we cannot even see, how it would be possible to recognize whether this is so or not.
>
> (Jung, 1954d, p. 476)

Rather than to speculate about indemonstrables, Jung was content to address subsidiary matters that, he felt, could be entertained with confidence.

> It ... seems to me, on the most conservative estimate, to be wiser not to drag the supreme metaphysical factor into our calculations, at all events not at once, but, more modestly, to make an unknown psychic or perhaps psychoid factor in the human realm responsible for inspirations and such like happenings.
>
> (Jung, 1970, pp. 550–1)

Jung's term "psychoid" was not a synonym for "psychic" or "psychical." It denoted the impossibility of conceptualizing an unconscious that could account for paranormal phenomena, by existing simultaneously in a person and in the external world. "It cannot be directly perceived or 'represented,' in contrast to the perceptible psychic phenomena, and on account of its 'irrepresentable' nature I have called it 'psychoid'" (Jung, 1969b, p. 436).

Jung's concept of the psychoid was an original variant of the traditional view that philosophers term "panpsychism" (Skrbina, 2005). "Spirit and matter may well be forms of one and the same transcendental being" (Jung, 1948c, p. 212).

> One can only conclude that the unconscious tends to regard spirit and matter not merely as equivalent but as actually identical, and this in flagrant contrast to the intellectual one-sidedness of consciousness, which would sometimes like to spiritualize matter and at other times to materialize spirit.
>
> (Jung, 1950, p. 313)

Jung evidently did not place much weight on his concept of the psychoid. Its contemplation led him rapidly into paradox.

> Does the psychic in general—the soul or spirit or the unconscious—originate in *us*, or is the psyche, in the early stages of conscious evolution, actually outside us in the form of arbitrary powers with the intentions of their own, and does it gradually take its place within us in the course of psychic development? Were the split-off "souls"—or dissociated psychic contents, as we would call them—ever parts of the psyches of individuals, or were they from the beginning psychic entities existing in themselves according to the primitive view as ghosts, ancestral spirits, and the like? Were they only by degrees embodied in man in the course of development, so that they gradually constituted in him that world which we now call the psyche?
>
> This whole idea strikes us as dangerously paradoxical, but at bottom, it is not altogether inconceivable.
>
> (Jung, 1931b, pp. 69–70)

The concept of the psychoid was presumably the most that he could assert as an empirical scientist. In interviews and personal correspondence, he instead maintained a sharply divergent position. Jung sparked a small controversy in 1958 when, in response to an interviewer's inquiry about his personal belief, he famously replied:

All that I have learned has led me step by step to an unshakable conviction of the existence of God. I only believe in what I know. And that eliminates believing. Therefore I do not take His existence on belief—I *know* that He exists.

(Jung, 1977, p. 251)

Repeatedly challenged over his remark, Jung (1976) explained himself to a correspondent:

I dislike belief in every respect, because I want to know a thing, and then I don't have to believe it if I know it. If I don't know it, it looks to me like an usurpation to say "I believe it," or the contrary. I think one ought to have at least some more or less tangible reasons for our beliefs.

(p. 445)

Jung (1977) was apparently expressing his empiricism when he told a further interviewer, "I *know*. I don't need to believe. I know" (p. 428).

On what basis did Jung claim to know that God exists? The evidence that he offered a further correspondent consisted of his experiences of the paranormal. Within his mind, he experienced "another and very often stronger will ... putting strange ideas into my head"; and in the world of sense perception, he found the same will "maneuvering my fate sometimes into most undesirable corners or giving it unexpected favourable twists, outside my knowledge and my intention." The full passage reads as follows:

When I say that I don't need to believe in God because I "know," I mean I know of the existence of God-images in general and in particular. I know it is a matter of a universal experience and, insofar as I am no exception, I know that I have such experience also, which I call God. It is the experience of my own will over against another and very often stronger will, crossing my path often with seemingly disastrous results, putting strange ideas into my head and maneuvering my fate sometimes into most undesirable corners or giving it unexpected favourable twists, outside my knowledge and my intention. The strange force against or for my conscious tendencies is well known to me. So I say, "I know Him." But why

82   Cure of souls

should you call this something "God?" I would ask: "Why not?" It has always been called "God."

(Jung, 1976, pp. 522–3)

The evidence of thought-transference led Freud to contemplate an impersonal intellectual power, an Aristotelian Intellect;[1] but he considered prophecy impossible. Jung (1973a), by contrast, had repeatedly experienced prophecy, beginning with symbolic dreams on the eve of the First World War; and the occurrences obliged him to contemplate a power that was not only intellectual, but both personal and actively intervening in human affairs. As an empiricist, he claimed to know God; but as a writer of scientific publications, he confessed that his knowledge was indemonstrable to others. He nevertheless maintained that religious experiences were synchronistic events—in religious terms, revelations or gifts of grace.

Religious experience is *numinous*, as Rudolf Otto calls it, and for me, as a psychologist, this experience differs from all others in the way it transcends the ordinary categories of space, time, and causality.... I have put a great deal of study into synchronicity (briefly, the "rupture of time"), and I have established that closely resembles numinous experiences where space, time, and causality are abolished. I bring no value judgments to bear on religious experience.

(Jung, 1977, p. 230)

There are various points in his scientific writings where Jung confessed himself a Protestant Christian, but overmuch weight ought not to be placed on his institutional affiliation. Leaving aside all of the many passages where he discussed the God image in the unconscious, I have found only a single passage where he wrote of God as distinct from the God image in a fashion that committed his psychological theories to theism. Jung (1952d) wrote:

---

1   Editor's note: Here Merkur is referring to Aristotle's notion of the Active Intellect, which is the determinate power of reason or Logos, as opposed to passive and acquired Intellects, which is receptive thinking and the product of experiential knowledge (see *De Anima*, bk. III, ch. 5, 430a10–25; *Metaphysics*, book xii, chs 7–10).

It would be going perhaps too far to speak of an affinity; but at all events the soul must contain in itself the faculty of relationship to God, i.e., a correspondence, otherwise a connection could never come about. *This correspondence is, in psychological terms, the archetype of the God-image.*

(p. 11; italics in original)

For the God image to be one term in a correspondence, the God who is the other term must have a reality independent of the "unknown psychic or perhaps psychoid factor in the human realm." All that he could argue as a scientist, however, was the centrality of the God image in human psychological experience.

Just as man, as a social being, cannot in the long run exist without a tie to the community, so the individual will never find the real justification for his existence and his own spiritual and moral autonomy anywhere except in an extramundane principle capable of relativizing the overpowering influence of external factors. The individual who is not anchored in God can offer no resistance on his own resources to the physical and moral blandishments of the world. For this he needs the evidence of the inner, transcendent experience which alone can protect him from the otherwise inevitable submersion in the mass.

(Jung, 1957b, p. 258)

Jung here argued that an "inner, transcendent experience" leads people to become "anchored in God." Because his phrasing was equivocal, he can be misunderstood to have affirmed the existence of a transcendent God. Readers familiar with his thought will know, however, that he implicitly referred to the God image.

Jung's client population

Jung devised his practice of analytical psychology not to rival Freud's psychoanalysis and Adler's individual psychology, but to complement and augment them. Jung (1943e) maintained that "the neuroses of the young generally come from a collision between the forces of reality and an inadequate, infantile attitude," and that these neuroses were best treated through "the reductive methods of Freud and Adler" (Jung, 1943c,

84   Cure of souls

p. 59; see also Jung, 1929a, pp. 38–9). "For young people a liberation from the past may be enough: a beckoning future lies ahead, rich in possibilities. It is sufficient to break a few bonds; the life-urge will do the rest" (Jung, 1943c, p. 60). Jung's (1938a) original contribution to psychotherapy "has scarcely any meaning before the middle of life (normative between the ages of thirty-five and forty), and if entered upon too soon can be decidedly injurious" (p. 14). It was also inappropriate for deeply troubled individuals. "The severer neuroses usually require a reductive analysis of their symptoms and states.... So long as one is moving in the sphere of genuine neurosis one cannot dispense with the views of either Freud or Adler" (Jung, 1935b, pp. 19–20).

Jung offered analytical psychology to several different client populations. First were

> people who have left a large part of their life behind them, for whom the future no longer beckons with marvelous possibilities, and nothing is to be expected but the endless round of familiar duties and the doubtful pleasures of old age.
>
> (Jung, 1943b, p. 60)

> We are speaking not of people who still have to prove their social usefulness, but of those who can no longer see any sense in being socially useful and who have come upon the deeper and more dangerous question of the meaning of their own individual lives.
>
> (Jung, 1929a, pp. 47–8)

> We are no longer concerned with how to remove the obstacles to a man's profession, or to his marriage, or do anything that means a widening of his life, but are confronted with the task of finding a meaning that will enable him to continue living at all—a meaning more than blank resignation and mournful retrospect.
>
> (Jung, 1943b, p. 74)

In some discussions of patients in middle age, Jung described the psychological syndrome that is today termed "mid-life crisis" (Jacques, 1965).

> There are many neuroses which either appear only at maturity or else deteriorate to such a degree that the patients become incapable of

work. Naturally one can point out in these cases that an unusual dependence on the parents existed even in youth, and that all kinds of infantile delusions were present; but all that did not prevent them from taking up a profession, from practicing it successfully, from keeping up a marriage of sorts until that moment in riper years when the previous attitude suddenly failed.

(Jung, 1943b, pp. 59–60)

The transition from morning to afternoon means a revaluation of the earlier values. There comes the urgent need to appreciate the value of the opposite of our former ideals, to perceive the error in our former convictions, to recognize the untruths in our former truth, and to feel how much antagonism and even hatred lay in what, until now, had passed for love. Not a few of those who are drawn into the conflict of opposites jettison everything that had previously seem to them good and worth striving for; for they try to live in complete opposition to their former ego. Changes of profession, divorces, religious convulsions, apostasies of every description, are the symptoms of this swing over to the opposite. The snag about a radical conversion into one's opposite is that one's former life suffers repression and thus produces just as unbalanced a state as existed before, when the counterparts of the conscious virtues and values were still repressed and unconscious.

(Jung, 1943b, p. 75)

A second client population for analytical psychology consisted of patients who were themselves religious, and for whom a non-religious method of treatment was neither credible nor meaningful.

Why should he bother his head about science? If he is a religious person, his relationship to God will mean infinitely more to him than any scientifically satisfactory explanation, just as it is a matter of indifference to a sick man *how* he gets well so long as he does it well. Our patient, indeed any patient, is treated correctly only when he is treated as an individual. This means entering into his particular problem and not giving him an explanation based on "scientific" principles that goes clean over his head although it may be quite correct biologically.

(Jung, 1918, p. 24; see also Jung, 1970, p. 366)

86   Cure of souls

Other clients who could benefit from analytical psychology were people who suffered from a lack of meaning in their lives, owing to life choices that had left them unsatisfied.

> I have frequently seen people become neurotic when they content themselves with inadequate or wrong answers to the questions of life. They seek position, marriage, reputation, outward success or money, and remain unhappy and neurotic even when they have attained what they were seeking. Such people are usually confined within too narrow a spiritual horizon. Their life has not sufficient content, sufficient meaning. If they are enabled to develop into more spacious personalities, the neurosis generally disappears. For that reason the idea of development was always of the highest importance to me.
>
> (Jung, 1973b, p. 140)

In his *Visions* seminar, Jung suggested that the problem of insufficient meaning was not neurotic in the medical sense of the term, but should instead be regarded as a kind of underachievement.

> The people who have not the power to live in a higher consciousness are not really neurotic; they are only neurotic if they put up against a certain task, say just this task of reaching a higher condition which would enable them to overcome a particular difficulty. You see, many people who are supposed to be neurotic are not exactly that, they suffer from nothing in particular, they are just not efficient. And then something comes along and they are upset because they are called upon to make an effort to reach the more comprehensive con-sciousness which they *ought* to reach.
>
> (Jung, 1997, p. 1327)

A further clientele to whom Jung offered analytical psychology were genuine neurotics, whom he treated with Freudian or Adlerian approaches, as cases warranted, but whose treatment had become stalled.

> When the thing becomes monotonous and you begin to get repeti-tions, and your unbiased judgment tells you that a standstill has been

reached, when mythological or archetypal contents appear, then is the time to give up the analytical-reductive method and to treat the symbols anagogically or synthetically, which is equivalent to the dialectical procedure and the way of individuation.

(Jung, 1935b, p. 20)

Jung expected that psychoanalytic treatments would sooner or later inevitably bog down, because Freud artificially limited psychoanalysis when he excluded pedagogy from its procedures.

Freud has often been compared to a dentist, drilling out the carious tissue in the most painful manner. So far the comparison holds true, but not when it comes to the gold-filling. Freudian psychology does not fill the gap. If our critical reason tells us that in certain respects we are irrational and infantile, or that all religious beliefs are illusions, what are we to do about our irrationality, what are we to put in place of our exploded illusions?

(Jung, 1939b, p. 47)

Jung also expected that "mythological or archetypal contents" would inevitably appear sooner or later, as the "reductive" methods emptied the "personal unconscious" and gave the "collective unconscious" the opportunity to manifest. Jung's formulation may be translated meaningfully into Freudian terms. Jung identified the collective unconscious with the superego (Jung, 1951b, p. 120; 1958a, p. 348; 1958b, pp. 439–40; 1970, p. 473), and he discussed the individual archetypes within it in terms appropriate to individual ego ideals. "The archetype as an image of instinct is a spiritual goal toward which the whole of nature of man strives" (Jung, 1954b, p. 212). From a psychoanalytic perspective, we may expect that in resolving or at least reducing fixations, analysis will free symbolic materials for sublimated uses as ego ideals. Every successful analysis will shift in its concerns from mostly id materials to mostly ego ideals—in Jung's terms, from mostly personal unconscious to mostly collective. Although subsidiary theoretical differences remain to be resolved, there can be no serious question as to Jung's clinical observations—and to his priority. Jung (1948a, p. 472) discovered the collective unconscious in "about 1912."

Apologies for irrationalism

Pragmatic, clinical considerations motivated Jung's accommodation of religion. "The essential question is: what will pierce through this fog of verbiage to the conscious personality of the patient, and what must be the nature of his attitude?" (Jung, 1934d, p. 174). "What is rationally correct is too narrow a concept to grasp life in its totality and give it permanent expression" (Jung, 1921, p. 189). "Certain religious convictions not founded on reason are a vital necessity for many people. Again, there are psychic realities which can cause or cure diseases" (Jung, 1931b, p. 356).

> For thousands of years the religious symbol proved a most efficacious device in the moral education of mankind. Only a prejudiced mind could deny such an obvious fact. Concrete values cannot take the place of the symbol; only new and more effective symbols can be substituted for those that are antiquated and outworn and have lost their efficacy through the progress of intellectual analysis and understanding. The further development of the individual can be brought about only by means of symbols which represent something far in advance of himself and whose intellectual meanings cannot yet be grasped entirely. The individual unconscious produces such symbols, and they are of the greatest possible value in the moral development of the personality.
>
> (Jung, 1916c, p. 293)

Jung considered scientific values to be an unrealistic expectation and intolerable burden for many and perhaps most patients.

> Our age is afflicted with a blindness that has no parallel. We think we have only to declare an accepted article of faith incorrect and invalid, and we shall be psychologically rid of all the traditional effects of Christianity or Judaism. We believe in enlightenment, as if an intellectual change of front somehow had a profounder influence on the emotional processes or even on the unconscious. We entirely forget that the religion of the last two thousand years is a psychological attitude, a definite form and manner of adaptation to the world without and within, that lays down a definite cultural pattern and creates an atmosphere which remains wholly uninfluenced by any intellectual denials. The change of front is, of course, symptomatically important

as an indication of possibilities to come, but on the deeper levels the psyche continues to work for a long time in the old attitude.

(Jung, 1921, p. 185)

Clinicians were obliged, Jung insisted, to meet their patients at whatever cultural level had psychic reality for them.

The physician's recognition of the spiritual factors in their true light is vitally important, and the patient's unconscious comes to the aid of this vital need by producing dreams whose content is essentially religious. Not to recognize the spiritual source of such contents means faulty treatments and failure.

(Jung, 1931b, p. 356)

The psychotherapist who takes his work seriously must come to grips with this question. He must decide in every single case whether or not he is willing to stand by a human being with counsel and help upon what may be a daring misadventure. He must have no fixed ideas as to what is right, nor must he pretend to know what is right and what not—otherwise he takes something from the richness of the experience. He must keep in view what actually happens—for only that which acts is actual. If something which seems to me an error shows itself to be more effective than a truth, then I must follow-up the error, for in it lie power and life which I lose if I hold to what seems to me true.

(Jung, 1932b, p. 343)

In keeping with his view of the intrinsic and inalienable religiosity of the psyche, Jung maintained that no effort to eliminate patients' religiosity could actually succeed. When clinicians exploit the psychoanalytic situation to suppress their patients' religiosity, they never accomplish more than to oblige the religiosity to undergo displacement.

You can take away a man's gods, but only to give him others in return. The leaders of the mass states could not help being deified, and wherever crudities of this kind have not yet been put over by force, obsessive factors arise in their stead, charged with demonic energy—money, work, political influence, and so forth.

(Jung, 1957b, p. 280)

90 Cure of souls

Jung's example of the deification of leaders of mass states made his point vivid; but attention should also be paid to the authority that classical psychoanalysts wielded over the patients, which included the passive aggressive and obsessive aspects of the classical psychoanalytic set-up.

At the same time, Jung's recourse to pragmatism had a negative consequence to which pragmatism is inevitably always liable. When does compromise go too far? My guess is that most psychoanalysts would feel that the following recommendation went too far, and that Jung was advocating that clinicians collude with their patients' illness.

> Our patient is confronted with the power of will and suggestion more than equal to anything his consciousness can put against it. In this precarious situation it would be bad strategy to convince him that in some incomprehensible way he is at the back of his own symptom, secretly inventing and supporting it. Such a suggestion would instantly paralyse his fighting spirit, and he would get demoralized. It is far better for him to understand that his complex is an autonomous power directed against his conscious personality. Moreover, such an exclamation fits the actual facts much better than a reduction to personal motives. An apparently personal motivation does exist, but it is not made by his will, it just happens to him.
>
> (Jung, 1938b, p. 16)

In order to avoid what he called "bad strategy," Jung here advocated lying to patients in order not to demoralize them. Rather than to encourage patients—gently, gradually—to take ownership of their defenses, to recognize the ego-dystonicity of the latter, and to inquire after their own unconscious motives for engaging in habitual self-deceptions, Jung supported his patients' disavowal of responsibility. By neglecting to mention that archetypes were defense mechanisms, he allowed patients to personify split-off parts of their personalities as autonomous archetypes for which the ego bore no responsibility.

The continuation of the same passage indicates that Jung was well aware that he was crossing swords with psychoanalysis on this particular issue. He made bold to suggest that Freud's sexual theories were a defense against numinous experiences.

If, therefore, a patient is convinced of the exclusively sexual origin of his neurosis, I would not disturb him in his opinion because I know that such a conviction, particularly if it is deeply rooted, is an excellent defence against an onslaught of immediate experience with its terrible ambiguity. So long as such a defence works I shall not break it down, since I know that there must be cogent reasons why the patient has to think in such a narrow circle. But if his dreams should begin to destroy the protective theory, I have to support the wider personality.

(Jung, 1938b, pp. 44–5)

Jung (1970, 1996) wrote and lectured on the sexual theories of the Kabbalah, the Tantric practice of kundalini yoga, and the incest motifs of Western alchemy. He assuredly knew that he was writing nonsense in this passage. Sexual ideas do not inhibit numinous experiences, but may instead infuse and be made ecstatic by them. In calling Freud's ideas "a narrow circle" and boasting himself a "wider personality," he was winking at his readers while having sport.

Jung's limited therapeutic ambitions

Jung penned several severe criticisms of analytical psychology. Above all, he did not aim at cure. He aimed not to end suffering, but to reconcile people to their suffering.

The patient has not to learn how to get rid of his neurosis, but how to bear it. His illness is not a gratuitous and therefore meaningless burden; it is *his own self,* the "other" whom, from childish laziness or fear, or for some other reason, he was always seeking to exclude from his life.

(Jung, 1934d, pp. 169–70, italics in original)

Jung's enlargement of these striking statements make them somewhat less extraordinary, but what was not said continues to be alarming.

We should not try to "get rid" of a neurosis, but rather to experience what it means, what it has to teach, what its purpose is. We should even learn to be thankful for it, otherwise we pass it by and miss the opportunity of getting to know ourselves as we really are. A neurosis is truly removed only when it has removed the false attitude of the ego. We do not cure it—it skewers us. A man is ill, but the illness is nature's attempt to heal him. From the illness itself we can learn so much for our recovery, and what the neurotic flings away as absolutely worthless contains the true gold we should never have found elsewhere.

(Jung, 1934d, p. 170)

Jung made two statements here. In keeping with his synthetic method of dream interpretation, he conceptualized neurotic symptoms not as so much nonsense to be discarded in favor of their latent content, but as invaluable sources of information concerning the directions of healthy growth. However, he did not begin by agreeing with Freud's assertion that the illness is a failed attempt to heal, and then add that the failure can be corrected by re-directing the healing process toward health. He instead contradicted Freud flatly, with the remark that "the illness is nature's attempt to heal." His phrasing implied that nothing was amiss, that the trajectory of the illness was to be continued. He took for granted, of course, that archetypal manifestations were immutable. Neurotic symptoms consisted precisely of archetypal materials that had become conscious. All that was variable was whether consciousness handled them badly or well. There was nothing unconscious for the therapist to help make conscious. Neither was a cure to be sought in any such direction.

Jung offered his patients the possibility of what he called "individuation" through a "transcendent function." The therapeutic achievement amounted to a cultivation of psychological-mindedness regarding the vicissitudes of the archetypes, much as psychoanalytic ego-psychology's aim at "self-observation" (Sterba, 1934) amounts to a cultivation of psychological-mindedness regarding the ego's defense mechanisms and the unconscious Oedipus complex. Jung was of two minds, however, as to whether psychological-mindedness was desirable.

Then of course the question comes: Which is better—what should be? Well, obviously there are two opinions. The God of the Old Testament says: "Don't be an 'I,' don't eat of that tree, or you will see how unconscious and pitiful you are, how pitiful is the thing I have made." And the other point of view is: "Be as conscious as you can, be responsible to your self, for you will thereby spare much evil not only to yourself but also to your surroundings." Now, we don't know which is right. The decision is always the particular task of the time—whether we are forced this way or that, to be a collective people or a more individual people. I cannot decide it in many cases. I have said to quite a number of people that they had better go another way. If you are interested in Catholicism, or are a Catholic, remain in the fold of the church. Or join this or that other movement, where you are no longer "I." I am quite convinced that there are numbers of people who are not meant to be "I," but to live in the world of old Jehovah where everything is perfect. But there are numbers of people who are not meant to be perfect and who cannot live in the world of old Jehovah.

(Jung, 1988, p. 676)

In stating that individuation was not for everyone, Jung tacitly acknowledged that his therapy had limited effectiveness. "A number of my patients have joined this [Oxford Group] movement with my entire approval, just as others have become Catholics, or at least better Catholics than they were before" (Jung, 1935b, p. 16). When patients found their way to an institutional religious outlet, Jung did not introduce them to the "dialectical procedure" on which the transcendent function depended.

There is no point in promoting individual development beyond the needs of the patient. If he can find the meaning of his life and the cure for his disquiet and disunity within the framework of an existing credo—including a political credo—that should be enough for the doctor.

(Jung, 1935b, pp. 16–17)

A patient's failure to find an institutional outlet for the collective unconscious was, in Jung's view, reason to encourage individuation. "Then the impersonal factors have no receptacle, and so the patient falls back into the transference, and the archetypal images spoil the human relation to the analyst" (Jung, 1936a, p. 165). Other categories of patient to whom Jung offered individuation were the irreligious and the eccentrically religious.

94   Cure of souls

There are, however, very many patients who have either no religious convictions at all or highly unorthodox ones. Such persons are, on principle, not open to any conviction. All rational therapy leaves them stuck where they were, although on the face of it their illness is quite durable. In these circumstances nothing is left but the dialectical development of the mythological material which is alive in the sick man himself, regardless of history and tradition.

(Jung, 1935b, p. 17)

By "rational therapy," Jung referred to approaches, such as psychoanalysis and individual psychology, that aspire to promote rationality through a reduction of irrationality. Jung considered any such effort improper, unethical, and a boundary violation.

To replace a Christian view of the world by a materialistic one is, to my way of thinking, just as wrong as the attempt to argue with the convinced materialist. That is the task of the missionary, not of the doctor.

(Jung, 1951b, p. 117)

Ethics aside, pragmatic clinical issues were at stake. It was no use attempting to produce a spiritual awakening or religious conversion experience in a patient who was already religious. Active imagination would not then be effective.

There are many normal cases in which, under certain circumstances, a character opposed to the conscious personality suddenly manifests itself, causing a conflict between the two personalities.

Take the classic case of the temptation of Christ, for example. We say that the devil tempted him, but we could just as well say that an unconscious desire for power confronted him in the form of the devil...

Naturally, these experiences appear only in people without religious convictions. For where there is a definite belief there are also definite concepts from among which a symbol can be chosen. Thus conflict is avoided, or rather the opposite does not appear, being hidden beneath a dogmatic image.... If any conflict appears, it is immediately repressed or resolved by a definite religious idea. That is why the transcendent function can be observed only in people who no longer have their original religious conviction, or never had any, and who, in consequence, find themselves directly faced with their unconscious.

(Jung, 1973a, pp. 267–8)

Religious people have adequate compromise formations available to them in the form of traditional religious symbolism. Their dreams and imaginations do not need to go through the laborious procedure of first producing symbols of their conflicts or opposite, before arriving at original compromise formations. Instead, their unconscious draws directly on compromise formations to which they already subscribe. For this reason, analytical psychology is not a means to correct morbidities in already existing religiosity. It is as powerless as Freud and Reik found psychoanalysis, but for different reasons.

The advanced phases of analytic psychology constituted, in Jung's term, an "irrational" therapy. Their goal was the production of compromise-formations.

In practice, opposites can be united only in the form of a compromise, or *irrationally*, some new thing arising between them which, although different from both, yet has the power to take up their energies in equal measure as an expression of both and of neither.

(Jung, 1921, p. 105)

Jung agreed with Freud that compromise-formations often took the form of symbols. Where, however, Freud considered compromise-formation symptomatic of unresolved conflicts, Jung valued the process positively, as the necessary precondition of psychological-mindedness of the neurosis or other complaint that cannot be cured, but only endured.

The much-needed union of conscious and unconscious ... cannot be accomplished either intellectually or in a purely practical sense, because in the former case the instincts rebel and in the latter case reason and morality. Every dissociation that falls within the category of the psychogenic neuroses is due to a conflict of this kind, and the conflict can only be resolved through the symbol. For this purpose the dreams produce symbols which in the last analysis coincide with those recorded throughout history.

(Jung, 1948d, p. 191)

Jung's testimony is persuasive. His practice of analytical psychology did not produce cures of psychopathology. It produced numinous experiences that could be interpreted in manners that culminated in spiritual awakenings to the self or image of God. These awakenings were irrational and cast in the form of symbols. They aspired neither to rationality nor to the resolution of compromise formations.

Jung (1973a) was naive in his disclaimer, "If you have formed the peculiar notion that I am proclaiming a religion, this is due to your ignorance of psychotherapeutic methods" (p. 361). His original formulations of comparative mythology and religion, included not a little dilettantism, errors in fact, Eurocentric, male chauvinist, and Christian prejudice, etc. His position did not fit honestly within the Protestant tradition that he claimed, nor did he make a clean break with dogmatism in order to aspire, so far as possible, to a pure empiricism. For all of its limitations, his work, integrating the Protestant cure of souls within the modern development of depth psychotherapy, was a stunning achievement.

Writing twenty years after his break with Jung, Freud discerningly summarized some major differences between the therapeutic techniques.

Suppose, for instance, that an analyst attaches little value to the influence of the patient's personal past and looks for the causation of neuroses exclusively in present-day motives and in expectations of the future. In that case he will also neglect the analysis of childhood; he will have to adopt an entirely different technique and will have to make up for the omission of the events from the analysis of childhood by increasing his didactic influence and by directly indicating certain particular aims in life. We for our part will then say: "This may be a school of wisdom; but it is no longer analysis."

(Freud, 1933, p. 143)

Freud's preoccupations kept him from appreciating that Jung did not begin with a disinterest in the patient's personal past. Jung interpreted the transference in terms of parental memories; but when independence was achieved of the parents, he regarded the remaining transference onto the therapist not as a good parent transference, but as the transference of a numinous archetype. The task of transference interpretation had moved, in his model, from the personal to the collective unconscious. If psychoanalysts insist that the shift proceeds from fixation to sublimation, the formulation remains an unearned assumption.

The balance of Freud's remarks remains judicious, however. Jung's technique of "amplification" involves selectively teaching patients a goodly amount of comparative mythology, as a means to guide their understanding of their dreams, visions, and other symbolic productions away from their own associations to accommodate the scholasticism of their therapists. The procedure requires the therapist to teach the patient about the desirable or normative relations to each of several archetypes. Jung was also guilty of pedagogy in a further respect. As he acknowledged, "the soul possesses by nature a religious function, and ... it is the prime task of all education (of adults) to convey the archetype of the God-image, or its emanations and defects, to the conscious mind" (Jung, 1952d, pp. 12–13). Freudian patients arguably do not need to be taught as much in order to recognize and self-regulate their autonomy. A measure of didacticism comparable to Jungian analysis is inevitable, however, of any other modern cure of souls. Didacticism becomes unavoidable whenever therapy addresses not the route by which the patient has come, but the very different route by which the patient may best travel in the future.

Freud's characterization of analytical psychology as "a school of wisdom" involved a play on words. *Schule der Weisheit*, "School of Wisdom," was the name that Count Herman von Keyserling gave his teaching academy in Darmstadt, which opened in 1919. Keyserling intended his school to be a "breeding ground of higher culture" that would connect soul and spirit (*Seele und Geist*). He aspired to an ecumenism that would unite the East and the West and positioned his approach near Anthroposophy, despite its rejection by Rudolf Steiner as "mental shortness of breath." In addition, once or twice each year Keyserling hosted week-long conferences, called *Tagungen*, that offered lectures by an international array of spiritual luminaries and drew hundreds of attendees, including royalty and aristocracy; the latter were of keener interest to many attendees than the lecturers were (Landau, 1935). Keyserling was psychoanalyzed by several analysts, beginning in 1922 with Oscar A. H. Schmitz, author of *Psychoanalysis and Yoga*, and

98   Cure of souls

continuing with Hans von Hattingberg. According to Karl Abraham, Freud referred Keyserling to him at a psychoanalytic meeting in 1925 (Feuchtner, 2011, pp. 91–2).

Jung attended occasional conferences at Darmstadt from 1923 onward; it was there that he first met Richard Wilhelm, the Sinologist with whom he collaborated on the "The Secret of the Golden Flower" and the *I Ching* (Jung, 1973b, p. 373). A letter from May 1923 recorded Jung's evaluation of Keyserling's project at the time.

> Though it would be wrong to draw a parallel between Darmstadt and theosophy, it does seem to me that the same danger exists in both cases: a new house being built on the old shaky foundations, and of new wine being poured into old bottles. Though the old damage is covered up, the new building does not stand firm. Man must after all be changed from within, otherwise he merely assimilates the new material to the old pattern.
>
> (Jung, 1973a, p. 40)

By 1930 Jung was lecturing at the School of Wisdom (Jung, 1973a, p. 313, n. 2), and Freud, writing in 1933, announced the fact.

Concluding reflections

Antoine Vergote (1998), an orthodox psychoanalyst and a Jesuit, criticized Jung's cure of souls on the grounds that its methodological agnosticism was so far from being a concession to religious faith as to constitute its mockery and betrayal. "The therapist cannot use religion to cure under the penalty of inducing in his patient a spirit of calculation that, in any event, does not cure the true pathology but falsifies religious faith" (p. 271). Because therapy is not the *raison d'être* of religion, a spiritual director or curer of souls who deploys religion not for its own sake, but for the purpose of therapy, necessarily falsifies the religion. Vergote allowed, however, that qualified individuals might undertake the dual procedure.

> The principles that I have affirmed do not prevent combining therapy and spiritual direction in the proper sense in certain cases where the person asks for two forms of help from someone sufficiently trained

Cure of souls 99

in both areas. Obviously, in this case, it is necessary that the properly spiritual assistance fit a properly religious intention and that it not be proposed with any other purpose than that of bringing about a relationship to God in greater truth. Of course, in this case, the therapy will not be the psychoanalytic treatment, even though the therapist may work from this model.

(Vergote, 1998, p. 272)

The interdisciplinary limitations and boundaries that Freud, Pfister, and Jung articulated in the 1910s and 1920s, and that Vergote reaffirmed in the 1990s, remain valid. As psychoanalysts we should not be asking, as most of the contemporary "spiritually integrated" literature is content to do, how far clinicians can accommodate existing religions. It is one thing to explore, as the psychoanalytic mystics have done, the spirituality inherent in psychoanalysis: the unitive principles (Eros) of wholeness, integration, and individuation; the moral principles of truth and integrity, and so forth. It is quite another to interpolate selected elements of non-analytic spiritualities within psychoanalysis just because a patient or an analyst happens to like the Buddhist, Christian, Jewish, or whatever interpolation. We should be doing psychoanalysis and not compromising it for the purposes of diplomacy and market-share. In the pious rush of religious analysts to speak piously with their patients, the scientific task is being shirked. The current *Zeitgeist* may make the brand name of psychoanalysis more acceptable to the pious, but spiritually supportive psychotherapies regularly proceed at the cost of debasing the product.

Psychoanalysis without a compatible cure of souls may well be analogous to surgery without post-operative rehabilitation. Compromising psychoanalysis is not, however, an appropriate foundation for developing a contemporary cure of souls. A therapist who will not say hard words when they are warranted can never master Freud's art. If analysts are to widen the scope of psychotherapy beyond psychoanalysis into the domain of spirituality, it will remain the analytic task not to cater politely to religions, but to follow Freud and Fromm in exposing idolatries wherever they are found.

As Freud wrote Ludwig Binswanger on October 8, 1936, psychoanalysis, if it is to be psychoanalysis, must address the topic of spirituality by building its data base and theories from the bottom up.

I have never ventured beyond the ground floor and basement of the building.—You maintain that if one changes one's point of view one can also see a higher floor, in which there live such distinguished guests as religion, art, etc. You are not alone in this; most cultivated specimens of *homo natura* think likewise. You are the conservative in this respect, and I the revolutionary. If I still had a lifetime of work ahead of me, I should dare to assign a home in my lowly little house to those highborn personages. I have already done so for religion since coming across the category "neurosis of mankind." But we are probably speaking at cross purposes and it will take centuries before our differences are settled.

(Freud and Binswanger, 2003, p. 212)

Freud was not here making a claim to reduce what he called spirituality to something else, although he suspected that Binswanger would mistake his meaning that way. Fromm's claim that psychoanalysis is a humanistic religion was not incompatible with Freud's claim that psychoanalysis is a part of science. Assuming that there is truth to spirituality, it must necessarily be possible to conduct a spirituality, so far as possible, along scientific lines. Philosophers find problems, of course, with the concept of a *natural spirituality*. Owing to the history of theology, the phrase only too easily gives rise to a category mistake that implies a claim to timeless and universal truths, like the laws of physics. A natural spirituality would, however, warrant classification among the semiotic sciences, such as linguistics, aesthetics, anthropology, the sociology of knowledge, and selected portions of psychology (D'Andrade, 1986). The semiotic sciences are concerned not with the relations among empirical things, but with the relations among signifiers, the things signified, and the process of signification. Semiotic science might be concerned, for example, with what makes a good television show, where physical science addresses how to make a functioning television set. Granting that the details of a *natural spirituality* remain to be worked out, the premise that Freud and Fromm shared remains tenable. What Freud wrote Binswanger was that if we are to talk psychoanalytically of higher mental functions and their cultural achievements, we shall have to approach the cultural achievements from the bottom up in keeping with the procedures of science. The psychoanalytic mystics (Merkur, 2010) have begun this project but have drawn, as I have shown, overly freely on traditional spiritualities in order to fill gaps in their psychoanalytic procedures. As befits pioneers, they are both to be commended and acknowledged to have had limitations. The psychoanalytic mystics offer a variety of would-be natural spiritualities; but we also need clinical procedures, as Reik remonstrated, for working with morbid spiritualities. Neither philosophy nor theology nor speculative scientific theorizing can provide serviceable shortcuts.

Chapter 3

The creativity of dreams

On November 24, 1912, at a meeting in Munich of the presidents of the local branch societies of the International Psychoanalytic Association, Jung proposed that the Fourth International Psychoanalytic Congress, which was to be held in Munich on September 7–8, 1913, be devoted to the theme of "The Teleological Function of Dreams." The presidents decided that the theme would instead be "The Function of Dreams" (Freud and Jung, 1974, pp. 522, 547). What was at stake in the deleted emphasis on teleology?

Freud, Adler, Jung, Maeder and others debated the issue in lectures and/ or publications of 1912–13, whose experience-distant formulations make it rather difficult to understand the controversy.[1] The underlying clinical issue can be identified, I suggest, through passages in two of Jung's seminars that went unpublished during his lifetime: *Dream Analysis*, which he taught in 1928–30; and *Visions*, given in 1930–34. In both passages, Jung stressed the importance for dream interpretation to be based on the choice of manifest symbolism. In *Dream Analysis*, Jung (1984) stated:

> This is where I differ from Freud. You cannot say the symbol in a dream is merely a façade behind which you can hide and then say what the dream is. The symbol is a fact, as in this dream it is a sewing-machine, and we can only go on with the dream by understanding what the sewing-machine means. We cannot merely say that the sewing-machine

---

1 Editor's note: The controversy was likely influenced by the inherent Aristotelianism implied in the notion of *telos*, hence a final end, goal, or purpose, that was seen by many as incompatible with the scientific viewpoint of the day that assumed causality was governed by material-efficient reductive explanations, while teleology was deemed an obstacle to such a deterministic model. This was further compounded by the bias against freewill and choice that challenged reductive arguments.

The creativity of dreams   103

means a method of getting new clothes, for you can get new clothes in a number of ways: in a mystical way, a magical way, etc. The point of the sewing-machine method would mean a mechanical way, purely of cause and effect, a soulless way. You get the idea of what this mechanical way can be by studying the patient's associations. A symbol in a dream is meant to be what is.

(pp. 93–4)

Jung routinely objected to Freud's (1925, p. 131) analogy of the manifest dream to a façade. Here alone he provided a clarifying illustration. He referred to what may be called the dream's choice of the manifest content. Jung expressed the same opinion in his *Visions* seminar, but without a clarifying illustration his meaning remained obscure.

It is always advisable to enter into the detail of the symbolism; it is by no means indifferent what symbol the dream chooses. In this respect I take a different standpoint from the Freudian school to whom the particular character of the symbolism is absolutely indifferent; ten thousand things can mean the same thing—the genitals, say. But I insist that what the dream actually says is all-important, rather than the interpretation which we put into it. We might go astray with our interpretation, but the dream is a natural fruit, a product of nature, and we have not organized or produced it.

(Jung, 1997, p. 23)

Let me immediately provide an example from my own clinical practice. A patient, whose son was five months old, dreamt: *I was meeting Georgia and her daughter for the first time. I was surprised that the girl was three years old, very beautiful, with long blonde hair. I very much enjoyed seeing her.* The patient's associations to the dream all concerned the day residue. Georgia is a woman whom my patient met and befriended in an expectant mothers' group. They were well on their way to becoming close friends; but when she gave the woman unsolicited advice, Georgia's husband took offense and forbade Georgia to have further contact with her. Recently, however, the two women found themselves in a new mothers' group that each joined independently, and they struck up an e-correspondence in advance of meeting. But once again Georgia stopped all contacts without explanation; my patient guessed that the husband may again have intervened. At the time of the dream, Georgia's daughter was two months old; the dream inexplicably represented her as of preschool age.

My patient had no further associations. In a previous session she had said that she would like to have a second child; and in each of the last two sessions, we had discussed the residue of distrust that she continues to feel toward me, after seven or eight years of productive and amicable therapy, as a father-transference. Earlier in the session in which she had related the dream, I had addressed the fearful father-transference a third time, now in reference to her former employer. Then she told me the dream. So I suggested to her that the manifest content of her enjoyment of Georgia's daughter represented her genuine feelings. According to Freud (1900), the manifest and latent affects in a dream are always the same. If so, the dream might be a wish-fulfillment, depicting her own desire specifically for a girl-child, additional to her son. My patient found this interpretation close to her heart. And so I added: "Perhaps the dream portrays you as Georgia in order to imply a comparison between Georgia's husband and your husband." My patient immediately understood the transference implication, that she was delaying talking with her husband about how much she wants another child, because she was treating him in this regard as though he were a fearful father figure.

Now, for present purposes it is not significant whether my interpretation was accurate, that her dream was helping her work-through the insight that she had gained regarding her father-transference. The dream applied the principle that she had learned in our work on the transference onto me, to the parallel circumstance of her father-transference onto her husband. Here I want to stress her dream's choice of symbolism. The wish for a girl-child was uncensored and manifest. The identity of the mother was conflicted and symbolic. Among all of the possible symbols for the mother, the dream portrayed a specific woman, whose particular husband was unconsciously a forbidding father-figure for my patient. In this way the choice of symbolism expressed an intellectual insight, a self-observation of my patient's father-transference.

Because the manifest symbol was created through the condensation of my patient's sense of self with the pictorial image of Georgia, we are dealing with an aspect of the unconscious dream-work whose existence Freud and mainstream psychoanalysts have always flatly denied. Freud (1900) wrote:

The dream-work is not simply more careless, more irrational, more forgetful and more incomplete than waking thought; it is completely different from it qualitatively and for that reason not immediately comparable with it. It does not think, calculate or judge in any way at all; it restricts itself to giving things a new form.

(p. 507)

This claim was wrong. The dream-work often makes its thinking and judging evident through its choice of the manifest content. The thinking and judging are not manifest, nor otherwise part of the manifest content. The thinking and judging cannot reasonably be attributed, as Freud alleged, to preconscious materials that the dream-work has merely cast into pictures. The thinking and judging only become evident through the act of interpretation, when the manifest contents are understood as symbols of latent contents, and the dream's interpreter becomes aware of the intelligence—the thinking and judging—that went into the dream's choice of symbolism.

Jung (1997) was accordingly not extrapolating from unearned theoretic assumptions about archetypes, but proceeding from easily replicable clinical experience, when he stated that "the unconscious has its own ideas and can produce the most amazing changes in the conscious, by extracting things or inserting things into the conscious, and the conscious can do precious little about it" (p. 209). In so far as the choice of the manifest content of the dream is made through the unconscious process of condensation, the thinking or judging that we find in dreams must be counted as unconscious and not, as Freud insisted, as preconscious alone.

For the pre-war psychoanalysts who acknowledged the existence of the clinical phenomenon, the logical theoretical options were two. Either the unconscious has a capacity for higher thought, in which event the topographic hypothesis of the psyche had to be seriously flawed; and/or Freud was wrong to assign condensation to the primary process. In *Unconscious Wisdom* (Merkur, 2001), I noted that Freud's (1923a) concept of the superego pertained to a portion of the unconscious, separate from the id, that has a capacity for higher thought (see also Merkur, 2009). Freud (1900, pp. 489, 491–2, 514; 1916–17, pp. 140, 168, 233, 249) credited some and perhaps all of the dream-distortion to the unconscious censor, which, from 1923 onward, Freud (1923b, p. 262; 1933, pp. 27–8; 1914a, p. 97) termed the superego; and Freud (1923c) acknowledged that although some dreams are mostly disguised id materials "from below," others proceed "from above" and are mostly symbolic of superego materials. There is no logical obstacle to extending Freud's conclusions into a general rule that embraces the creativity of dreams.

Because Jung was making a clinical claim about clinical interpretations of dreams' choices of symbolism; and because Freud, reasoning independently, eventually replaced his topographic model of the mind with a more sophisticated hypothesis that accommodated Jung's clinical findings, I think it obligatory to conclude that disinterested scientific considerations were not responsible for the pre-war controversies about the dream. Insuperable interpersonal conflicts complicated the scientific discussion; and *ad hominem* criticisms replaced the debate of ideas. By the time that psychoanalytic histories began to be written (Freud, 1914b), Stekel, Adler, Maeder, and Jung had been expelled from the psychoanalytic movement, and their views ceased to be discussed by Freud's followers. A generation later the very existence of the pre-war controversy about dreams was forgotten. Where, in 1912, Jung had asserted that "psychoanalysis, considered as a therapeutic technique, consists in the main of numerous dream-analyses" (Jung, 1966a, p. 265), a decade later dream interpretation had yielded to transference analysis as the royal road to the unconscious, and the exceptional position of the dream in psychoanalysis had become a minority point of view.

The theories that I shall be examining in the balance of this chapter nevertheless repay psychoanalytic attention. They form a repressed portion of our history, whose recovery and critical integration is long overdue.

Wilhelm Stekel

The crisis in dream theory began, as Rand and Torok (1997) have appreciated, in the period 1909–14. Freud's original psychoanalytic method had patients associate freely to each of their dream's symbols. In the pre-war period, Freud added a different clinical practice that bypassed patients' associations and relied instead on a catalogue of what, from 1914 onward, he called "typical symbols." Freud suggested that most occurrences of these symbols had the same meaning, so they might be used when patients had no associations, or there was no time in a session to elicit associations. Rand and Torok (1997) concluded:

Freud did not draw the necessary logical conclusion, namely that the two modes of interpretation are mutually exclusive. His desire to combine them seems inexplicable to us, since it leads to a fundamental incompatibility that debilitates all of psychoanalytic theory and practice.

(p. 23)

The puzzle is not difficult to unriddle. In 1911, Wilhelm Stekel had published *The Language of Dreams*, in which he documented a considerable number of typical symbols and suggested that the motifs were universal, both in dreams and in "primordial" cultures. "The dream portrays its images in a secret symbolic language. Its language is the language of the primordial man. For man's aboriginal ancestor also expressed himself in symbolic form" (Stekel, 1922, p. 19). In Stekel's view, dream interpretation ought to have two phases, which began with attention to the symbolic language and secondarily followed Freud's advice, using free association to identify and interpret displacements.

Numerous examples have shown us that the dream speaks a symbolic language and that the unraveling of the symbols yields a partial explanation of the dream. I must underscore again, *a partial explanation only*, because in addition to the symbolism various processes involved in the *dream distortion* play a rôle.

(Stekel, 1922, p. 107)

Consider, for example, Stekel's (1922) pioneering conceptualization of symbolic equations. "All bodily openings (in the dream) are equal to each other and may substitute one another. Thus, mouth, eyes, ears, nasal opening, penis, vagina, urethra and navel may substitute each other" (p. 139). On the basis of the manifest content, an analyst may immediately know a variety of possible solutions to the meaning of a particular dream; but only free association completes the work of interpretation, by determining which of several possible meanings happens to be unconsciously intended. Stekel emphasized that his findings were based on the manifest dream content. Once the symbolic language of dreams is understood, "the manifest dream material itself displays the most important content, the latent dream thoughts" (p. 56)—*displays*, as distinct from *conceals*, in a universally shared symbolic manner.

When Freud introduced his catalogue of typical symbols in the 1914 edition of *The Interpretation of Dreams*, he was accommodating the incontrovertible evidence that Stekel had amassed, without knowing what to do theoretically with the new data. Freud dealt with Stekel himself less generously, expelling him from the psychoanalytic movement in 1911. The problem of the dream-work's choice of manifest symbolism may be appreciated as a sequel to Stekel's contribution. If, as classical analysis held, almost all symbols' latent contents are a small set of erogenous zones, what accounts for the extraordinary versatility of symbols' manifest contents? The problem is not solved, but only rephrased, by the object relations, interpersonal, and relational schools that replace a small set of erogenous zones with a small set of interpersonal relationships as the latent contents of symbols in general. The human species does not get by with a correspondingly small set of manifest symbols. We are enormously creative in our symbol-forming, and Freud's denial that the dream-work thinks or judges disallowed contributions on the topic.

I would like to suggest that the dream-work's choice of manifest symbolism was both clinically important and an intriguing theoretical puzzle whose solution offered the possibility of bridging the gap between Freud's theory and Stekel's findings. Freud did not solve the problem, as he claimed, but instead made it more acute when he concluded *Totem and Taboo* (1913b) with the grandiose claim:

> At the conclusion, then, of this exceedingly condensed inquiry, I should like to insist that its outcome shows that the beginnings of religion, morals, society and art converge in the Oedipus complex. This is in complete agreement with the psychoanalytic finding that the same complex constitutes the nucleus of all neuroses, so far as our present knowledge goes. It seems to me a most surprising discovery that the problems of social psychology, too, should prove soluble on the basis of one single concrete point—man's relation to his father.
>
> (pp. 156–7)

Let us allow, for the sake of argument, that Freud's claim was valid. To tell us that a million million different things all come down to the same one thing is to tell us that the same one thing is utterly uninteresting. What is significant is how the million million things come to be. Or to

The creativity of dreams 109

put the same issue clinically: I have never heard of a patient who was cured of anything by insights regarding the Oedipus complex. Insights regarding the patient's relations with his or her own mother and father can be transformative; but the universal biological insight, that is, the awareness that all people have both a mother and a father, cures no one of anything.

Freud was still arguing the universality of Oedipus when his ablest followers had granted him the theoretic point and then moved on to the puzzle of the relation between the latent and the manifest. Because Freud expelled them from the movement, psychoanalysis has been permanently impoverished. The puzzle remains unsolved, the history of the pre-war controversies is everywhere told incorrectly, and one can become a pariah for raising the very topic. But Freud's embarrassment, his narcissistic wound, should not be inhibiting our research today.

Alfred Adler

Adler was expelled before Stekel. He had been working on a different set of issues that included the teleological function of the dream. When Jung proposed the congress topic in November 1912, he was implying that psychoanalysts who remained with Freud would do well to evaluate how much of Adler's contribution might be retained. A limited review of Adler's position will help clarify what analysts meant by teleology in 1912.

In *The Neurotic Constitution*, first published in German in 1912, Adler presented the basic ideas of his system. He maintained that all people have feelings of inferiority that commenced with the inferiority of the baby and child to the adult (Adler, 1917, pp. 13, 35, 46–7, 51–3), and may have secondarily been influenced by further constitutional occasions for realistic inferiority. Neurotics fantasize additional inferiority, over and above the realistic feelings of inferiority that all people share (p. 13). "This feeling must always be understood in a relative sense, as the outgrowth of the individual's relation to his environment or to his strivings" (p. 13). In order to compensate for feelings of inferiority, the individual develops as "a guiding principle" the ambition "to raise himself to the level of his (all-powerful) father, even to the point of surpassing the latter" (p. 14). In this way, the individual acquires "the aim to be great, to be strong, to be a man, to be 'above'" (p. 36). Owing to their positions in society, women feel categorically inferior to men (pp. 99–100), boys and junior men feel inferior to senior men (p. 104), and everyone engages in a "masculine protest," that seeks to deny inferiority by asserting superiority (pp. 42–4). Adler's theory was predicated on sociology, conscious experience, and gender, where Freud had premised his thinking on biology, unconscious motivation, and sex. The two could easily have been harmonized, with Adler's "masculine protest" being treated as a conscious attitude that manifested what Freud had conceptualized as an unconscious wish to kill the father; but Adler claimed that his own theory made that of Freud superfluous. For Adler, it was Adler or Freud, not both together (pp. 62, 64, 69–70, 76–7, 106); and Freud obliged Adler by agreeing to part ways.

The teleological component in Adler's theory followed as a corollary to the masculine protest. Every sense of inferiority implies at least some concept of superiority, and the achievement of superiority is "a guiding principle" (Adler, 1917, p. 14) or "guiding fiction" (p. 56) that is also a "final purpose" (p. viii), "goal" (p. xii) or *telos*. Because a guiding fiction is always responsive both to the particular sense of inferiority and to the individual's social and physical environment, the guiding fiction is never generic. It is always highly individualistic. At the same time, its intensity is predictable. "The greater the feeling of inferiority, the more imperative and stronger will be the necessity for a steadying, guiding principle" (p. 56). Neurotics pursue "an impossible ideal" (p. xvi), "an imaginary goal" (p. xvii), and "a fantastic goal" (p. 54) where non-neurotics are realistic in their aims. Adler's clinical strategy was to analyze the patient's goals, together with the habitual attitudes and practices that subserved the goals.

> He remains the plaything of his emotions and affects until such time as the mechanism becomes revealed to him and set to rights, until such time as the predispositions and neurotic plan of life are shattered; a plaything of emotions and affects the interaction of which becomes further complicated because of a constant admixture of traits of character intended to negate his sense of inferiority, such as pride, envy, greed, cruelty, courage, revenge fullness, irritability, etc., traits of character which are constantly being excited through his craving for security.
>
> (Adler, 1917, p. 61)

Because Adler's clinical practices anticipated aspects of defense analysis, he is often dismissed by mainstream psychoanalysts as having been superseded by ego psychology; but the trivializing of his contribution does everyone a disservice. He regarded "the guiding ideal of the ego as a fiction" (Adler, 1917, p. 75) whose "combative, not to say hostile character" (p. 80) was integral to its fictitiousness. Well into the book, Adler several times used the phrase "ego-ideal" (pp. 132, 150) and "compensatory ego-ideal" (p. 136). Adler noted the personification of the ideal as an inner voice: "Sometimes in a situation of psychic uncertainty the personified, deified guiding idea is met with as a second self, as an inner voice like the Daemon of Socrates which warns, encourages, punishes, accuses" (p. 96). He found "self-observation and self-esteem always excited and reënforced by the guiding fiction" (p. 97). Freud did not acknowledge his debt to Adler when in 1914 he adopted the term "ego ideal" and attributed self-observation, conscience, and the maintenance of ideals to a single psychic agency (renamed "superego" in 1923); but the fact of Freud's debt in 1914 to the teleological component in Adler's thinking provides an appropriate perspective from which to view Jung's proposal in 1912 to discuss the teleological function of the dream.

Adler discussed dreams only briefly in his book, but he devoted a lecture to dreams the same year. In his book, Adler (1917) claimed that the extremism of neurotics' ideals made the dreams of neurotics easier to interpret than those of non-neurotic people (p. 110). He also claimed that patients' ideals were easily detected in their dreams' manifest contents.

> The tendency of the neurotically reënforced guiding idea will be revealed regularly in the dreams of a neurotic person, usually in the form of a striving to attain a position "above" or the masculine protest. The feminine or "under" base of operation is always indicated.
>
> (Adler, 1917, p. 110)

Because the 1912 lecture referred its audience to the book, it was presumably delivered later in the same year. Adler (1912) began by noting that people are constantly thinking about the future, expecting it, fearing it, planning for it, presuming to know it. He maintained that this same orientation is also found in dreams (p. 216); and the dreamer's concerns with the future always inevitably involve his or her ideals. "The *anticipatory, prescient function of the dream* is always clearly discernible; it foreshadows *the preparations developed in connection with actual difficulties encountered by the dreamer's life-line*, and the safe-guarding purpose is never lost sight of" (p. 217). He distinguished two types of anticipation in dreams: dreams that solve problems, and dreams that address problems that remain unsolved.

> We find consequently in dreams two types of attempts of pre-interpreting, of solving a problem, and of initiating what the dreamer desires to put into a given situation. This he will seek to accomplish along lines best adapted to his personality, his nature and character. The dream may depict the situation which is anticipated in the future as already existing ... in order in the waking state to put this arrangement into effect either openly or surreptitiously.
>
> (Adler, 1912, pp. 219–20)

In order to account for "the apparent lack of intelligibility in the dream," its manifest incoherence, Adler (1912) proposed that dreams are not means of solving-problems. Rather, they are by-products of problem-solving, but "an accessory phenomena," "a synchronous movement of our thought, one running in the same direction as the character and the nature of the personality demands and expressing itself in a difficult language which even when understood, is not at all clear" (p. 221). This formulation agreed with Freud's assertion that the dream-work neither thinks nor judges. If the dream anticipates, it does so because the entire personality does so. "*In dreams all the transitional phases of anticipatory thinking occur as if directed by some previously determined goal and by the utilization of personal experiences*" (p. 222). Dreams express more than the wishes that Freud acknowledged. The "previously determined goal" might be a wish, but the "utilization of personal experiences" embeds the goal, or wish, in a body of memory that contextualizes the wish in realistic circumstances.

Adler was apparently unaware that his further effort to account for "the initially unintelligible details" in dreams arrived him at a formulation of dreams' creativity.

> The dream rarely gives a presentation of facts—not even and even when it does, this is conditioned by a specific trait of the dreamer—in

which recent happenings or pictures of the present occur. For the solution of an undecided question simpler, more abstract and infantile comparisons are at hand, comparisons frequently suggesting more expressive and more political images.

(Adler, 1912, p. 222)

Dreams produce "comparisons" that Adler earlier in his lecture had called "analogical ... characterizations" (p. 217). These descriptions of the effects of condensation agreed with the account of wish-fulfillment in Freud's article "Creative Writers and Day-Dreaming" (1908).

Mental work is linked to some current impression, some provoking occasion in the present which has been able to arouse one of the subject's major wishes. From there it harks back to a memory of an earlier experience (usually an infantile one) in which this wish was fulfilled; and it now creates a situation relating to the future which represents a fulfilment of the wish. What it thus creates is a day-dream or phantasy, which carries about it traces of its origin from the occasion which provoked it and from the memory.

(Freud, 1908b, p. 148)

A wish that is not presently being satisfied is associated with the memory of a wish that was satisfied. When the two wishes are unconsciously equated, the satisfaction of the past wish becomes the fantasied satisfaction of the present wish. A condensation of this kind is the beginning of all creativity. Whether a creative analog develops into a viable or tenable achievement, or remains within the realm of fantasy, is a secondary consideration. Adler recognized clinically that some dreams portray solutions to problems, either manifestly or latently; while others portray attempts at solutions—but in keeping with Freud's denial of the intellectuality of dreams, Adler declined to attribute the creativity to the dreams. At the same time, Adler insisted that dreams' simplifications of complex situations, leading sometimes to creative solutions and at other times to over-simplicity, owed to their reliance on ego ideals.

The simplicity of the dream scenes—simple in comparison with the complex situations of life—represent ... the attempts of the dreamer to find some outlet by excluding the confusing multiplicity of powers present in any given situation [by being] … willing to pursue a guiding-line that resembles these simple situations.

(Adler, 1912, p. 223)

Alphonse Maeder

Jung twice credited Alphonse Maeder, a Zurich psychoanalyst who followed Jung upon his break with Freud (Jung, 1973b, pp. 167–8), with having introduced two ideas about dreams that he had adopted as his own: the notion that the dream has a "prospective and finally-oriented function" (Jung, 1913b, p. 238) and is "a spontaneous self-portrayal, in symbolic form, of the actual situation in the unconscious" (Jung, 1948a, p. 263). Responding in 1913 to charges that he had plagiarized Adler, Maeder asserted the independence of his own thinking. He had published papers in 1909 and 1911, proposing that dreams are attempts at conflict solution (Shamdasani, 2003, p. 143). Maeder originally presented his controversial views in a German-language lecture and article on the "Function of the Dream." When Jung broke with Freud in 1913, Maeder was one of the Zurichers who sided with Jung. He later summarized and extended his position for an English audience in *The Dream Problem* (1916), prefacing that "no real or necessary differences exist between us, for what we of the Zürich school have accomplished is a natural outcome of what Freud gave us."

In *The Dream Problem*, Maeder (1916) stated explicitly that he "place[d] great importance on the choice of the pictures and expressions in the manifest dream content" (p. 20) and that he "value[d] the composition of the manifest dream content more highly than does Freud" (p. 21). Unfortunately, because Maeder offered no clinical examples to illustrate his assertions, it is possible to read his pamphlet—I did so three or four times!—thinking that he was talking about the manifest dream content and not, as he explicitly stated, about the *choice* or *composition* of the manifest dream content. He was talking about the dream-work, which is an unconscious process.

Maeder's clinical acumen exceeded his ability to formulate his findings in theoretical abstractions. He relied, as also Jung did, on a distinction that the Viennese analyst Herbert Silberer had introduced in connection with myths (1910, 1912) and secondarily extended to the literature of alchemy (1914, Engl. tr. 1917). Silberer asserted that the symbols of myths and alchemical texts each have two levels of meaning. The one is psychoanalytic and unconscious; the other is anagogical and conscious. Even though Abraham (1909) had demonstrated parallels between myths and dreams, Silberer limited his initial presentations to the circumstances of conscious symbolism, and Freud had no objection to his thesis. When, however, Silberer (1955) addressed the circumstances of dreams in 1918, Freud (1922) took sharp exception, emphasizing, as he had done from 1913 onward, that intellectual contributions to latent dream contents owe to the preconscious day residue and must be distinguished theoretically from the unconscious processes of the dreamwork. Freud did not retract his criticism of Silberer, who was then deceased, when he introduced his concept of dreams "from above" (Freud, 1923c), tacitly acknowledging that some intellectual contributions are unconscious, because tracing to the superego rather than the preconscious ego (for a discussion of Silberer, see Merkur, 2005, pp. 86–94).

Writing in the pre-war period, Maeder applied Silberer's concept of two types of symbol to the circumstance of dreams. Where Silberer had written of the psychoanalytic and the anagogical meanings of single symbols, Maeder spoke of "the cathartic and the preparing function" (p. 2), "the sexually symbolic" and "the intellectual content." As further designations of the second level of meaning, Maeder wrote of "the prospective function" (p. 4) and the "teleological side of the unconscious function." In this way, Maeder linked Silberer's concept of two types of meaning with Adler's concept of teleology. He further linked them to Freud's (1911) metapsychology: "The connection between pleasure and displeasure principle and the cathartic function, on the one hand, and between the reality principle and the preparatory function on the other can here be merely indicated" (Maeder, 1916, p. 43). Maeder similarly sought to integrate Stekel's work, when he regarded "the dream as a means of expression of the unconscious, as a true language" (p. 4). The dream "pictures in symbolic speech, a typical psychic reaction of the dreamer to a given stimulus from the outer world" (p. 41).

Silberer had achieved fame among psychoanalysts and a permanent place in later editions of Freud's *Interpretation of Dreams*, through an early paper that reported his efforts to autosuggest hypnagogic hallucinations. When he entertained abstract ideas immediately before he fell asleep, Silberer (1909) found that the images that arose as he was falling asleep were often metaphoric or allegorical presentations of the same ideas. "Autosymbolic" symbols of this kind were easily replicable experimental proof, he asserted, of the part of the dream-work that Freud had termed "considerations of representability." Maeder (1916) invoked Silberer's concept in his own presentation. Anticipating Kohut's concept of a self-state dream, Maeder (1916) remarked that "[d]reams give autosymbolic representations of the actual condition of the libido, which are transmitted to the consciousness" (p. 4). "The dream renders an autosymbolic presentation of the psychological situation of the unconscious" (p. 20). Maeder claimed that the dream provides the dreamer with "insight into his situation, the correct evaluation of his adventure" that is "emotional, not merely intellectual" and guarantees that a person "is really acting on his own principles and conviction" (pp. 13–14). Dream interpretation that is sensitive to the phenomenon alters the status of the analyst:

> The physician is no longer one who asserts this or that; something which one accepts or rejects, according to the predominance of the positive or negative attitude, but he has become a leader who sees and points out what one carries in oneself and only recognizes with difficulty; the physician is now he who helps one to know oneself better and how to rule oneself.
>
> (Maeder, 1916, p. 14)

The preparing, prospective, or teleological function of the dream combined with the autosymbolic function to produce "a symbolic expression of the future and as yet insufficiently elaborated material" (p. 15). "The dreams which are specially plastic and well constructed (in which Freud assumes a particularly intense secondary dream work) represent a clearly grasped and intensely felt situation" (p. 21). "There exists a direct relation between the plastic-figurative or vaguely outlined manifest dream-content, and the clarified-mature or confused state of the unconscious conflict" (p. 17). Maeder considered the dream-work process artistic. "Dream analyses have given me repeatedly the impression that genuine artistic talents lie latent in all men, of which only little reaches manifestation" (p. 5). "I see in all this a really artistic work, a real art of expression, which I would like to place in some relation to art in general. The dream is perhaps the primitive work of art" (p. 21).

Recognition of the unconscious artistry that is involved in the dream-work's choices of the manifest symbolism led Maeder to contemplate the dream's ability to portray an open-ended type of aspiration that eclipses both self-knowledge and the limited goal-orientation that can be produced through reaction-formation, as Adler imagined. Maeder wrote: "Dreams also contain a progressive side.... We want something more of life than the longing for the past; the poet wishes to make something of the life that still remains in him" (p. 29). He imagined a "prospective outlook; dreams which are not so much an actual picture of the situation but rather a vision of the future striven for, and potentiality contained in the individual" (pp. 29–30). "We are not dealing with the prophetic vision but with a foresight, with a clue to the direction which is suited to the reaction and strength of the patient in question" (p. 30). We should perhaps not be surprised that Maeder, in 1934, had abandoned psychotherapy and was "devoting himself entirely to the Christian work of conversion in the Oxford Movement" (Jung, 1973a, p. 147).

Freud's "An Evidential Dream"

Freud did not understand Maeder's position. In a short article titled "An Evidential Dream" that responded to the analysts who wanted to expand his theory of dreams, Freud (1913a) restated his customary position while emphasizing the distinction between the preconscious and the unconscious aspects of dream formation.

> Must we really concede that in addition to wishful (and anxiety) dreams, there are also dreams of admission, as well as of warning, reflection, adaptation, and so on?
>
> I must confess that I still do not quite understand why the stand I took against any such temptation in my *Interpretation of Dreams* has given rise to misgivings in the minds of so many psycho-analysts, among them some well-known ones.
>
> (p. 273)

Freud (1913a) suggested that the apparent variations among types of dreams reflect variations in the "so-called 'day's residues'" that disturbed sleep and construct dreams.

118   The creativity of dreams

In accordance with the multiplicity of thought-processes in the conscious and preconscious, these day's residues have the most numerous and varied meanings: they may be wishes or fears that have not been disposed of, or intentions, reflections, warnings, attempts at adaptation to current tasks, and so on.

(pp. 273–4)

Freud insisted, however, that in contrast with the day's residues that originate in consciousness and preconsciousness, the dream work is an unconscious process.

The present state of our knowledge leads us to conclude that the essential factor in the construction of dreams is an unconscious wish—as a rule an infantile wish, now repressed—which can come to expression in this somatic or psychical material (in the day's residues too, therefore) and can thus supply these with a force which enables them to press their way through to consciousness even during the suspension of thought at night. The dream is in every case a fulfillment of *this* unconscious wish, whatever else it may contain— warning, reflection, admission, or any other part of the rich content of preconscious waking life that has persisted undealt-with into the night. It is *this* unconscious wish that gives the dream-work its peculiar character as an unconscious revision of preconscious material. A psychoanalyst can characterize as dreams only the products of the dream-work: in spite of the fact that the latent dream-thoughts are only arrived at from the interpretation of the dream, he cannot reckon them as part of the dream, but only as part of preconscious reflection. (Secondary revision by the conscious agency is here reckoned as part of the dream-work. Even if one were to separate, this would not involve any alteration in our conception. We should then have to say: dreams in the analytic sense comprise the dream-work proper together with the secondary revision of its products.) The conclusion to be drawn from these considerations is that one cannot put the wish-fulfilling character of dreams on a par with their character as warnings, admissions, attempts at solution, etc., without denying the concept of a cyclical dimension of depth—that is to say, without denying the standpoint of psycho-analysis.

(pp. 274–5)

The creativity of dreams 119

In a letter to Freud on July 29, 1913, Jung complained that Freud's (1913a) article had misunderstood and misrepresented the views of Jung and others. Jung wrote:

> This misunderstanding turns on the conception of the actual conflict, which for us is *not the petty vexation of the moment* but the problem of adaptation. A second misunderstanding seems to be that you think we deny the wish-fulfilment theory of dreams. We fully admit the soundness of the wish-fulfilment theory, but we maintain that this way of interpreting dreams touches only the surface, that it stops at the symbol, and that further interpretation is possible. When, for instance, a coitus wish appears in a dream, this wish can be analysed further, since this archaic expression with its tiresome monotony of meaning needs re-translating into another medium. We recognize the soundness of the wish-fulfilment theory up to a certain point, but we go beyond it. In our view it does not exhaust the meaning of the dream.
>
> (Freud and Jung, 1974, p. 548)

Jung's letter did not make matters any more clear to Freud. And I confess that I read my way through the eighteen volumes of Jung's collective works and both read and re-read Maeder's article several times without finding any further clarity. It was, as I said previously, only the case illustration in Jung's *Dream Analysis* seminar that led me to appreciate what Jung and Maeder were arguing. They were not talking of the manifest dream per se. They were talking of the manifest dream precisely as Freud did, as evidence of latent dream-forming processes. Maeder did not discuss whether the latent processes were unconscious or preconscious. What mattered to Maeder was the clinical utility of interpreting patients' materials.

Rather than to speculate why Freud was unable to understand Maeder and Jung, I will ask what in Freud's system of psychoanalysis he would have had to change if he had accepted the clinical findings of Maeder and Jung in 1912? The answer is not far to seek. If Maeder and Jung were correct that the manifest dream contents imply an unconscious choice of the manifest content, a deliberate, purposive, intentional selection of which image to deploy as a symbol for the latent content, two of Freud's (1900) theoretical claims were wrong: (a) that unconscious symbol-forming proceeds at random, through "unbound cathexes" of "psychical energy," and (b) that the system Unconscious does not think (Freud,

120 The creativity of dreams

1900, p. 617) or, at most, engages in no more abstraction than pattern perception (Freud, 1911, p. 221). Because Freud (1923c) later reversed himself on the second of the two claims, when he allowed that the superego has an unconscious reach that contributes to dreams "from above," what was ultimately at stake for Freud's theories in 1912–13 were his ideas about psychical energy. Freud had adopted the antithesis of free and bound energy from Breuer, calling them "the deepest insight we have gained up to the present into the nature of nervous energy" (Freud, 1915, p. 188). Had Freud allowed himself to understand Maeder and Jung and been persuaded to confirm their clinical observations with his own, he would have been obliged by the evidence to conclude that the dreamwork does not proceed at random, forming associations haphazardly, but instead proceeds purposively. With the collapse of the idea of "free" or "unbound" cathexis, all of Freud's ideas about psychical energy would have been at risk. A major theoretic link between the neurological and the psychical would have been severed; and it would not have awaited the 1960s for the psychoanalytic mainstream to question (Holt, 1962; 1967; Apfelbaum, 1965), and a generation later, to abandon (Gill, 1983; Greenberg and Mitchell, 1983), the concept of psychical energy.

Jung on dreams

Jung's pre-war formulations about the dream largely duplicated Maeder's findings. In *Psychology of the Unconscious*, whose original German publication in 1911–12 was the occasion of his break with Freud, Jung (1916b) both praised Silberer by name (p. 6) and echoed his distinction between psychoanalytic and anagogical levels of meaning when he generalized, "All that is psychologic has an under and an over meaning" (p. 63). Jung attributed the generation of the second level of meaning to "thinking in analogies" (1946a, p. 24; see also 1913c, p. 436; 1916b, pp. 156, 171). In a refutation of Tausk, first published in 1913, Jung echoed Maeder regarding the choice of symbolism but, in his own meandering way of thinking, he no sooner made his point than confused his readers by bringing up a second.

> In a discussion of the historical fish-symbol, one of those present remarked that the fish vanishing in the sea was simply the father's penis vanishing in his wife's vagina. This kind of interpretation, which I

consider sterile, is what I call sexual concretism. It seems to me that psychoanalysts are confronted with the much greater and more important task of understanding what these analogies are trying to say. What did man of many different races and epochs mean by this symbol of the fish? Why—in the present case too, for that matter—were these infantile channels of interest reactivated? What does this fetching up of infantile material signify? For this obviously is the problem.

(Jung, 1913c, p. 434)

The question, "What did man of many different races and epochs mean by this symbol of the fish?," was extraneous to his discussion, but causes the balance of the paragraph to be misread. Jung was asserting that by telling us that a fish symbolizes a penis is to tell us a truism that is rarely if ever curative. The clinically relevant question is always why did this dreamer on this night make use of a fish symbol in this particular dream? Jung's sentence-length digression onto the topic of the wide historical and geographical distribution of fish symbols, and his unearned assumption of their biologically determined availability to the particular dreamer, distracts his readers from the clinical relevance of his further remarks. Speaking in generalities created ambiguity that contributed further to his readers' confusion.

The Zurich school naturally recognizes that the material is reducible to simpler infantile patterns, but it is not content to let it go at that. It takes these patterns for what they are, that is, images through which the unconscious mind is expressing itself.

(Jung, 1913c, p. 434)

Indeed, Jung miswrote. He did not take "these patterns for what they are," but instead treated them as analogies. For example, he did not treat fish as fish, but as fish that the unconscious had selected from all the myriad other penis symbols at the dream's disposal.

Another writing of the same period makes a closely similar point. Discussing a clinical situation in which a patient, discussing a dream, free-associated to a particular fairytale, Jung commented:

The unconscious came out with just this example, and this cannot be mere chance but is somehow characteristic of the situation at that moment. In analysing dreams we have to look out for these seeming accidents, for in psychology there are no blind accidents, much as we are inclined to assume that these things are pure chance.

(1913b, p. 216)

Jung's attunement to unconscious intellectual expression by means of free association during the clinical situation was a second instance of his attunement to unconscious intellectual expression, the first being the unconscious choice of the manifest dream imagery.

Following his break with Freud, Jung maintained much the same position, modifying it only slightly as the decades and his own thinking advanced. In late 1913, he was agreeing with Freud in giving Stekel's overstatements a mixed review. "There can be no dream-symbols whose meanings are fixed in every detail, but, at most, a frequent occurrence of symbols with fairly general meanings" (Jung, 1913b, p. 238; see also p. 236; 1948b, pp. 247, 263–4). Jung (1913b) continued to follow Maeder in applying Silberer's two levels of symbolic meaning, not only to consciously produced symbols, as Silberer had done, but also to the symbols of dreams. "Every symbol has at least two meanings. The very frequent sexual meanings of dream-symbols is at most one of them" (p. 237; see also 1989, p. 159). Jung (1913b) continued to use the term "analogy" (p. 239) in reference to the second level of meaning; and he agreed with both Adler and Maeder in asserting that sexual motifs, no differently than any other, may sometimes be analogical rather than literal (pp. 237, 239). Jung cited Maeder by name in connection with "the prospective and finally-oriented function of dreams in general" (p. 238) and echoed his regard for the dream as autosymbolic. "The dream is, in the first instance, a subliminal picture of the actual psychological situation of the individual in his waking state. It gives us a résumé of the subliminal associative material constellated by the psychological situation of the moment" (p. 240). Importantly, Jung already in 1913 referred to the goal of psychoanalysis as "the progress of the development of [the] personality" (p. 239).

Jung expanded on Maeder's position by adding a key bit of theory that reconciled the Zürichers' clinical practices with Freud's view of creativity.

Consciousness tries to adjust itself to the necessities of the moment, or, to put it differently: there are tasks ahead which the individual must overcome. In many cases the solution is, in the nature of things,

The creativity of dreams 123

unknown, for which reason consciousness always tries to find the solution by way of analogous experiences. We try to grasp the unknown future on the model of our experience in the past. We have no reason to suppose that the subliminal psychic material obeys other laws than the "supraliminal" material.... This is the way we always recognize things, and it is also the essential reason for the existence of symbolism: it is a process of comprehension by means of analogy. The dream is a *subliminal* process of comprehension by analogy.

(Jung, 1913b, p. 240)

Jung neglected to credit Freud (1908) with the formulation that problem solving proceeds, in daydreams and literary composition, by reverting to memories of analogous problems that were solved successfully in the past, and developing a fantastic or realistic solution to the present problem on their model. Jung wrote as though he were discussing a generally embraced truth about conscious problem solving, rather than a contribution specifically by Freud. In this passage, Jung nevertheless claimed that the same process of problem solving through analogy occurs unconsciously in dreams.

Signs and symbols

The further development of Jung's thought on dreams can be seen as a gradual deepening of his understanding of the position that he had already developed before his break with Freud. In his writings after 1913, Jung habitually exaggerated the differences between Freud's views and his own; and for me, at least, it came as an astonishment to realize that Jung's theory of archetypes—easily the least congenial of his ideas for psychoanalysts—was an attempt to solve a problem that Jung had taken over from Freud. To criticize Jung fairly, one must sometimes simultaneously criticize the antecedents of Jung's arguments in Freud. The theory of dreams is a case in point.

Freud's (1900, p. 617; 1911, p. 221; 1915, p. 202) allocation of thinking to consciousness imposed a fundamental constraint on dream theory. "The conscious presentation comprises the presentation of the thing plus the presentation of the word belonging to it, while the unconscious presentation is the presentation of the thing alone" (Freud, 1915, p. 201). Freud's categorical limitation of the unconscious to thing-presentations, while crediting all verbal productions to consciousness alone, was integral to Freud's effort to develop a model of the mind that began with biology and unconsciousness, and ended with consciousness and culture. The unconscious, including the dream-work, depends exclusively on thing-presentations, with the possible exception of the perceptions of relations among thing-presentations.

Jung was consequently conforming to Freud's metapsychology when he objected to Freud's theory of dreams, as he frequently did, with the following argument:

> We have no right to accuse the dream of, so to speak, a deliberate man-oeuvre calculated to deceive. Nature is often obscure or impenetrable, but she is not, like man, deceitful. We must therefore take it that the dream is just what it pretends to be, neither more nor less. If it shows something in a negative light, there is no reason for assuming that it is meant positively.... The dream itself wants nothing; it is a self-evident content, a plain natural fact like the sugar in the blood of a diabetic or the fever in a patient with typhus. It is only we who, if we are clever and can unriddle the signs of nature, turn it into a warning.
>
> (Jung, 1943c, pp. 100–1; compare 1918, p. 23; 1926a,
> pp. 88, 103; 1930a, p. 32; 1936a, p. 86; 1938a,
> p. 27; 1973b, pp. 161–2; 1997, p. 26)

If the unconscious content of the dream consists exclusively of thing-presentations, there can be no difference between their latent and mani-fest contents. Thing-presentations necessarily portray what they appear to portray, neither more nor less. For example, as a thing-presentation the mental image of an orange signifies neither more nor less than an orange, regardless of whether it is used in memory or in imagination; if it signi-fies anything else, it is no longer a thing-presentation alone. Accordingly, if dream images have latent meanings that differ from their manifest meanings, as Freud maintained they did, they cannot be thing-presentations. They must be symbols, as Freud (1900) indeed called them. Freud seems never to have noticed the interior contradiction between his metapsychology and his theory of dreams. If Freud's method of dream interpretation is correct, *dream images cannot be thing-presentations of the unconscious; they cannot constitute a primary process that accomplishes the transition between the body and the mind, and between neurology and psychology.* For dreams to constitute a primary process, the images of dreams must be thing-presentations. They cannot signify more or other than what they portray. To be the type of symbol that Freud alleged, dream-images had to be mixed thing-and-word presentations of the conscious system; the dream-work had to constitute a tertiary process, that mediated between and reconciled the truly primary process and consciousness. Jung did not dwell on this inconsistency in Freud's position, but his own ideas about dreams often make sense as an implicit attempt to correct Freud's oversight.

Because Jung's clinical findings required him to postulate that in forming each dream the dream-work makes choices among the images that are available for it to deploy, he amended Freud's position as little as was necessary, by postulating that thing-presentations somehow already possess meanings. He expressed his position by drawing a distinction, on the one hand, between signs and semiotics, which he attributed to Freud and, on the other, between symbols and symbolism, which he claimed for himself. Jung introduced the distinction as early as 1916.

> The Viennese School adopts an exclusively sexualistic standpoint while that of the Zurich School is symbolistic. The Viennese School interprets the psychological symbol semiotically, as a sign or token of certain primitive psychosexual processes.... The Zurich School recognizes the scientific possibility of such a conception but denies its exclusive validity, for it does not interpret the psychological symbol semiotically only but also symbolistically, that is, it attributes a positive value to the symbol.
>
> The value of the symbol does not depend merely on historical causes; its chief importance lies in the fact that it has a meaning for the actual present and for the future, in their psychological aspects. For the Zurich School the symbol is not merely a sign of something repressed and concealed, but is at the same time an attempt to comprehend and to point the way to the further psychological development of the individual. Thus we add a prospective meaning to the retrospective value of the symbol.
>
> (Jung, 1916a, p. 291)

Apart from Jung's introduction of a special sense of the term *symbol* that he contrasted with *sign*, Jung here re-stated the position that he shared with Maeder concerning the genetic orientation of psychoanalysis and the forward looking, teleological, or prospective orientation of the Zurich school. The choice of the terms *symbol* and *sign* was unfortunate, however, because it led Jung into self-contradiction. In writings of the 1910s, Jung kept closely to Silberer's ideas of the two levels of symbolic meanings. Silberer (1910, 1912) had contrasted symbols that expressed verbal formulations in imagistic form, with symbols whose corresponding verbal formulations had never been attained. Silberer (1917) later added that single symbols might have both levels of meaning, and Jung built on the second formulation. "Silberer distinguishes between the psychoanalytic and the anagogic interpretation, while I distinguished between the analytical-reductive and the synthetic-hermeneutic interpretation" (Jung, 1935b, p. 8). In early writings, Jung (1913c, pp. 434, 436; 1913a, p. 239; 1916b, pp. 156, 171; 1946a, p. 24) described the second category of symbols as analogies.

> The symbol is not a sign that disguises something generally known. Its meaning resides in the fact that it is an attempt to elucidate, by a more or less apt analogy, something that is still entirely unknown or still in the process of formation. If we reduce this by analysis to something that is generally known, we destroy the true value of the symbol.
>
> (Jung, 1966b, p. 290)

In *Psychological Types* (1921), he used terms differently.

> Every view which interprets the symbolic expression as an analogue or an abbreviated designation for a *known* thing is *semiotic*. A view which interprets the symbolic expression as the best possible formulation of a relatively *unknown* thing, which for that reason cannot be more clearly or characteristically represented, is *symbolic*.
>
> (p. 474)

The term "analogue" here referred to the analytical-reductive symbol, where it had previously named the synthetic-hermeneutic. Jung used terms similarly in an article first published in 1940–41: "Symbols are never simple—only signs and allegories are simple. The symbol always covers a complicated situation which is so far beyond the grasp of language that it cannot be expressed at all in any unambiguous manner" (Jung, 1954b, p. 254).

Not only did Jung have difficulty deciding on technical terms for the phenomena that he contrasted as symbols and signs, but his writings contain a great many references to symbols that treat them precisely as signs. Jung referred repeatedly to the "language" of dreams or the unconscious (Jung, 1913b, p. 209; 1921, p. 422; 1936a, p. 82; 1948b, pp. 263–4; 1964, pp. 206–8, 227; 1984, p. 525), and he occasionally remarked on its lexicon. No differently than Freud's symbols, Jung's symbols are actually signs of a linguistic and semiotic nature. They are not thing-presentations. Like Freud's signs, Jung's symbols have latent contents that differ from their manifest meanings. Jung's symbols tend to refer to the psyche and its processes, where Freud's tend to refer to sexuality; but their semiotic nature is unmistakable. "Water is the commonest symbol for the unconscious. The lake in the Valley is the unconscious" (Jung, 1954a, p. 18). "The idea of the *anima mundi* ... coincides with that of the collective unconscious whose centre is the self. The symbol of the sea is another synonym for the unconscious" (Jung, 1952d, p. 188). "'The bottom of the sea' is a metaphor for the collective unconscious, the great collectivity at the bottom for the sea" (Jung, 1984, p. 198). Referring to alchemical water, Jung (1946b) stated: "this fluid substance, with all its paradoxical qualities, really signifies the unconscious" (p. 209). "The snake, as a chthonic and at the same time spiritual being, symbolizes the unconscious" (Jung, 1950, p. 363). "There is hardly anything under God's sun that does not mean the unconscious—a forest, the sea, a river, a house, the mother, the aunt, a church—there are ten thousand things which express the unconscious" (Jung, 1997, p. 73). "Fishes and snakes are favourite symbols for describing psychic happenings or experiences that suddenly dart out of the unconscious and have a frightening or redeeming effect" (Jung, 1969a, p. 186). "Animals mean unconscious movements or tendencies towards what you are going to do, or what is going to happen to you" (Jung, 1988, p. 896). "Pieces of furniture mean contents, either of the conscious or of the unconscious. And baggage, pieces of luggage, very often mean complexes" (Jung, 1997, p. 903). "Symbols of a reconciling and unitive nature do in fact turn up in dreams, the most frequent being the motif of the child-hero and the squaring of the circle, signifying union of opposites" (Jung, 1952a, p. 454). "A snake for a man is eternally a woman" (Jung, 1984, p. 18). "The pearl

128   The creativity of dreams

symbolizes the uniqueness of the individual, the imperishable individual that is always there. It is the hero, really, who is swallowed by the dragon yet always reappears, having destroyed the dragon from within" (Jung, 1997, p. 358). "The snake, particularly the green snake, very often means the path of life, as the river means the flow of life, or the path of fate; it has a source, it follows a potential, and it finally ends in the infinite sea" (Jung, 1997, p. 381). "Fire always symbolizes emotion, passion" (Jung, 1997, p. 407). "The fire means a great outburst of passion" (Jung, 1997, p. 638).

> The Phoenix is a symbol of rebirth, like the eagle in alchemy that rises from the fire. That means that out of this glowing center of passions, from down in the solar plexus, something can rise into the kingdom of the air, into consciousness.
>
> (Jung, 1997, p. 409)

"Water usually means the water of life, the medium through which one is reborn; it symbolizes the baptismal ceremony, or initiation, a healing bath that gives rebirth" (Jung, 1997, p. 1091). "The pyramid represents the Self in its transformation" (Jung, 1997, p. 1345). "Dwarfs mean the innate spirit in things" (Jung, 1997, p. 446). "The golden ball is the sun which represents our libido" (Jung, 1997, p. 542). "Wherever the cauldron appears it indicates the alchemistic process, the process of transformation" (Jung, 1997, p. 562).

Although Jung's clinical work ignored his distinction between symbols and signs, the theoretic distinction was apparently intended to solve Freud's problem with unconscious thing-presentations. Jung's concept of the symbol was inspired, I suggest, by his readings of Friedrich Creuzer's four-volume *Symbolik und Mythologie der alten Völker, besoders der Griechen* [*Symbolism and Mythology of Ancient People*] (1810–12). Jung read Creuzer with great excitement around 1910 and mentioned him both in *Psychology of the Unconscious* (1916b, pp. 268–9) and in his memoirs (Jung, 1989, p. 23, n. 16). With the exception of Noll (1994, pp. 179–81), scholars writing on Jung have nevertheless failed to discuss Creuzer at any length. Creuzer is generally said to have been Jung's introduction to comparative mythology; but Creuzer had even more impact, I suggest, on Jung's theory of symbolism.

For Creuzer, the symbol is a means, above all, by which the divine becomes manifest. Any and all physical phenomena, and any and all thing-presentations, may serve as symbols by betokening the divinity or sacrality that is immanent within them. Creuzer wrote:

> The symbol that was primarily born from sculpture but which, bodied forth through words, through meaningful syllables, through the totality and compact vitality of its essence, could interpret the unity and inexpressibility of religion in a way legend could not.
>
> (In Feldman and Richardson, 1972, p. 392)

"There, the invisible and incorporeal is gradually portrayed as a corporeal image to the eye of the soul. In letters they are as an image of sound, and in hieroglyphs a visible image of a concept" (p. 394). The divine gains expression in symbols; myths string symbols together into sequences that are linguistic by contrast, for example, with painting and sculpture.

> In symbol a universal concept takes on earthly garment, and steps meaningfully before the eye of the soul as an image. In myth the pregnant soul expresses its presentiments or knowledge in a living word. It is also an image but of the kind that, in a way different from symbol, goes through the ear to attain inner meaning.
>
> (p. 396)

The historian of religion Mircea Eliade's (1961) theory of the symbol as a *hierophany*, or manifestation of the sacred, may be treated as an updated assertion of Creuzer's thesis.

For Creuzer, symbols were symbolic because they betokened the divine. For Jung, symbols were similarly natural facts whose implications exceeded the facts themselves; but Jung psychologized Creuzer's metaphysics, leaving the implications unknown and open-ended. "The true symbol ... should be understood as an expression of an intuitive idea that cannot yet be formulated in any other or better way" (Jung, 1922, p. 70). "Symbols are tendencies whose goal is as yet unknown.... This does not contradict the statement that symbols are the best possible formulation of an idea whose referent is not clearly known" (Jung, 1970, p. 468 and n. 54). Jung's formulations agreed with Silberer's secular, psychological phrasing; but Jung could also be read in a sense that comprehended the unknown with a capital "U," that is, as the Mystery or Unknown that is divine.

130   The creativity of dreams

Jung encouraged religious interpretations. Building on Freud's (1914a) ideas of primary narcissism and object cathexis, Jung proposed a systematic interpretation of dreams that tinged them with unitive thinking—with mysticism. Jung (1943c) wrote:

> I call every interpretation which equates the dream images with real objects an *interpretation on the objective level*. In contrast to this is the interpretation which refers every part of the dream and all the actors in it back to the dreamer himself. This I call *interpretation on the subjective level*. Interpretation on the objective level is analytic, because it breaks down the dream content into memory-complexes that refer to external situations. Interpretation on the subjective level is synthetic, because it detaches the underlying memory-complexes from their external causes, regards them as tendencies or components of the subject, and reunites them with that subject.
>
> (p. 14)

Jung's objective level was the level of object-cathexis, his subjective level imagined the perspective of primary narcissism. Where Freud (1930) interpreted mystical states as regressions to primary narcissism, Jung offered dream interpretations that disclosed the primary narcissism that, he assumed, was always inevitably at the deepest unconscious level of dreams. For Jung, disclosing the mystical significance of dreams through their subjective interpretations was intrinsically synthetic. "The synthetic or constructive process of interpretation is interpretation on the subjective level" (p. 85). Because Jung followed Freud in psychologizing mysticism, his claim about subjective interpretations was not metaphysical but naturalistic. Subjective interpretations might be illusions, but they were psychologically necessary all the same. "There is nothing for it but to recognize the irrational as a necessary, because ever-present, psychological function, and to take its contents not as concrete realities—that would be a regression!—but as psychic realities" (p. 95).

A criticism may be offered in passing. Here again Jung was misled by his adherence to a theory of Freud's that has turned out to be mistaken. Direct infant observation has falsified Freud's theory of a discrete stage of infancy when primary narcissism prevails. Mystic states are not regressions to primary narcissism; there is no such stage to which to regress. Mystic states are better appreciated as complex, intellectual achievements of developmentally later construction (for extended discussions, see Merkur, 1998, 1999, 2010). Jung's "subjective interpretations" taught his patients to think like mystics. They did not provide insights into a deeply unconscious mystical awareness that his patients already possessed, for none such existed.

Jung's statements on the creativity of dreams attest to his consciousness of a quandary. Some formulations agree with the Freudian position, that the unconscious supplies irrational images whose endowment with meaning is a conscious interpolation by the creative personality.

> The creative process, so far as we are able to follow it at all, consists in the unconscious activation of an archetypal image, and in elaborating and shaping this image into the finished work. By giving it shape, the artist translates it into the language of the present, and so makes it possible for us to find our way back to the deepest springs of life.
>
> (Jung, 1922, p. 82)

Jung found it difficult, however, to reconcile this theory with the fact of creativity's novelty.

> Thus the unconscious is seen as the collective predisposition to extreme conservativism, a guarantee, almost, that nothing new will ever happen.
>
> If this statement were unreservedly true, there would be none of that creative fantasy which is responsible for radical changes and innovations. Therefore our statement must be in part erroneous, since creative fantasy exists and is not simply the prerogative of the unconscious psyche. Generally speaking, it is an intrusion from the realm of the unconscious, a sort of lucky hunch, different in kind from the slow reasoning of the conscious mind. Thus the unconscious is seen as a creative factor, even as a bold innovator, and yet it is at the same time the stronghold of ancestral conservativism. A paradox, I admit, but it cannot be helped.
>
> (Jung, 1930a, p. 34)

Although theory might lead one to expect unconscious creativity to subsist on repetitions of the unconscious's meagre stock of motifs, the actual scope of creativity is highly impressive.

It is, however, far from my intention to give the impression that the unconscious is merely reactive in all cases. On the contrary, there is a host of experiences which seem to prove that the unconscious is not only spontaneous but can actually take the lead.

(Jung, 1938b, p. 184)

Faced with clinical evidence of more creativity than his theory of dreams could explain, Jung appreciated that alternate possibilities merited mention. Conforming dogmatically to Freud's metapsychology without mentioning his name, Jung rejected the possibility that the dream-work involves thought. "The dream, being essentially a subliminal process, cannot produce a definite thought, unless it should cease to be a dream by instantly becoming a conscious content" (Jung, 1964, p. 223). The theoretic option that remained tenable for Jung was a mechanical model of dreams' creativity. "We may talk about the *unconscious goal orientation* of the dream process, in noting that these are not conscious goals, not intentions like those of consciousness, but ... purposive automatisms that, like cell reactions, cannot be other than purposive" (Jung, 2008, p. 4).

Jung named compensation as dreams' primary function, that is, their "unconscious goal orientation" or "purposive automatisms." "Dreams are the compensators of consciousness. If it were not so we would have to regard them as a source of knowledge superior to consciousness" (Jung, 1966b, p. 290). Jung's practice of dream interpretation privileged the concept of compensation. "There is no rule, let alone a law, of dream interpretation, although it does look as if the general purpose of dreams is *compensation*" (Jung, 1964, p. 220; see also 1918, p. 20; 1921, p. 423; 1926a, p. 101; 1928a, p. 163; 1931a, pp. 153–4; 1934b, p. 152; 1936a, p. 110; 1943c, p. 104; 1948b, pp. 244, 250, 252; 1948h, pp. 287–8, 290, 296; 1973b, p. 133; 1984, p. 457). The term *compensation* made Jung seem more original than he was. It referred to the clinical evidence that Freud had called the unconscious becoming conscious. What is unconscious strives for consciousness and, in doing so, compensates for the one-sidedness of consciousness. In Jung's view, compensation was an automatic, mechanical process, akin to a rheostat reacting to changes in room temperature by turning a furnace or air conditioning on or off.

Though dreams contribute to the self-regulation of the psyche by automatically bringing up everything that is repressed or neglected or unknown, their compensatory significance is often not immediately apparent because we still have only a very incomplete knowledge of the nature and the needs of the human psyche.

(Jung, 1948g, p. 250)

The more one-sided his conscious attitude is, and the further it deviates from the optimum, the greater becomes the possibility that vivid dreams with a strongly contrasting but purposive content will appear as an expression of the self-regulation of the psyche.

(p. 253; see also 1936a, p. 110)

Jung (1948g) accounted for the compensatory function by invoking the theory that dreams are autosymbolic. "I hold with my friend and collaborator Alphonse Maeder that the dream is a spontaneous self-portrayal, in symbolic form, of the actual situation in the unconscious. Our view coincides at this point with the conclusions of Silberer" (p. 263; see also 1938c, p. 131).

The driving force, so far as it is possible for us to grasp it, seems to be in essence only an urge towards self-realization. If it were a matter of some general teleological plan, then all individuals who enjoy a surplus of unconsciousness would necessarily be driven towards higher consciousness by an irresistible urge. That is plainly not the case.

(Jung, 1938c, p. 184)

When consciousness is one-sidedly one way, unconsciousness is one-sidedly the opposite, and a dream that portrays the unconscious situation manifests unconscious materials that unwittingly function as compensations for conscious one-sidedness.

Over and over again I have seen how thoughts that were not thought and feelings that were not felt by day afterwards appeared in dreams, and in this way reached consciousness indirectly. The dream as such is undoubtedly a content of consciousness, otherwise it could not be an object of immediate experience. But in so far as it brings up material that was unconscious before, we are forced to assume that these contents already had some kind of psychic existence in an unconscious state and appeared to the "remnant" of consciousness only in the dream.

(Jung, 1948i, p. 144)

Jung recognized that the compensation is seldom appreciated by consciousness, but he postulated a kind of "psychic equilibrium" that had psychic reality. "Dreams try to re-establish the equilibrium by restoring the images and emotions that express the state of the unconscious" (Jung, 1964, p. 209; see also 1958a, p. 388; 1980, p. 608).

Jung's theory of dreams was tidy, but Jung was aware that it was incomplete. Clinically Jung knew what he sometimes denied in his theories. "The unconscious is capable at times of manifesting an intelligence and purposiveness superior to the actual conscious insight" (Jung, 1938a, p. 39). "All the activities ordinarily taking place in consciousness can also proceed in the unconscious. There are numerous instances of an intellectual problem, unsolved in the waking state, being solved in a dream" (Jung, 1948i, p. 144). For Jung, the intellectual activities in dreams remained an unsolved puzzle.

Chapter 4

Having it out with the unconscious

In 1916, Jung wrote an article entitled "The Transcendent Function" that remained unpublished until 1957, when it was printed privately by students at the Zurich institute. It was included in Jung's Collected Works in 1958. The text speaks briefly of several different ways in which people may consciously cultivate manifestations of the unconscious that are suitable foundations for the transcendent function.

> Critical attention must be eliminated. Visual types should concentrate on expectation that an inner image will be produced. As a rule such a fantasy-picture will actually appear—perhaps hypnagogically—and should be carefully observed and noted down in writing. Audio-verbal types usually hear inner words, perhaps mere fragments of apparently meaningless sentences to begin with, which however should be carefully noted down too. Others at such times simply hear their "other" voice. There are, indeed, not a few people who are well aware that they possess a sort of inner critic or judge who immediately comments on everything they say or do. Insane people hear this voice directly as auditory hallucinations. But normal people too, if their inner life is fairly well developed, are able to reproduce this inaudible voice without difficulty, though as it is notoriously irritating and refractory it is almost always repressed. Such persons have little difficulty in procuring the unconscious material and thus laying the foundation of the transcendent function.
>
> There are others, again, who neither see nor hear anything inside themselves but whose hands have the knack of giving expression to the contents of the unconscious. Such people can profitably work with plastic materials. Those who are able to express the unconscious by means of bodily movements are rather rare.
>
> (Jung, 1958c, pp. 83–4)

136   Having it out with the unconscious

Jung warned that giving the unconscious the opportunity to manifest, in any of these manners, runs the risk of destabilizing consciousness.

> Just as the conscious mind … has a restrictive effect on the unconscious, so the rediscovered unconscious often has a really dangerous effect on the ego. In the same way that the ego suppressed the unconscious before, a liberated unconscious can thrust the ego aside and overwhelm it. There is a danger of the ego losing its head, so to speak that it will not be able to defend itself against the pressure of affective factors—a situation often encountered at the beginning of schizophrenia.
> (Jung, 1958c, p. 87; see also 1936–37, p. 49; 1941, p. 190; 1950a, p. 351; 1966, pp. 282–3)

When unconscious materials have manifested, however, consciousness is not only in danger of being overwhelmed by them, but is also in a position to engage them in an interaction, for example, in a dialogue; and it is the outcome of the interaction that constitutes the transcendent function.

> The psychological "transcendent function" arises from the union of conscious and unconscious contents.
> Experience in analytical psychology has amply shown that the conscious and the unconscious seldom agree as to their content and their tendencies. This lack of parallelism is not just accidental or purposeless, but is due to the fact that the unconscious behaves in a calm compensatory or complementary manner.
> (Jung, 1958c, p. 69)

As an example of the process of "having it out with the unconscious" (Jung, 1958c, p. 88), Jung discussed the experience of an "inner voice."

> The way this can be done is best shown by those cases in which the "other" voice is more or less distinctly heard. For such people it is technically very simple to note down the "other" voice in writing and to answer its statements from the standpoint of the ego. It is exactly as if a dialogue were taking place between two human beings with equal rights, each or else to distinguish them clearly from one another. Since the way to agreement seldom stands open, in most

cases a long conflict will have to be borne, demanding sacrifices from both sides ...

The shuttling to and fro of arguments and affects represents the transcendent function of opposites.

(Jung, 1958c, pp. 87–8, 90)

The transcendent function also operates through dreams and normal waking consciousness, as a process of assertion and reversal over the course of days or weeks, in thinking a problem through.

In the unconscious he must submit to the slow progress of to and fro; to a sort of balancing deliberation, a sort of torture. One day you think you have come to a clear decision, next day it is gone. You feel like a fool and curse it until you learn that this thing is pairs of opposites, and you are not the opposite. If you learn that, you have got your lesson.

(Jung, 1984, p. 149)

When the unconscious is manifesting amid resistance, the overall thought process has a cumulative aspect that is analogous to a zig-zag motion, or tacking a sailboat into the wind. Small forward gains are made in the midst of considerable sideways movement. Each shift from consciousness to the unconscious, or vice versa, makes the waste obvious, while the modest gain is unaffected by the criticism and persists. The analogies to zig-zagging and tacking imply, of course, that there is a goal toward progress that is slowly being made. In the case of the transcendent function, the goal is unconscious and its direction is unknown until it is discovered.

In many cases, the ego's admission of unconscious materials to consciousness places the ego on the defensive and requires it to undergo much-needed growth. "Nothing so promotes the growth of consciousness as this inner confrontation of opposites. Quite unsuspected facts turn up in the indictment, and the defense is obliged to discover arguments hitherto unknown" (Jung, 1973b, p. 345). In other cases, when consciousness and the unconscious engage in a dialectic, forming thesis and its "compensatory or complementary" antithesis, consciousness holds its own against the unconscious. The impasse is resolved when the unconscious not only manifests but develops new and original positions.

In each instance, the novelties that the unconscious produces constitute a third position that exceeds both the thesis and the antithesis by reconciling the opposites in a unity.

> The confrontation of the two positions generates a tension charged with energy and creates a living, third thing—not a logical stillbirth in accordance with the principle *tertium non datur* but a movement out of the suspension between opposites, a living birth that leads to a new level of being, a new situation. The transcendent function manifests itself as a quality of conjoined opposites. So long as these are kept apart—naturally for the purpose of avoiding conflict—they do not function and remain inert.
>
> (Jung, 1958c, p. 90)

Jung's initial formulation of the transcendent function was implicitly indebted to Hegel's ideas of dialectic.[1] However, the transcendent function is not an automatic, predicable compromise of thesis and antithesis. It is not a mathematical halving of the distance between the conscious and the unconscious. Rather, the transcendent function frequently accomplishes creative innovation. Jung nevertheless attempted to reduce creativity to a species of uncreative automaticity. "In whatever form the opposites appear in the individual, at bottom it is always a matter of a consciousness lost and obstinately stuck in one-sidedness, confronted with the image of instinctive wholeness and freedom" (Jung, 1958c, p. 90). Jung's idea that the transcendent function arrives the psyche at wholeness was not an empirical observation but an inference from his theories. The interpretation of wholeness rests on the prior assumption of unconscious compensation. If it is true that the unconscious invariably

---

1 Editor's note: Jung was critical of Hegel in his Collective Works, although he likely purloined various aspects of his philosophy when it suited him. Hegel's dialectic is often misunderstood and inaccurately captured by the pedestrian phrase "thesis-antithesis-synthesis," when this phrase comes from Fichte's *Wissenschaftslehre*, which Jung would have likely read along with Kant and other German Idealists of his day. For Hegel, the dialectic is much more complicated and involves a complex movement of mediating opposition while surpassing its immediate shape, which constitutes a simultaneous threefold process as the act of negation or annulment, transcendence or supersession, while at the same time subsuming or preserving opposition within a higher structural unity of mind (see Mills, 2002, for a review).

compensates for the one-sidedness of consciousness and does not engage, for example, only in wish-fulfilments or the return of the repressed, then and only then might we take for granted that the transcendent function necessarily arrives precisely and always at wholeness. For clinical purposes, it suffices that it enriches the ego by manifesting previously unknown, unconscious materials.

Jung first referred to the transcendent function in print in 1917, in an article titled "The Psychology of the Unconscious Processes," whose 1943 revision appears in Jung's Collected Works. The nature of the process was only vaguely mentioned in the original version of the article; the 1943 additions were as confusing as they were helpful.

> The point is not conversion into the opposite but conservation of previous values together with recognition of their opposite. Naturally this means conflict and self-division. It is understandable enough that one should shrink from it, philosophically as well as morally; hence the alternative sought, more often than conversion into the opposite, is a convulsive stiffening of the previous attitude.
>
> (Jung, 1943c, p. 76)

Even at a descriptive level, Jung remained mysterious and suggestive, rather than adequately explanatory.

> A general account of this process, which may extend over a long period of time, would be pointless—even if such a description were possible—because it takes the greatest imaginable variety of forms in different individuals. The only common factor is the emergence of certain definite archetypes.
>
> (Jung, 1943c, pp. 109–10)

At the same time, in a passage that discussed therapeutic progress from the personal to the collective unconscious, Jung (1943c) asserted that similar experiences of images explained the appeal of Theosophy and its offshoot, Anthroposophy.

> When, on the other hand, psychic energy regresses, going beyond even the period of early infancy, and breaks into the legacy of ancestral life, the mythological images are awakened: these are the

archetypes. An interior spiritual world whose existence we never suspected opens out and displays contents which seem to stand in sharpest contrast to all our former ideas. These images are so intense that it is quite understandable why millions of cultivated persons should be taken in by theosophy and anthroposophy.

(p. 77)

Jung acknowledged that he was employing mental imagery techniques for therapeutic purposes that occultists deployed to attain magical ends. "Analytical psychology ... now seeks to investigate scientifically the phenomena of the unconscious—the same phenomena which the theosophical and Gnostic sects made accessible to the simple-minded in the form of portentous mysteries" (Jung, 1918, p. 16). Jung acknowledged the parallelism without explanation; but his practice of secrecy, together with his admission of the proximity of the visions to occult practices, raises the question, impossible to answer, whether Jung *discovered* his visualization practices, as Jungian hagiography maintains (Hannah, 1976, p. 108), or instead modified visualization practices that he had originally encountered in an occult milieu. Perhaps he was taught occult visualization on condition of secrecy. He was definitely practicing yoga as early as visualization (Jung, 1973a, p. 177), and we are equally ignorant of his introduction to meditative practices. At any rate, a generation prior to Jung the Theosophist Franz Hartmann (1885, p. 210) had discussed an occult mental imagery practice under the very name that Jung favored from 1936 onward, *active imagination*.

Whatever may have been Jung's motives for secrecy about his visualization practice, as late as 1956 he acknowledged: "I myself have said little about it and have contented myself with hints" (Jung, 1970, p. 530). He provided a good overview of the transcendent function only toward the end of his life. The Hegelian structure of the process, as a dialectic between consciousness and the unconscious, remained prominent in his understanding of it.

In the cases with which we are here concerned it is tacitly agreed that the apparently incompatible contents shall not be suppressed again, and that the conflict shall be accepted and suffered. At first no solution appears possible, and this fact, too, has to be borne with patience. The suspension thus created "constellates" the unconscious—in other words, the unconscious suspense produces a new compensatory reaction in the unconscious. This reaction (usually manifested in dreams) is brought to conscious realization in its turn. The conscious mind is thus confronted with a new aspect of the psyche, which arouses a different problem or modifies an old one in an unexpected way. The procedure is continued until the original conflict is satisfactorily resolved.... The function is called "transcendent" because it facilitates the transition from one psychic condition to another by means of the mutual confrontation of opposites.

(Jung, 1954d, p. 489)

The transcendent function and symbol-formation

Years earlier, in his book *Psychological Types* (1921), Jung offered a simple and helpful entry to the topic. "This function of mediation between the opposites I have termed the *transcendent function*, by which I mean nothing mysterious, but merely a combined function of conscious and unconscious elements" (Jung, 1921, p. 115). The concept of mediation must be added to and reconciled with the idea of a dialectical process. Unfortunately, Jung went on to confound issues by drawing on Freud's ideas of symbol-formation. "The mediatory condition is characterized as producing 'something positive,' namely the symbol. The symbol unites antithetical elements within its nature" (Jung, 1921, pp. 128–9).

We know from daily experience in the treatment of neurotic patients what an eminently practical importance the interventions from the unconscious possess. The greater the dissociation, i.e., the more the conscious attitude becomes alienated from the individual and collective contents of the unconscious, the more harmfully the unconscious inhibits or intensifies the conscious contents. For quite practical reasons, therefore, the symbol must be credited with a not inconsiderable value. But if we grant it a value, whether great or small, the symbol acquires a conscious motive force—that is, it is *perceived*, and its unconscious libido-charge is thereby given an opportunity to make itself felt in the conscious conduct of life. Thus, in my view, a practical advantage of no small consequence is gained, namely, the *collaboration of the unconscious*, its participation in the conscious psychic performance, and hence the elimination of disturbing influences from the unconscious.

This common function, the relation to the symbol, I have termed the *transcendent function*.

(Jung, 1921, p. 126)

Drawing on Freud's ideas about neurotic symptom-formation in order to conceptualize symbol-formation in the transcendent function had the unintended effect of pathologizing creativity. Freud's (1900) account of the suppression or repression of unpleasure, leading to symbol-formation and the return of the repressed, may be *analogous* to the transcendent function; but it is a mistake to equate the spontaneous occurrence of symbol-formation that occurs in psychopathology, with the voluntary stimulation of the unconscious and its deliberate provocation to symbol-formation in the case of the transcendent function. Compromise-formation and mediation may be analogized, but they are not equivalent. Jung nevertheless obliterated the difference between the two processes, possibly because he was constrained by his ideas about psychic energy. In Jung's formulation, the voluntary initiation of the transcendent function invigorates the unconscious while de-stabilizing consciousness. The resultant symbols are indeed symptoms, and are not merely analogous to symptoms, because the introverted psychic state is, in effect, a voluntary pathology.

The more the libido is invested—or, to be more accurate, invests itself—in the unconscious, the greater becomes its influence or potency: all the rejected, disused, outlived functional possibilities that have been lost for generations to come to life again and begin to exert an ever-increasing influence on the conscious mind, despite its desperate struggles to gain insight into what is happening. The saving factor is the symbol, which embraces both conscious and unconscious and unites them. For while the consciously disposable libido gets gradually used up in the differentiated function and is replenished more and more slowly and with increasing difficulty, the symptoms of inner disunity multiply and there is a growing danger of inundation and destruction by the unconscious contents, but all the time the symbol is developing that is destined to resolve the conflict. The symbol, however, is so intimately bound up with the dangerous and menacing aspect of the unconscious that it is easily mistaken for it, or its appearance may actually call forth evil and destructive tendencies.

(Jung, 1921, p. 264)

In keeping with Herbert Silberer's (1912) distinction between the psychoanalytic and anagogical interpretations of single symbols, Jung (1921, p. 252) maintained that there were "two methods of treatment: 1. the reductive, and 2. the synthetic."

The synthetic method elaborates the symbolic fantasies resulting from the introversion of libido.... This produces a new attitude to the world, whose very difference offers a new potential. I have termed this transition to a new attitude the transcendent function.

(Jung, 1921, p. 252)

The synthetic level of interpretation, and method of treatment, treated the manifest content of the symbol as its point of departure. It was, in Freud's terminology, a "secondary elaboration" of the symbolism.

If the mediatory product remains intact, it forms the raw material for a process not of dissolution but of construction, in which thesis and antithesis both play their part. In this way it becomes a new content that governs the whole attitude, putting an end to the division and forcing the energy of the opposites into a common channel. The standstill is overcome in life and can flow on with renewed power toward new goals.

I have called this process in its totality the *transcendent function*, "function" being here understood not as a basic function but as a complex function made up of other functions, and "transcendent" not as denoting a metaphysical quality but merely the fact that this function facilitates a transition from one to another. The raw material shaped by thesis and antithesis, and in the shaping of which the opposites are united, is the living symbol.

(Jung, 1921, p. 480)

Jung's subsequent formulations of the transcendent function regularly emphasized the production of symbols. "Symbols were never devised consciously, but were always produced out of the unconscious by way of revelation or intuition" (Jung, 1928b, p. 48). "The union of opposites on a higher level of consciousness is not a rational thing, nor is it a matter of will; it is a process of psychic development that expresses itself in symbols" (Jung, 1938a, p. 21).

Amplification

It would be a mistake, however, to neglect the idiosyncrasy in Jung's use of the words *rational* and *irrational*. Consider, for example, the following statement: "This continual process of getting to know the counterposition in the unconscious I have called the 'transcendent function,' because the confrontation of conscious (rational) data with those that are unconscious (irrational) necessarily results in a modification of standpoint" (Jung, 1970, p. 200). The transcendent function is not a product of logical thinking, performed consciously by the ego, that utilizes syllogisms in order to arrive at conclusions. It cannot be attributed to what the medievals called *ratio*, reason, the rational faculty of the Aristotelian soul. Its symbols manifest spontaneously, as intuitions, having implicitly been produced by the unconscious. They are accordingly irrational, which is to say, not of conscious origin. They are not necessarily illogical, however, nor lacking in wisdom. "The transcendent function ... is the discursive co-operation of conscious and unconscious factors or, in theological language, of reason and grace" (Jung, 1958b, p. 454).

How the harmonizing of conscious and unconscious data is to be undertaken cannot be indicated in the form of a recipe. It is an irrational life-process which expresses itself in definite symbols. It may be the task of the analyst to stand by this process with all the help he can give. In this case, knowledge of the symbols is indispensable, for it is in them that the union of conscious and unconscious contents is consummated. Out of this union emerge new situations and new conscious attitudes. I have therefore called the union of opposites the "transcendent function." This rounding out of the personality into a whole may well be the goal of any psychotherapy that claims to be more than a mere cure of symptoms.

(Jung, 1939a, p. 289)

By the help that the analyst provides, Jung referred to the procedure that he called *amplification*, which amplifies the patient's production of symbols with further instances of the same symbols, known to the therapist through studies of the world's mythologies and religions. The therapist's knowledge of comparative symbolism provides "intellectual categories and moral feelings" that place the symbols in a coherent or logical context.

In my experience it is of considerable practical importance that the symbols aiming at wholeness should be correctly understood by the doctor. They are the remedy with whose help neurotic associations can be repaired, by restoring to the conscious mind a spirit and an attitude which from time immemorial have been felt as solving and healing in their effects. They are "représentations collectives" which facilitate the much-needed union of conscious and unconscious. This union cannot be accomplished either intellectually or in a purely practical sense, because in the former case the instincts rebel and in the latter case reason and morality. Every dissociation that falls within the category of the psychogenic neuroses is due to a conflict of this kind, and the conflict can only be resolved through the symbol. For this purpose the dreams produce symbols which in the last analysis coincide with those recorded throughout history. But the dream-images can be taken up into the dreamer's consciousness, and grasped by his reason and feeling, only if his conscious mind possesses the intellectual categories and moral feelings necessary for their assimilation. And this is where the psychotherapist often has to perform feats that tax his patience to the utmost. The synthesis of conscious and unconscious can only be implemented by a conscious confrontation with the latter, and this is not possible unless one understands what the unconscious is saying. During this process we come upon the symbols investigated in the present study, and in coming to terms with them we re-establish the lost connection with ideas and feelings which make a synthesis of the personality possible. The loss of gnosis, i.e., knowledge of the ultimate things, weighs much more heavily than is generally admitted. Faith alone would suffice too, did it not happen to be a charisma whose true possession is something of a rarity, except in spasmodic form. Were it otherwise, we doctors could spare ourselves much thankless work.

(Jung, 1948d, pp. 191–2)

Active imagination

Jung maintained that the transcendent function is a naturally occurring developmental process that sometimes occurs spontaneously. To illustrate his contention, Jung cited the New Testament narrative of the three temptations of Christ.

> There are many normal cases in which, under certain circumstances, a character opposed to the conscious personality suddenly manifests itself, causing a conflict between the two personalities.
>
> Take the classic case of the temptation of Christ, for example. We say that the devil tempted him, but we could just as well say that an unconscious desire for power confronted him in the form of the devil. Both sides appear here: the light side and the dark. The devil wants to tempt Jesus to proclaim himself master of the world. Jesus wants not to succumb to the temptation; then, thanks to the function that results from every conflict, a symbol appears: it is the idea of the Kingdom of Heaven, a spiritual kingdom rather than a material one. Two things are united in this symbol, the spiritual attitude of Christ and the devilish desire for power. Thus the encounter of Christ with the devil is a classic example of the transcendent function. It appears here in the form of an involuntary personal experience. But it can be used as a method too; that is, when the contrary will of the unconscious is sought for and recognized in dreams and other unconscious products. In this way the conscious personality is brought face to face with the counter-position of the unconscious. The resulting conflict— thanks precisely to the transcendent function—leads to a symbol uniting the opposed positions. The symbol cannot be consciously chosen or constructed; it is a sort of intuition or revelation. Hence the transcendent function is only usable in part as a method, the other part always remains an involuntary experience.
>
> (Jung, 1973a, pp. 267–8)

Similar crises of personality development may be expected toward the end of the first major phase of analytical psychology. When the shadow or personal unconscious becomes conscious, consciousness of the personality is widened, and the ego is obliged to integrate previously conscious shadow materials within itself. Jung described this phase of the work as "the ego-personality's coming to terms with its own background, the shadow" (Jung, 1970, p. 497). The process inevitably involves the ego giving ground. The persona, or social presentation of oneself with which the ego has identified as its self-image, is invariably falsified by its newly acquired knowledge of the shadow, leading the ego to abandon its persona. At the same time, the archetypes of the collective unconscious have the opportunity to manifest consciously, among other means, in both fantasies and dreams.

> One result of the dissolution of the persona is the release of fantasy, which is apparently nothing less than the specific activity of this collective psyche. This outburst of fantasy throws up into consciousness materials and impulses whose existence one had never before suspected. All the treasures of mythological thinking and feeling are unlocked.
>
> (Jung, 1966b, p. 282; see also p. 283)

> In most cases it is contents of an archetypal nature, or the connections between them, that exert a strong influence of their own whether or not they are understood by the conscious mind. This spontaneous activity of the psyche often becomes so intense that visionary pictures are seen or inner voices heard—a true, primordial experience of the spirit.
>
> (Jung, 1932, p. 346)

Archetypal content could also manifest in consciousness through a technique Jung developed (using himself) called "active imagination," which was an "indispensable" part of his form of analysis "that is really meant to go to the roots" (Jung, 1973a, p. 459). Here we would summon visions and voices through autosuggestion or the free-reign of fantasy, but they are far from being psychotic states. Jung explains: "These 'visions' are far from being hallucinations or ecstatic states; they are spontaneous, visual images of fantasy or so-called *active imagination*. The latter is a method (devised by myself) of introspection for observing the stream of interior images" (Jung, 1941, p. 190). Jung devised different techniques or methods for inducing active imaginary states that could apply to waking consciousness, dreams, daydreaming, fantasy elaboration, and so forth by focusing on internal images in one's mind. Here he experienced his methodology could "get a grasp of contents that also find expression in dream life. The process ... [is] an irrigation of the conscious mind by the unconscious, and ... ultimately ... the process of individuation" (Jung, 1952d, p. 346). Other variations of active imagination produced a sequence of fantasies "by deliberate concentration" (Jung, 1936–37, p. 49). The goal of the process was to integrate unconscious productions into conscious understanding, without which could result in remaining unconscious of the imaginary material played out in fantasy.

> This process can begin and run its course without any special knowledge having to stand sponsor to it. But if one wants to understand anything of it and assimilate it into consciousness, then a certain amount of knowledge is needed. If the process is not understood at all, it has to build up an unusual intensity so as not to sink back again into the unconscious without result.
>
> (Jung, 1950a, p. 351)

But Jung was careful to note certain indications for the use of active imagination as a therapeutic measure as well as its potential dangers.

When appropriate fantasies did not occur spontaneously, Jung intervened with procedures that would circumvent the inhibition. "If there is no capacity to produce fantasies freely, we have to resort to artificial aid. The reason for invoking such aid is generally a depressed or disturbed state of mind for which no adequate cause can be found" (Jung, 1958c, p. 82). Here Jung seems to be suggesting that certain recalcitrant symptoms require more of a guided procedure to get at the underlying disturbance rather than relying on a spontaneous stream of consciously producing fantasies. But he was also careful about whom he could use the procedure with:

> I don't use active imagination as a panacea; there have to be definite indications that the method is suitable for the individual, and there are a number of patients with whom it would be wrong to force it upon them. But often in the later stages of analysis, the objectification of images replaces the dreams. The images anticipate the dreams, and so the dream-material begins to peter out. The unconscious becomes deflated insofar as the conscious mind relates to it. Then you get all the material in a creative form and this has great

advantages over dream-material. It quickens the process of maturation, for analysis is a process of quickened maturation.

(Jung, 1936a, p. 172)

This passage suggests that active imagination can get to the heart of the matter and supersede other therapeutic approaches common to clinical psychoanalysis that may take time due to the free-associative method. He also warns against imposing interpretations on patients, which may have unintended consequences.

Stiffnecked and violent interpretations should under all circumstances be avoided, likewise a patient should never be forced into a development that does not come naturally and spontaneously. But once it has set in, he should not be talked out of it again, unless the possibility of a psychosis has been definitely established.

(Jung, 1950a, p. 351)

Jung is sensitive to the observation that this procedure could go too far and even contribute to inducing psychosis in certain patients. But his main goal is to form a union of oppositions between the unconscious and conscious dimensions of the personality, which can only be accomplished by an open confrontation between these two split-off aspects of mind.

As a rule it occurs when the analysis has constellated the opposites so powerfully that a union or synthesis of the personality becomes an imperative necessity. Such a situation is bound to arise when the analysis of the psychic contents, of the patient's attitude and particularly of his dreams, has brought the compensatory or complementary images from the unconscious so insistently before his mind that the conflict between the conscious and the unconscious personality becomes open and critical.

(Jung, 1970, pp. 494–5)

There are many places in his writings where Jung warns of the dangers of active imagination, something he insists "ought not to be minimized" because the psyche can easily become overwhelmed (Jung, 1966b, p. 282; see also p. 283). He cautions the practitioner against its "thoughtless application" because it "may carry the patient too far away from reality" (Jung, 1936–37, p. 49). The worst-case scenario is a renegade psychosis (see Jung, 1950a, p. 351).

> With slightly pathological individuals, and particularly in the not infrequent cases of latent schizophrenia, the method may, in certain circumstances, prove to be rather dangerous and therefore requires medical control. It is based on the deliberate weakening of the conscious mind and its inhibiting effect, which either limits or suppresses the unconscious.
>
> (Jung, 1941, p. 190)

Jung pointed out that the tendency to "unleash a psychosis" usually presented itself at the beginning of the treatment, but "if it has got so far that the patient can do active imagination and shape out his fantasies, and there are no suspicious incidents, then there is as a rule no longer any danger" (Jung, 1970, p. 530).

In various places in his writings, Jung offered instruction on how to conduct and induce active imagination in patients. "You begin by concentrating upon a starting point" (Jung, 1936a, p. 171). The starting point often involved concentrating on inner images or pictures, and allowing them to unfold naturally in fantasy, which "produce a series of images which make a complete story" (Jung, 1936a, p. 172). But active imagination also culled from classical psychoanalysis' use of free-association:

> In cases of this sort, the patient is simply given the task of contemplating any one fragment of fantasy that seems significant to him—a chance idea, perhaps, or something he has become conscious of in the dream—until its context becomes visible, that is to say, the relevant associative material in which it is embedded.
>
> (Jung, 1936–37, p. 49)

In addition to focusing on inner pictures, visions, dream-images, and the like, Jung also gave great weight to spontaneous visual impressions and changes in the mind's eye. Observing such changes is part of the evolving story. But at the same time, he adopted the stance from phenomenology and tried to bracket out ontological questions by simply staying focused on the developing material: "all criticism must be suspended and the happenings observed and noted with absolute objectivity" (Jung, 1941, p. 190). Jung also noted that with sustained concentration, the spontaneous generation of images or pictures in the mind would start to "talk."

> Often, when a patient has a tendency to remain static, if you concentrate upon it, it begins to move or to talk. It might remain quite silent and mute, but if you concentrate sufficiently, the picture begins to talk. The more you concentrate upon that creative energy, the image, the more you animate it with actual life. Of course, the more you fill the image with life, the more you lose your own consciousness, and therefore the *dhyana* condition, the trends, as the effect of a contraction of the field of vision, a sort of *abaissement du niveau mental*, or a *rétrécissement de la conscience*. There is a loss of realization of your self while you realize the life of the object all the more.
>
> (Jung, 1997, p. 122)

Here Jung focuses upon how a certain dissociability of psyche operates when consciousness of oneself is suspended in becoming absorbed in and animating the life of the fantasy scenario. In fact, Jung encouraged many different forms of experimentation with methodologies that were peculiar to each patient and their dispositions and predilections.

> I therefore took up a dream-image or an association of the patient's, and, with this as a point of departure, set him the task of elaborating or developing his theme by giving free rein to his fantasy. This, according to individual taste and talent, could be done in any number of ways, dramatic, dialectic, visual, acoustic, or in the form of dancing, painting, drawing, or modelling.
>
> (Jung, 1954b, p. 202)

Jung implicitly realized the creative tendency or urge that active fantasies could be played out that communicated something specific about patients' personal unconscious processes. Where personalities had difficulty visualizing images, he would then focus on affect or emotional states that became the starting point for his procedure. He would then systematically guide the patient or instruct through self-analysis to focus upon and become fully conscious of the mood one is in so as to amplify and clarify the affect and bring it into the forefront along with conscious content, which makes it more clear, "understandable," and sets the stage for integration.

> At all events, it creates a new situation, since the previously unrelated affect has become a more or less clear idea, thanks to the assistance and co-operation of the conscious mind. This is the beginning of the transcendent function, i.e., of the collaboration of conscious and unconscious data.
>
> The emotional disturbance can also be dealt with in another way, not by clarifying it intellectually but by giving it visible shape. It is not important for the picture to be technically or aesthetically satisfying, but merely for the fantasy to have free play and for the whole thing to be done as well as possible. Patients who possess some talent for drawing or painting can give expression to their mood by means of a picture.
>
> (Jung, 1958c, pp. 82–3)

Recall, this is exactly what Jung did in his Red Book.

Jung wrote in other places on the internal resistances and defenses that are evoked which create inhibitions and impasses to entering into active imagination, with some strategies on how to overcome them.

> To begin with, the task consists solely in observing objectively how a fragment of fantasy develops. Nothing could be simpler, and yet right here the difficulties begin. Apparently one has no fantasy fragments—or yes, there's one, but it is too stupid! Dozens of good reasons are brought against it. One cannot concentrate on it—it is too boring—what would come of it anyway—it is "nothing but" this or that, and so on. The conscious mind raises innumerable objections, in fact it often seems bent on blocking out the spontaneous fantasy activity in spite of real insight and in spite of the firm determination to allow the psychic process to go without interference. Occasionally there is a veritable cramp of consciousness.
>
> If one is successful in overcoming the initial difficulties, criticism is still likely to start in afterwards in the attempt to interpret the fantasy, to classify it, to accept this, size it, or to devalue it. The temptation to do this is almost irresistible.
>
> (Jung, 1928b, pp. 16–17)

Having it out with the unconscious   153

But Jung says one must go back to fixing attention and concentrating on the given image, vision, inner picture, affect, etc. as a means of overcoming the resistance and creating one's own internal reality.

> It is an undeniable psychological fact that the more one concentrates on one's unconscious contents the more they become charged with energy; they become vitalized, as if it illuminated from within. In fact they turn into something like a substitute reality.
>
> (Jung, 1954d, p. 496)

Although Jung believed that our psychologies conform to certain "irrational" laws of human nature (Jung, 1984, p. 79), they nevertheless acquire their own psychic reality that at times can blur all distinctions between what is real and not.

> Each time the fantasy material is to be produced, the activity of consciousness must be switched off again.
>
> In most cases the results of these efforts are not very encouraging at first. Usually they consist of tenuous webs of fantasy that give no clear indication of their origin or their goal. Also, the way of getting at the fantasies varies with individuals. For many people, it is easiest to write them down; others visualize him, and others again draw or paint them with or without visualization. If there is a high degree of conscious cramp, often only the hands are capable of fantasy; they model or draw figures that are sometimes quite foreign to the conscious mind.
>
> These exercises must be continued until the cramp in the conscious mind is relaxed, in other words, until one can let things happen, which is the next goal of the exercise. In this way a new attitude is created, an attitude that accepts the irrational and the incomprehensible simply because it is happening.
>
> (Jung, 1928b, p. 17)

For Jung, it is necessary to suspend reality-testing, lose the resistance of reality-concerns, and habituate to fantasy. What Jung called "the cramp in the conscious mind" is the objection of reality-testing to his effort to become embedded in fantasy material. He wanted people not only to play, but also to lose themselves in play, that is, to mistake fantasy for reality.

Jung provided further elaboration on the techniques of active imagination by reinforcing the patient practice of concentration and suspension of a critical faculty:

> Take the unconscious in one of its handiest forms, say a spontaneous fantasy, a dream, and irrational mood, an affect, or something of the kind, and operate with it. Give it your special attention, concentrate on it, and observe its alterations objectively. Spare no effort to devote yourself to this task, follow the subsequent transformations of the spontaneous fantasy attentively and carefully. Above all, don't let anything from outside, that does not belong, get into it, for the fantasy-image has "everything it needs." In this way one is certain of not interfering by conscious caprice and of giving the unconscious a free hand.
>
> (Jung, 1970, p. 526)

Jung believed that a sustained patient approach to the method would eventually bring about a series of dramas in one's fantasy life that "brings a mass of unconscious material to light" (Jung, 1941, p. 190). Whether the process is spontaneous or artificially induced, there actually is a variety of starting points that get at the unconscious material, whether you focus on a dream-image, a fantasy, vision, mood, or mechanical activity, which requires fixed attention and concentration on the object of thought. Once this is accomplished, imagination takes over and the scene or internal affective state shifts, moves, becomes animated, and takes on a life of its own.

> In this way conscious and unconscious are united, just as a waterfall connects above and below. A chain of fantasy ideas develops and gradually takes on a dramatic character: the passive process becomes an action. At first it consists of projected figures, and these images are observed like scenes in the theatre. In other words, you dream with open eyes.
>
> (Jung, 1970, p. 495)

Another technical maneuver that assists the process is to simply adopt the role of an observer or spectator, as if you are watching a movie or the landscape pass before you during a country drive.

The point is that you start with any image, for instance fully observe how the picture begins to unfold or to change. Don't try to make it into something, just do nothing but observe what its spontaneous changes are. Any mental picture you contemplate in this way will sooner or later change to a spontaneous association that causes a slight alteration of the picture. You must carefully avoid impatient jumping from one subject to another. Hold fast to the one image you have chosen and wait until it changes by itself. Note all these changes and eventually step into the picture yourself, and if it is a speaking figure at all then say what you have to say to that figure and listen to what he or she has to say.

Thus you can not only analyse your unconscious but you also give your unconscious a chance to analyse yourself, and therewith you gradually create unity of conscious and unconscious without which there is no individuation at all.

(Jung, 1973a, p. 460)

Here Jung introduces the notion of a shift from observer to participant, to actually engaging the inner fantasies or personifications by relating and speaking to them, which holds a key to both unconscious communication and inner dialogue.

Inner dialogues

When the act of imagination is successful, it further includes introducing a process of dialoguing with inner figures as an active participant in engaging the spontaneous productions of the unconscious.

As a rule there is a marked tendency simply to enjoy this interior entertainment and to leave it at that. Then, of course, there is no real progress but only endless variations on the same theme, which is not the point of the exercise at all. What is enacted on the stage still remains a background process; it does not move the observer in any way, and the less it moves him the smaller will be the cathartic effect of this private theatre. The piece that is being played does not want merely to be watched impartially, it wants to compel his participation. If the observer understands that his own drama is being performed on this theater stage, he cannot remain indifferent to the plot and its dénouement. He will notice, as the actors appear one by one and the plot thickens, that they all have some purposeful relationship to his conscious situation, that he is being addressed by the unconscious, and that *it* causes these fantasy-images to appear before him. He therefore feels compelled, or is encouraged by his analyst, to take part in the play and, instead of just sitting in a theatre, really have it out with his alter ego. For nothing in us ever remains quite uncontradicted, and consciousness can take up no position which will not call up, somewhere in the dark corners of the psyche, a negation or a compensatory effect, approval or resentment. This process of coming to terms with the Other in us is well worth while, because in this way we get to know aspects of our nature which we would not allow anybody else to show us and which we ourselves would never have admitted. It is very important to fix this whole procedure in writing at the time of its occurrence, for you then have ocular evidence that will effect-ively counteract the ever-ready tendency to self-deception. A running commentary is absolutely necessary in dealing with the shadow, because otherwise its actuality cannot be fixed. Only in this painful way is it possible to gain a positive insight into the complex nature of one's own personality.

(Jung, 1970, p. 495)

Here we may see how Jung turns his technique from passively observing actors or players in the private theatre of one's mind toward being the unconscious playwright that orchestrates a confrontation with alterity—the Other within. Within this context, we may say that active imagination is ultimately a means for dealing with the shadow, hence a moral enterprise.

In several places Jung emphasizes the notion that fantasy is real, and is a fact of the psyche: "It is a psychic fact that this fantasy is happening, and it is as real as you—as a psychic entity—are real" (Jung, 1970, p. 529). With the introduction of the conscious ego dialoguing with the fantasy images, a certain "counterbalance" is created and the work of individuation advanced.

For what is now happening is the decisive rapprochement with the unconscious. This is where insight, the *unio mentalis*, begins to become real. What you are now creating is the beginning of individuation, whose immediate goal is the experience and production of the symbol of totality.

(Jung, 1970, p. 529)

Jung delineates the task of individuation to be ultimately about unification within a totality, and this is very much a moral endeavor, as a "moral standpoint is introduced by consciousness" (Jung, 1977, p. 30), but the counterbalancing or compensation that eventually takes place is achieved by interpreting the concrete visualizations in the fantasies (see Jung, 1970, pp. 517–18). In order to obtain meaning, an "intellectual and emotional understanding is needed; they require to be not only rationally integrated with the conscious mind, but morally assimilated. They still have to be subjected to a work of synthetic interpretation" (Jung, 1928b, p. 51). As the transcendent function gives rise to high forms of symbolism and integration, understanding of their meaning leads to knowledge over the unconscious productions (Jung, 1970, p. 529), which implies the resolution of the transference, i.e., through its displacement onto God or the Self. Inner dialoguing with alien forces within helps accomplish this aim.

Starting from the fact that in a state of affect one often surrenders involuntarily to the truths of the other side, would it not be far better to make use of an asset so as to give the other side an opportunity to speak? It could therefore be said just as truly that one should cultivate the art of conversing with oneself in the setting provided by an affect, as though the affect itself was speaking without regard to our rational criticism. So long as the affect is speaking, criticism must be withheld. But once it has presented its case, we should begin criticizing as conscientiously as though the real person closely connected with us were our interlocutor. Nor should the matter rest there, but statement and answer must follow one another until a satisfactory end of the discussion is reached. Whether the result is satisfactory or not, only subjective feeling can decide. Any humbug is of course quite useless. Scrupulous honesty with oneself and no rash anticipation of what the other side might conceivably say are the indispensable conditions of this technique for educating the anima.

(Jung, 1938c, pp. 202–3)

Jung seems never to have remarked that the occurrence of inner dialogues falsifies his model of the psyche, according to which the unconscious subsists on imagery (Jung, 1913c, p. 434; 1918, p. 23; 1954a, p. 28; 1954d, pp. 479–81; 1989, p. 4; 2008, pp. 182–3), and language is an exclusively conscious function (Jung, 1988, pp. 437, 447). Jung was instead concerned with the circumstance that inner dialogues, along with a number of other expressive procedures, "make the unconscious content conscious" (Jung, 1989, p. 101) in a manner that involves a personification—a phenomenon that psychoanalysts term "psychic presences" (Grotstein, 2000). "The unconscious appears personified: mostly it is the anima who in singular or plural form represents the collective unconscious. The personal unconscious is personified by the shadow. More rarely, the collective unconscious is personified as a Wise Old Man" (Jung, 1970, p. 106). In Jung's view, the personifications are analogous to projections and transferences in their potential vulnerability to therapeutic interpretation.

> The essential thing is to differentiate oneself from these unconscious contents by personifying them, and at the same time to bring them into relationship with consciousness. That is a technique for stripping them of their power. It is not too difficult to personify them, as they always possess a certain degree of autonomy, a separate identity of their own. Their autonomy is a most uncomfortable thing to reconcile oneself to, and yet the very fact that the unconscious present itself in that way gives us the best means of handling it.
>
> (Jung, 1973b, p. 187)

The primary value of inner dialogues and active imagination is not contingent on the interpretations that may be placed on the unconscious materials that manifest. Rather, priority belongs to the very experience of unconscious manifestations. "The light that gradually dawns on him consists in his understanding that his fantasy is a real psychic process which is happening to him personally" (Jung, 1970, pp. 528–9). In other words, what is most important is to allow the presence of the fantasy to appear and to experience them as such (see Jung, 1938c, pp. 212–13).

Jung's emphasis on the experiential dimension of inner dialogues, active imagination, and the like, concerned neither the pleasure of creative expression, nor any catharsis arising from making the unconscious

conscious. Rather, the experiences were valuable therapeutically for their ego-alien quality. "This means not only bringing the conflict to consciousness; it also involves an experience of a special kind, namely, the recognition of an alien 'other' in oneself, or the objective presence of another will" (Jung, 1945a, p. 348).

Jung (1938c) called the transcendent function "the aim of our analysis of the unconscious" (p. 223), which accomplishes "the transformation of personality through the blending and fusion of the noble with the base components, of the differentiated with the inferior functions, of the conscious with the unconscious" (Jung, 1938c, p. 220). These statements imply that the other major aims of analytical psychology—the realization of the shadow, the expansion of consciousness, and individuation through the integration of the self—are subsidiary to the transcendent function and can be accomplished as its by-products.

Jung offered the interpretive procedure when working with patients who were already involved with expressive fantasy techniques. At the same time, Jung denied that he required patients to engage in inner dialogues, active imaginations, or other functionally equivalent techniques.

> I must ... expressly emphasize that my method of treatment does not consist in causing my patients to indulge in strange fantasies for the purpose of changing their personality, and other nonsense of that kind. I merely put it on record that there are certain cases where such a development occurs, not because I force anyone to it, but because it springs from inner necessity.
>
> (Jung, 1938c, p. 223)

Here we must conclude that Jung was flexible, open-minded, experimental, and sensitive to the unique personalities of his patients when deciding how to conduct analysis, which more classical forms of psychoanalysis deny by virtue of their prescriptive methods.

Chapter 5

Jung's individuation process

In discussing Jung's individuation process, I have tried, above all, to make it comprehensible to a psychoanalytic readership and, where appropriate, to indicate how Jung's technical terms can be translated into Freudian terms, and at what costs of imprecision. Unfortunately, as Paul Roazen (2002) remarked, "Jung's recommendations ... are so encased in such an alien vocabulary for those of us educated conventionally in Freud's school, that Jung's ideas on clinical matters have scarcely gained much currency within the so-called mainstream" (p. 51). I hope I have made some leeway in making Jung more accessible to psychoanalytic audiences.

On several occasions, over a period of twenty-five years, Jung identified the collective unconscious with the superego (1951b, p. 120; 1958a, p. 348; 1958b, pp. 439–40; 1970, p. 473), and he discussed the individual archetypes within it in terms appropriate to psychoanalytic ideas about individual ego ideals. "The archetype as an image of instinct is a spiritual goal toward which the whole of nature of man strives" (Jung, 1954b, p. 212). Jung's individuation process may be consequently evaluated as a contribution to the theory and clinical practice of *superego psychology*. Jung referred, of course, to the superego as Freud had formulated it and not to the truncated version in Hartmann's ego psychology (see Merkur, 2009).

Liberation from possession was the first meaning of Jung's term *individuation*. All human beings share the same instincts, the same archetypes, the same group psychology. Jung explicitly included the Oedipus complex within his formulations, as the only complex that Freud had recognized. It consisted of mother, father, and child in the personal unconscious; but at the archetypal level it involved a pair of complexes, the hero myth and the *heirosgamos*, or brother–sister incest. The failure to resolve the Oedipus complex, to which Freud traced all neurosis, was, in Jung's terms, possession by or *participation mystique* within it. At the level of *participation mystique*, none of us are individuals. We acquire individuality only insofar as we achieve differentiation from the group, which is to say, from instinctual behaviors and archetypal fantasies that are identical in each member of the group.

> The concept of individuation plays a large role in our psychology. In general, it is the process by which individual beings are formed and differentiated; in particular, it is the development of the psychological *individual* ... as a being distinct from the general, collective psychology. Individuation, therefore, is a process of *differentiation* ..., having for its goal the development of the individual personality.
>
> (Jung, 1921, p. 448)

Jung's goal was not to destroy or annul the complexes but to reclaim them for the ego.

The depersonification of archetypes

Jung's ideas of the collective unconscious departed from Freud's theories but not from his clinical procedures. Jung traced repetition-compulsions not to infantile fixations, but to allegedly universal archetypes. Otherwise the procedures were in agreement. Making the unconscious conscious remained the clinical goal. In orthodox psychoanalysis the clinical procedure consists of the patient learning through analysis to recognize the self-sabotaging Oedipal dynamics that underlie past behaviors, and thereby being empowered to recognize the ego-dystonicity of current desires and fantasies that conform to similarly Oedipal patterns. With the unconscious made conscious, the repetition-compulsion loses its automaticity, and conscious decisions may be made to refrain from further enactments. Departing from Freud, Jung extended Freud's program beyond neurotic repetition-compulsions, to deal additionally with the further patterns that may be found in healthy symbols. "Individuation ... is the transformation process that loosens the attachment to the unconscious" (Jung, 1950a, p. 293).

In Jung's procedure, an archetype is not depersonified merely as an intellectual proposition. To be therapeutic, depersonification must proceed in an experiential manner, through the patient's active engagement of the personified archetype during active imagination. "To the degree that the patient takes an active part, the personified figure of anima or animus will disappear. It becomes the functional relationship between conscious and unconscious" (Jung, 1938c, p. 224).

Jung often depicts active imagination in two phases, despite his various discussions on the process as we have seen. Watching a personified archetype in a vision or hearing a personified archetype speak in one's mind, allows the archetype to appear responsible for its activity. When, however, a person engages an interior image or voice with active responses, by speaking to it and demanding answers, the unconscious responses gradually make it apparent that the image or voice is not responsible for its activities. When this second, dialogical phase of "having it out with the unconscious" is repeated with a plurality of archetypes, two inferences become obvious. The unconscious complexes that manifest in possessions and projections match up with the attitudes, values, and ideas of the images and voices; but all of the complexes are animated, like so many puppets or masks, by a single ulterior agency.

> Although he is forced, for epistemological reasons, to postulate an indefinite number of distinct and separate archetypes, yet he is constantly overcome by doubt as to how far they are really distinguishable from one another. They overlap to such a degree and have such a capacity for combination that all attempts to isolate them conceptually must appear hopeless. In addition the unconscious, in sharpest contrast to consciousness and its contents, has a tendency to personify itself in a uniform way, just as if it possessed only one shape or one voice. Because of this peculiarity, the unconscious conveys an experience of unity.
>
> (Jung, 1954e, p. 288)

In the following discussion of depersonifying the anima and animus, Jung touched on two further features that merit emphasis. Once an archetype is depersonified, its skill set is available for conscious use as an impersonal function. Second, the contents of each archetype or complex become fully known only after they have been depersonified. As long as they are confused with the ulterior agency, and mistakenly perceived as "relatively independent personalities," their actual contents cannot be discerned accurately.

The autonomous complex of anima and animus is essentially a psychological function that has usurped, or rather retained, a "personality" only because this function is itself autonomous and undeveloped. But already we can see how it is possible to break up the personification, since by making them conscious we convert them into bridges to the unconscious. It is because we are not using them purposefully as functions that they remain personified complexes. So long as they are in this state they must be accepted as relatively independent personalities. They cannot be integrated into consciousness while their contents remain unknown. The purpose of the dialectical process is to bring these contents into the light; and only when this task has been completed, and the conscious mind has become sufficiently familiar with the unconscious processes reflected in the anima, will the anima be felt simply as a function.

(Jung, 1938c, p. 210)

To this point, Jung's individuation process was based on Freud's psychoanalytic process, as it stood during the years of their collaboration (1907–12). Jung enriched Freud's program with a "synthetic" method of dream interpretation that Maeder (1916) developed, his own innovation of active imagination, and his theory of the collective unconscious and its archetypes. The further portions of the individuation process, which concern the self, were unprecedented in Freud's work and have since remained largely unparalleled in the Freudian traditions.

The discovery of the self

What remains when an archetype is depersonified? Not only does the archetype become a depersonified function that is available for conscious use, but the depersonification process itself comes to conscious attention. Depersonification lays bare the mental state, detached from the archetype, from which depersonification proceeds. "All we can say rationally about this condition of detachment is to define it as a sort of centre within the psyche of the individual, but not within the ego. It is a non-ego centre" (Jung, 1936a, p. 167).

I call this ... *stage* of the therapy ... the *objectivation of impersonal images*. Its goal is to detach consciousness from the object so that the individual no longer places the guarantee of happiness, or of his life even, in factors outside himself, whether they be persons, ideas, or circumstances, but comes to realize that everything depends on whether he holds the treasure or not. If the possession of that gold is realized, then the centre of gravity is *in* the individual and no longer in an object on which he depends.

(Jung, 1936a, p. 166)

In these formulations concerning the psychic function that can observe, think about, and depersonify archetypes, Jung was discussing the activity that psychologists term *recursive* or *reflective thinking* and that Freud discussed as the superego's function of *self-observation*. In terming it "a sort of centre within the psyche," Jung employed a metaphor that he generally applied to *the self*. "Insofar as 'individuality' embraces our innermost, last, and incomparable uniqueness, it also implies becoming one's own self. We could therefore translate individuation as 'coming to selfhood' or 'self-realization'" (Jung, 1938c, p. 173). Much that Jung wrote about the self was poorly and confusingly formulated; he attempted, through his technique of amplification, to apply the term to a great deal of comparative mythology, religion, and mysticism, the resulting encyclopedism of which was far from edifying. In many cases, he interpolated comparative data that were themselves incoherent. For example, Jung appropriated the Hindu term *Atman*, "self," as a technical term for analytical psychology (Jung, 1921, pp. 198–9; 1938c, p. 191; 1950a, p. 325; 1959, pp. 463–4; 1970, p. 323; 1997, p. 1270; see also Coward, 1978, 1985). *Atman* is a paradoxical, mystical concept that means both the "self" of any human person and simultaneously the divine self of all existence. Restricting attention to experience-near formulations, we can nevertheless piece together Jung's clinical thinking.

> Knowledge of the unconscious is indispensable for every true self-investigation. Through its integration, the centre of the personality is displaced from the limited ego into the more comprehensive self, into that centre which embraces both realms, the conscious and the unconscious, and unites them with each other. This self is the mid-point about which the true personality turns. It has therefore been since remotest times the goal of every method of development based upon the principle of self-knowledge, as, for example, Indian yoga proves.

(Jung, 1943a, p. 819)

Jung was here discussing, I suggest, the attainment of an organizational shift within the personality. Rather than an ego commanding consciousness in ignorance or oblivion of the psyche's unconscious processes, the psyche, through life experience and/or analysis, becomes conscious of at least some unconscious processes, and seeks to integrate its psychological insights into a psychologically minded way of life. In Jung's view, this psychological project was not limited to a re-claiming of split-off, unorganized, and dysfunctional complexes. It also involved an encounter with the unappreciated organizing component of the unconscious, the process or processes that cause archetypal symbols to manifest in recurring patterns. The ego's awareness of, and attempts to work with, the organizing component of the unconscious creates a collaboration of the two, that shifts the executive function of the psyche from the ego to a mid-point, as it were, between consciousness and the unconscious. To the extent that the Freudian traditions have discussed this phenomenon, psychoanalysts have called it "regression in the service of the ego" (Kris, 1934) and left it, for the most part, to writers on art and creativity. In Jung's view, the phenomenon was much more important than the Freudian traditions have appreciated. "The centring process is, in my experience, the never-to-be-surpassed climax of the whole development, and is characterized as such by the fact that it brings with it the greatest possible therapeutic effect" (Jung, 1946b, p. 203).

The ego's surrender to the self

That Jung was concerned to cultivate something akin to creative personalities becomes clear from several passages in his writings where he unmistakably described the phenomenon that the psychoanalyst Marion Milner discussed as the creative personality's surrender to the unconscious (Field, 1934, 1937; Ehrenzweig, 1957, 1967). For example, Jung advised against attempting to master the unconscious through the strength of the ego. Because the unconscious would sooner or later gain the upper hand over even the most vigilant ego-consciousness, the ego is better served by surrendering in good grace.

The dissolution of the anima means that we have gained insight into the driving forces of the unconscious, but not that we have made these forces ineffective. They can attack us at any time in new form.

166 Jung's individuation process

> And they will infallibly do so if the conscious attitude has a flaw in it. It's a question of might against might. If the ego presumes to wield power over the unconscious, the unconscious reacts with a subtle attack, deploying the dominance of the mana-personality, whose enormous prestige casts a spell over the ego. Against this the only defense is full confession of one's weakness in face of the powers of the unconscious. By opposing no force to the unconscious we do not provoke it to attack.
>
> (Jung, 1938c, p. 234)

When the ego has made its adjustment, accommodating the unconscious rather than attempting to suppress it, it may make the happy discovery that the unconscious becomes a source of inspiration and guidance.

> The anima now becomes a life-giving factor, a psychic reality which conflicts strongly with the world of the father. Which of us could assert, without endangering his sanity, that he had accepted the guidance of the unconscious in the conduct of his life, assuming that anyone exists who could imagine what that would mean?
>
> (Jung, 1952d, pp. 73–4)

Other formulations discussed the same process but added value judgments to the description. Jung wrote of the ego's surrender to the unconscious as though it were unwanted and forced involuntarily on the ego.

> The clearly felt, ruthless setting aside of the so beloved and so important ego is no light matter. Not for nothing is this "letting go" the *sine qua non* of all forms of higher spiritual development, whether we call it meditation, contemplation, yoga, or spiritual exercises. But, as this case shows, relinquishing the ego is not an act of the will and not a result arbitrarily produced; it is an event, an occurrence, whose inner, compelling logic can be disguised only by willful self-deception.
>
> In this case and at this moment the ability to "let go" is of decisive importance. But since everything passes, the moment may come when the relinquished ego must be reinstated in its functions. Letting go gives the unconscious the opportunity it has been waiting for.
>
> (Jung, 1950a, pp. 318–19)

In another phrasing, Jung expressed ambivalence. He advised readers to tolerate as much of the unconscious as we can stand.

> Consciousness should defend its reason and protect itself, and the chaotic life of the unconscious should be given the chance of having its way too—as much of it as we can stand. This means open conflict and open collaboration at once. That, evidently, is the way human life should be. It is the old game of hammer and anvil: between them the patient iron is forged into an indestructible whole, an "individual."
>
> (Jung, 1939a, p. 288)

Other formulations characterized the transformative process in terms of the ego's subordination and defeat. "The advance to the third stage means something like a recognition of the unconscious, if not actual subordination to it" (Jung, 1948d, p. 183).

> The self, in its efforts at self-realization, reaches out beyond the ego-personality on all sides; because of its all-encompassing nature it is brighter and darker than the ego, and accordingly confronted with problems which you would like to avoid. Either one's moral courage fails, or one's insight, or both, until in the end fate decides. The ego never lacks moral and rational counter-arguments, which one cannot and should not set aside so long as it is possible to hold on to them. For you only feel yourself on the right road when the conflicts of duty seem to have resolved themselves, and you have become the victim of a decision made over your head or in defiance of the heart. From this we can see the numinous power of the self, which can hardly be experienced in any other way. For this reason *the experience of the self is always a defeat for the ego....* The ego enters into the picture only so far as it can offer resistance, defend itself, and in the event of defeat still affirm its existence.
>
> (Jung, 1970, pp. 545–6)

Elsewhere Jung emphasizes the supraordinate nature and organization of the self-individuating process as culminating in a totality figure or supraself.

168 Jung's individuation process

I doubt my ability to give a proper account of the change that comes over the subject under the influence of the individuation process; it is a relatively rare occurrence, which is experienced only by those who have gone through the wearisome but, if the unconscious is to be integrated, indispensable business of coming to terms with the unconscious components of the personality. Once these unconscious components are made conscious, it results not only in their assimilation to the already existing ego-personality, but in a transformation of the latter. The main difficulty is to describe the manner of this transformation. Generally speaking the ego is a hard-and-fast complex which, because tied to consciousness and its continuity, cannot easily be altered, and should not be altered unless one wants to bring on pathological disturbances. The closest analogies to an alteration of the ego are to be found in the field of psychopathology, where we meet not only with neurotic dissociations but also with the schizophrenic fragmentation, or even dissolution, of the ego. In this field, too, we can observe pathological attempts at integration—if such an expression be permitted. These consist in more or less violent irruptions of unconscious contents into consciousness, the ego proving itself incapable of assimilating the intruders. But if the structure of the ego-complex is strong enough to withstand their assault without having its framework fatally dislocated, then assimilation can take place. In that event there is an alteration of the ego as well as of the unconscious contents. Although it is able to preserve its structure, the ego is ousted from its central and dominating position and thus finds itself in the role of a passive observer who lacks the power to assert his will under all circumstances, not so much because it has been weakened in any way, as because certain considerations give it pause. That is, the ego cannot help discovering that the afflux of unconscious contents has vitalized the personality, enriched it and created a figure that somehow dwarfs the ego in scope and intensity. This experience paralyzes an over-egocentric will and convinces the ego that in spite of all difficulties it is better to be taken down a peg than to get involved in a hopeless struggle in which one is invariably handed the dirty end of the stick. In this way though will, as disposable energy, gradually subordinates itself to the stronger factor, namely to the new totality-figure I call the *self*. Naturally, in these circumstances there is the greatest temptation simply to follow the power-instinct and to identify the ego with the self outright, in order to keep up the illusion of the ego's mastery. In other cases the ego proves too weak to offer the necessary resistance to the influx of unconscious contents and is thereupon assimilated by the unconscious, which produces a blurring or darkening of the ego-consciousness and its identification with a preconscious wholeness. Both these developments make the realization of the self impossible, and at the same time are fatal to the maintenance of ego-consciousness they amount, therefore, to pathological effects.

(Jung, 1954b, pp. 223–5)

Individuation and numinosity

The acquisition of a creative personality, involving "regression in the service of the ego" and "creative surrender" to the unconscious, are the phenomena known to psychoanalysis that most closely approximate Jung's individuation process. Jung was nevertheless *not* talking about rare, creative personalities in the arts and sciences. Jung was explicitly discussing a widely occurring religious phenomena. "An experience of the self may be expected as a result of these psychotherapeutic endeavours, and quite often these experiences are numinous" (Jung, 1970, p. 547).

It is clear that these changes are not everyday occurrences, but are very fateful transformations indeed. Usually they have a numinous character, and can take the form of conversions, illuminations, emotional shocks, blows of fate, religious or mystical experiences, or their equivalents.

(Jung, 1948d, pp. 182–3)

The extraordinary difficulty in this experience is that the self can be distinguished only conceptually from what has always been referred to as "God," but not practically. Both concepts apparently rest on an identical numinous factor which is a condition of reality.

(Jung, 1970, pp. 545–6)

By individuation, here Jung was discussing the process of religious conversion. Jung psychologized the religious personality's submission to God by conceptualizing it as a devotion to an unconscious archetype, the

God within that is equivalent to the self. In his references to "individuation or rebirth" (Jung, 1984, p. 301; 1997, p. 871), Jung explicitly named the individuation process, that he produced clinically, as the same process that Christianity had traditionally called spiritual rebirth. What he offered clinically was a reductive psychologization of religious conversion, together with a psychological theory of conversion that was ostensibly applicable to a broad range of historical religious phenomena.

The wholeness archetype

In order to account for the numinosity of the individuation process, Jung postulated the existence of a wholeness archetype. This archetype has historically been identified in theistic religious systems as the sense of God; in Hinduism it was identified as the self. The self "might equally well be called the 'God within us'" (Jung, 1938c, p. 238; see also 1948d, p. 194; 1969a, pp. 22, 40; 1970, p. 546). When the archetype presses for conscious manifestation, it produces symbols of wholeness in both dreams and active imagination.

> The symbols used by the unconscious to this end are the same as those which mankind has always used to express wholeness, completeness, and perfection: symbols, as a rule, of the quaternity and the circle. For these reasons I have termed this the *individuation process*.
> This natural process of individuation served me both as a model and guiding principle for my method of treatment.
>
> (Jung, 1943c, p. 110)

Historically, rites of initiation were designed to produce individuation processes (Jung, 1973b, p. 342; 1997, p. 1302). Jung's clinical procedure sought to make scientific use of the individuation process for psychotherapeutic purposes. Both rested on the wholeness archetype.

> The "renewal" (... *reformation*) of the mind is not meant as an actual alteration of consciousness, but rather is the restoration of an original condition, an apocatastasis. This is in exact agreement with the empirical findings of psychology, that there is an ever-present archetype of wholeness which may easily disappear from the purview of

consciousness or may never be perceived at all until a consciousness illuminated by conversion recognizes it in the figure of Christ. As a result of this "anamnesis" the original state of oneness with the God-image is restored. It brings about an integration, a bridging of the split in the personality caused by the instincts striving apart in different and mutually contradictory directions.

(Jung, 1969a, p. 40)

Jung ordinarily confined his remarks about God either to the unconscious wholeness archetype within the psyche or, more frequently, to the God within, which was one among several manifest symbols of the archetype. The God within was natural and psychological. It had no implications, Jung claimed, for metaphysical claims concerning God.

It is only through the psyche that we can establish that God acts upon us, but we are unable to distinguish whether these actions emanate from God or from the unconscious. We cannot tell whether God and the unconscious are two different entities. Both are border-line concepts for transcendental contents. But empirically it can be established, with a sufficient degree of probability, that there is in the unconscious an archetype of wholeness which manifests itself spontaneously in dreams, etc., and a tendency, independent of the conscious will, to relate other archetypes to this centre. Consequently, it does not seem improbable that the archetype of wholeness occupies as such a central position which approximates it to the God-image. The similarity is further borne out by the peculiar fact that the archetype produces a symbolism which has always characterized and expressed the Deity.

(Jung, 1952a, pp. 468–9)

Because archetypes are, by definition, unconscious quiddities that form symbols, Jung's wholeness archetype does the same unconscious work, producing symbols of unity, that Freud's (1900) mechanism of condensation does. Jung's formulation is not consistent with the major trend of Freud's discussions of condensation but instead lends support to a minority trend. Although Freud most frequently discussed drives as the primary motivators of the dreamwork, he also recognized that the dream censorship is able to contribute original materials to the manifest dream.

The psychical agency which otherwise operates only as a censorship plays a *habitual* part in the construction of dreams.... There can be no doubt that the censoring agency, whose influence we have ... recognized in limitations and omissions in the dream-content, is also responsible for interpolations and additions in it.

(Freud, 1900, p. 489)

In his *Introductory Lectures on Psycho-Analysis*, Freud (1916–17) emphasized that "the dream-censorship itself is the originator, or one of the originators, of the dream-distortion" (p. 140; compare pp. 168, 233); and he expressly linked the motivation of the distortions to conscience (p. 429). Freud's (1923b, p. 262) identification of the dream censorship with the superego means that he credited the superego with the capacity to direct the unconscious process of condensation.

The substantive difference between Jung's and Freud's formulations pertains to whether the actualization of the human potential for individuation is a question of making unconscious unity conscious, or constructing a unity that never previously existed. Jung assumed that unity, in the form of a wholeness archetype, pre-exists its conscious manifestation. "The psychological individual, or his *individuality*..., has an a priori unconscious existence, but exists consciously only so far as a consciousness of his particular nature is present, i.e., so far as there exists a conscious distinction from other individuals" (Jung, 1921, p. 447). "Individuation appears ... as the revelation of something which existed before the ego and is in fact its father or creator and also its totality" (Jung, 1954e, p. 263). Freud's ways of thinking about unitive trends in the psyche, in terms of Eros and condensation (Merkur, 2010), instead left open a variety of constructivist possibilities.

Jung's theory of an inborn wholeness archetype precluded discussions of personal and cultural variations in the contents of wholeness. In Jung's writings, all symbols, all theologies, and all mystical doctrines, lead infallibly to the same concept of wholeness or, at minimum, to a one-sided and partial manifestation of the same. Wholeness for Jung is always paradoxical, self-contradictory, irrational, and transcendent.

Working instead with Freud's superego concept, we arrive at the very different conclusion that the ego's religious submission to the superego may proceed with superegos of very different sorts. A superego may be irrational, but it need not be. Its standard of integrity may resolutely oppose paradoxes, self-contradictions, and hypocrisies. It may embrace scientific concepts of law rather than claim to transcend them. People may undergo dramatic conversion experiences, not only to beliefs in gods, spirits, or a unique God, but also to atheism, communism, vegetarianism, environmentalism, and a host of other -isms. Conversions may be limited to beliefs and ideologies or they may extend to behaviors and ways of life. It all depends on what the conversion is to—which is to say, on the contents of the particular superego.

Individuation includes integration

The ego's depersonification of the archetypes leads, on the one hand, to the discovery of the self and the ego's submission to it. It also leads to a reclaiming of the depersonified complexes and their integration within a correspondingly enlarged ego-consciousness. "An integration process ... is characteristic of psychological individuation" (Jung, 1969a, p. 200). Formerly autonomous and capable of involuntary, unconscious control over the ego, the archetypes can, upon depersonification, be transformed into impersonal skill sets that are available to ego-consciousness. "To the degree that the patient takes an active part, the personified figure of anima or animus will disappear. It becomes the functional relationship between conscious and unconscious" (Jung, 1938c, p. 224). Jung attributed the process of integration to the action of the self on the archetypes.

> Conscious realization or the bringing together of the scattered parts is in one sense an act of the ego's will, but in another sense it is a spontaneous manifestation of the self, which was always there. Individuation appears, on the one hand, as the synthesis of a new unity which previously consisted of scattered particles, and on the other hand, as the revelation of something which existed before the ego and is in fact its father or creator and also its totality. Up to a point we create the self by making ourselves conscious of our unconscious contents.
>
> (Jung, 1954e, p. 263)

Just as Jung saw the ego's defeat by the self where Kris saw regression in the service of the ego, so here Jung conceptualized integration as proceeding through the self where psychoanalysts would be more likely to endorse Freud's (1919, p. 161) concept of the synthetic function of the

Jung's individuation process

ego (see also Nunberg, 1931), together with Hartmann's (1958) concept of an ego mechanism's change of function from defense to adaptation. Aristotle's distinction between the active and acquired intellects—in Freud's terms, between the superego and the internalization of its materials within the ego—might reduce the gap between the two points of view.

Revelation, vocation, and conscience

Freud (1911) had maintained that the unconscious subsists on mental imagery, and that only consciousness employs verbal language. Without acknowledging his debt to Freud, Jung ordinarily maintained the same theoretical distinction. He repeatedly argued, for example, that dreams could not possibly be the encoded messages that Freud maintained, because the unconscious is limited to mental images that have no meanings beyond their immediate appearance (Jung, 1926a, pp. 88, 103; 1930a, p. 35; 1938b, p. 27; 1943c, p. 101; 1973b, pp. 161–2; 1997, p. 23). Again, Jung insisted on the importance of intuition but carefully asserted that "intuition is the function of unconscious perception" (Jung, 1921, p. 366; see also 1936a, pp. 15, 28; 1939a, p. 282; 1948j, p. 132; 1952d, p. 137; 1973a, pp. 420–1; 1977, p. 307). Verbal thinking was not accomplished by the unconscious.

Jung took notice, however, of some psychological data that were inconvenient to Freud's generalizations regarding the location of verbal language in the psyche. In connection with active imagination, Jung repeatedly discussed the phenomena of inner voices, belonging to archetypal symbols in dream and visions, and inner dialogues that consciousness can have with them (Jung, 1934a, pp. 184–5; 1938b, pp. 38–41, 45; 1950b, pp. 131–3; 1954a, 40–1; 1952d, pp. 274–5, 277–9; 1954e, pp. 226, 289; 1958c, pp. 87–8, 90; 1970, p. 497; 1984, pp. 512–13. 516, 638–40, 642). Recall that Jung's procedure of "having it out with the unconscious" involved visualizing a normally silent imaginal vision and, while it was occurring, deliberately directing verbal thoughts at one of its images, demanding that a question be answered, until the character began to speak. Due presumably to the role played by autosuggestion in producing the verbalizations, Jung did not treat inner dialogues as exceptions to Freud's allocation of language to consciousness.

In other cases, however, Jung acknowledged that verbal inspirations apparently emerged from the unconscious. He remarked, for example, that revelation proceeds from the self to the ego and is consequently attributed to God.

> Despite the fact that we cannot help seeing in the positing of such a concept a product of human reflection, this reflection need not necessarily have been a conscious act. It could equally well owe its existence to a "revelation," i.e., to an unconscious reflection, and hence to an autonomous functioning of the unconscious, or rather of the self, whose symbols, as we have already said, cannot be distinguished from God-images. A religious interpretation will therefore insist that this hypostasis was a divine revelation.
>
> (Jung, 1948d, p. 160)

Jung's understanding of revelation allowed him to assert, with qualifications, that a person might achieve individuation in a culture or era where no one had achieved consciousness (see Jung, 1977, p. 211). But consistent with Jung's understanding of revelation were his discussions of two further religious phenomena: vocation and conscience. Jung suggested that "personality" entails vocation and involves experience of an inner voice.

> True personality is always a vocation and puts its trust in it as in God, despite its being, as the ordinary man would say, only a personal feeling. But vocation acts like a law of God from which there is no escape. The fact that many a man who goes his own way ends in ruin means nothing to one who has a vocation. He *must* obey his own law.... Anyone with a vocation hears the voice of the inner man: he is *called*.
>
> (Jung, 1934a, pp. 175–6)

Vocation may be understood as a demand for fidelity that the self or, in Freudian terms, the superego's ego ideal function imposes on the ego. Vocation was always contingent on individuation. Jung (1934a) contrasted vocation to acquiescence to "the voice of the group" and its "collective necessities" (p. 176).

> But even in this unconscious social condition there are not a few who are called awake by the summons of the voice, whereupon they are at

once set apart from the others, feeling themselves confronted with a problem about which the others know nothing.

(p. 176)

In their post-Freudian periods, Otto Rank (1932) and Rollo May (1975) expressed closely similar views of the relation of the artist or, more generally, the creative personality to the social group. Jung, writing after Rank, attributed the social tension to individuation rather than creativity.

Jung's concept of a person's "own law" also figured prominently in his discussion of conscience. He rejected Freud's (1923a) assertion that conscience is a superego function that originates through the internalization of the societal moral code, through the mediation of the parents. In Jung's view, conscience differed. "He hears a voice whispering, 'There is something not right,' no matter how much his rightness is supported by public opinion or by the moral code" (Jung, 1931d, p. 40). In Jung's view, conscience was not necessarily ethical.

> The etymology of the word "conscience" tells us that it is a special form of "knowledge" or "consciousness." The peculiarity of "conscience" is that it is a knowledge of, or certainty about, the emotional value of the ideas we have concerning the motives of our actions. According to this definition, conscience is a complex phenomenon consisting on the one hand in an elementary act of the will, or in an impulse to act for which no conscious reason can be given, and on the other hand in a judgment grounded on rational feeling. This judgment is a value judgment, and it differs from an intellectual judgment in that, besides having an objective, general, and impartial character, it reveals the subjective point of reference. A value judgment always implicates the subject, presupposing that something is good or beautiful *for me*. If, on the other hand, I say that it is good or beautiful for certain other people, this is not necessarily a value judgment but may just as well be an intellectual statement of fact.

(Jung, 1958b, p. 437)

The moral evaluation of actions may proceed unconsciously (Jung, 1958b, pp. 438–9). If conscience is a kind of knowledge, and nevertheless unconscious, then it cannot be the ego that knows it (p. 439). "The ego has been replaced by an unconscious personality who performs the necessary act of conscience" (p. 439). People ordinarily compromise their adherence to their consciences.

> It needs unusual courage or—what amounts to the same thing—unshakable faith for a person simply to follow the dictates of his own conscience. As a rule one obeys only up to a certain point, which is determined in advance by the moral code.
>
> (Jung, 1958b, pp. 442–3)

Jung (1958b, p. 444) suggested that "the true and authentic conscience, which rises above the moral code and refuses to submit to its dictates, get its justification from" an archetype. "Since olden times conscience has been understood by many people less as a psychic function than as a divine intervention; indeed, its dictates were regarded as *vox Dei*, the voice of God" (p. 444). "Conscience is, in itself, an autonomous psychic factor" (p. 446).

After "reducing the notion of the *vox Dei* to the hypothesis of the archetype" (Jung, 1958b, p. 449), Jung partially compensated for his reductionism by crediting it with "qualities of a parapsychological nature which I have grouped together under the term 'synchronicity'" (p. 450).

> When ... the psychologist explains genuine conscience as a collision of consciousness with a numinous archetype, he may be right but he will have to add it once that the archetype per se, its psychoid essence, cannot be comprehended, that it possesses a transcendence which it shares with the unknown substance of the psyche in general. The mythical assertion of conscience that it is the voice of God is an inalienable part of its nature, the foundation of the numen. It is as much a phenomenon as conscience itself.
>
> (Jung, 1958b, p. 453)

In Jung's formulation, the psychoid nature of reality, its constitution of both spirit and matter, accounts for the correspondence of external material events in the world with the human psyche's paranormal knowledge of them. Jung's term *psychoid* was a neologism that sought to account for paranormal phenomena, by postulating an unconscious that exists simultaneously in a person and in the external world. A collective unconscious within both the person and the cosmos, "it cannot be directly perceived or 'represented,' in contrast to the perceptible psychic phenomena, and on account of its 'irrepresentable' nature I have called it 'psychoid'" (Jung, 1969b, p. 436).

> The psychoid nature of the archetype ... points to the sphere of the *unus mundus*, the unitary world, towards which the psychologist and the atomic physicists are converging along separate paths, producing independently of one another certain analogous auxiliary concepts.
>
> (Jung, 1958b, p. 452)

Connecting the dots between Jung's explicit statements, we may infer that the linguistic character of conscience, vocation, and the voice of revelation did not necessarily controvert the general rule that the unconscious subsists of mental imagery, while language is restricted to consciousness. The voice of conscience, and presumably also the voices of revelation and vocation, were paranormal phenomena. In mythological terms, they might be credited to God; but in Jung's terms, they were better allocated to the self, which is incomprehensibly both personal and macrocosmic.

Psychoanalytic readers may instead attribute the voices of conscience, vocation, and revelation to the superego, while allowing that the superego may be the unconscious location of parapsychological activity in the psyche.

Symbols of individuation

Much that Jung wrote of the self flowed, not from his clinical observations, but from his extensive readings in comparative mythology, comparative religion, and theology. For example, Jung often cited the medieval formulation that God is a circle whose center is everywhere and circumference nowhere, and he applied the metaphor to the self.

> If the unconscious can be recognized as a co-determining factor along with consciousness, and if we can live in such a way that conscious and unconscious demands are taken into account as far as possible, then the centre of gravity of the total personality shifts its position. It is then no longer in the ego, which is merely the centre of consciousness, but in the hypothetical point between conscious and

unconscious. This new centre might be called the self. If the transposition is successful, it does away with the *participation mystique* and results in a personality that suffers only in the lower storeys, as it were, but in its upper storeys is singularly detached from painful as well as from joyful happenings.

(Jung, 1938a, pp. 45–6; see also 1938c, p. 221)

Jung's recourse to the metaphor of a center confused rather than clarified meaning. It is one thing to claim that the unconscious contains a wholeness archetype, whose manifestation produces a dramatic transformation of the psyche, freeing the ego of unconscious attachments, humbling the ego, empowering the ego through integrations of previously autonomous archetypes, and confronting the ego in consciousness as the self or God within. It is quite a different thing to claim that this same self is, in some sense, located between the unconscious and ego-consciousness, as the center of the psyche. Rather than to relinquish the metaphor, however, Jung compounded his incoherence by emphasizing that the unconscious, like God, is ineffable.

I have called this centre the *self*. Intellectually the self is no more than a psychological concept, a construct that serves to express an unknowable essence which we cannot grasp as such, since by definition it transcends our powers of comprehension.

(Jung, 1938c, p. 238)

In other passages, Jung abandoned his view that the self, like God, is unknowable and instead equated the self with the entire cosmos.

The collective unconscious is anything but an encapsulated personal system; it is sheer objectivity, as wide as the world and open to all the world. There I am the object of every subject, in complete reversal of my ordinary consciousness, where I am always the subject that has an object. There I am utterly one with the world, so much a part of it that I forget all too easily who I really am. "Lost in oneself" is a good way of describing this state. But this self is the world, if only a consciousness could see it. That is why we must know who we are.

(Jung, 1954a, p. 22)

Jung reverted to the same conception of the self as a divine macro-anthropos (Mills, 2013) in appropriating mythological imagery for his discussion of integration.

> Self-reflection or—what comes to the same thing—the urge to individuation gathers together what is scattered and multifarious, and exalted to the original form of the One, the Primordial Man. In this way our existence as separate beings, our former ego nature, is abolished, the circle of consciousness is widened, and because the paradoxes have been made conscious the sources of conflict are dried up.
>
> (Jung, 1954e, p. 265)

We may ignore Jung's efforts to make his theory of individuation account for more historical data than is plausible. It suffices that he offered a close analysis and clinical procedure for religious conversion. It is not necessary to attempt, as he did, to account for all religious phenomena in terms of conversions alone.

Concluding reflections

All in all, Jung's account of individuation is both fascinating and overly simple. Jung developed a clinical procedure by which to promote religious conversions, which he conceptualized as the ego's discovery of and submission to the Self. Jung postulated that individuations were caused by an inborn wholeness archetype, for which reason he assumed that all individuations were of a single type. All individuations, like all vocations, were true to the laws of the Self; and if a person's integrity demanded that his or her personal good was unethical, or otherwise tragically inconsistent with society, there was nothing clinical to be done about it. Approaching the same process in terms of superego theory provides us with considerably greater nuance. The contents of the superego are highly variable, owe much to education and epigenetic development, and mature with practice at insight and empathy. Individuations do not have to be as catch-as-catch-can as Jung assumed. But Jung's pioneering work may be appreciated for the fine beginning that it was.

The Freudian traditions have little comparable of which to boast. I would like to draw attention, however, to the work of James S. Grotstein, who blends ego psychology with Bion's approach to object relations theory.

Grotstein (1979, 1998, 2000) has arrived at several formulations that converge with Jung's concepts. Grotstein's experience of dreams whose powers of imagination exceeded by far anything he could attain consciously led him to favor Bion's concept of alpha-function, in augmentation of Freud's account of the dreamwork; and from these beginnings he arrived at a distinction between the Dreamer Who Dreams the Dream, and the ego that is the Dreamer Who Understands the Dream. In later phrasings he has distinguished the two dreamers, respectively, as "a numinous or ineffable subject of the unconscious" and the phenomenal subject of consciousness. These correspond in many ways with the self and the ego, respectively, of Jung's formulations. Working with the concept of internal objects in Kleinian theory, Grotstein emphasizes that they occur in dreams and visions as "psychic presences." There is no need to assume, as Klein did, from their manifest contents that internal objects are equally pluralistic unconsciously. Grotstein proposes that they are so many masks worn by the one Ineffable Subject; they manifest an autonomy and numinosity that belongs to the Ineffable Subject, and not to each psychic presence individually. Against Klein, and implicitly against Jung, Grotstein argues that psychic presences may be as many and varied as the unconscious happens to fantasize.

In several publications, Grotstein (1993, 1996, 2000) has proposed the existence of a "transcendent position," a developmental attainment analogous to the "depressive position" of Kleinian discussion.

> The "transcendent position" represents the achievement of the state of meditative-like grace in which one experiences a serenity that transcends conflict.... One has achieved the capacity for mourning, reparation, empathy, tolerance of ambivalence, and true love and caring. One must then continue his/her ontological pilgrimage to the next state, one of enlightenment and serenity where one is at peace with oneself and with the world, both internal and external.
>
> (Grotstein, 1996, pp. 127–8)

Grotstein (2000) conceptualized the transcendent position in mystical terms, "as becoming one with our *aliveness* ... or with our very *being-ness*" (p. 273). The elaboration of his understanding of the transcendent position and its clinical production will be necessary, however, before it will be possible to explore its points of contact with Jung's individuation process, something he never addressed in his scholarly writings.

Chapter 6

Consciousness and its expansion

Consciousness was the only reality that Jung considered empirical. "The only things we experience immediately are the contents of consciousness" (Jung, 1948i, pp. 139–40). "Consciousness is: *this* time, *this* here and now. Consciousness wants to let everything appear as a *here and now*" (Jung, 2008, p. 80). Jung's references to consciousness differed from those of Freud, who confusingly used the same term *consciousness* in reference both to a quality that different mental contents possess at some times, and also to a subdivision of the psyche having a great many functions, not all of which are qualitatively conscious at any single moment. Jung regularly employed the term in its qualitative sense alone.

> The conscious mind … is characterized by a certain narrowness. It can hold only a few simultaneous contents at a given moment. All the rest is unconscious at the time, and we only get a sort of continuation or a general understanding or awareness of a conscious world through the *succession* of conscious moments…. The area of the unconscious is enormous and always continuous, while the area of consciousness is a restricted field of momentary vision.
>
> (Jung, 1936a, p. 9)

Noting that consciousness never exists apart from the ego, Jung suggested that consciousness is a quality that psychic materials acquire when they are associated with the ego. "Anything psychic will take on the quality of consciousness if it comes into association with the ego" (Jung, 1926b, p. 323; see also 1936a, p. 11; 1939a, p. 275; 1954d, p. 484; 1970, p. 107; 1973a, pp. 254–5, 262; 1997, p. 154). Jung characterized the ego in terms of functions that Freud (1900) credited to the system Perception-Consciousness (Pcpt.-Cs.).

The ego is a complex datum which is constituted first of all by a general awareness of your body, of your existence, and secondly by your memory data; you have a certain idea of having been, a long series of memories.

(Jung, 1936a, p. 11)

Like Freud, Jung agreed with the medieval Muslim philosopher Ibn Sina's formulation of consciousness as a phenomenon that arises from the aggregation of the senses. "I ... think of ego-consciousness as a synthesis of the various 'sense-consciousnesses,' in which the independence of each separate consciousness is submerged in the unity of the overruling ego" (Jung, 1926b, p. 324).

Like Freud (1915), Jung attributed concrete imagery to the unconscious (Jung, 1913c, p. 434; 1918, p. 23; 1954d, pp. 479–81; 1989, p. 4; 2008, pp. 182–3) but abstract thought to consciousness. "A higher consciousness is a more abstract and impersonal consciousness" (Jung, 1997, p. 445; see also 1989, p. 49; 1997, pp. 664–6, 1324). "Consciousness is not only the *conditio sine qua non* of realization, it is realization in itself" (Jung, 1997, p. 1324). Like Freud (1900, 1911, 1915), Jung (1988, pp. 437, 447) allocated all linguistic function to consciousness. Jung additionally identified consciousness with reflexivity.

"Reflection" should be understood not simply as an act of thoughts, but rather as an attitude ... reflection is a spiritual act that runs counter to the natural process; an act whereby we stop, call something to mind, form a picture, and take up a relation to and come to terms with what we have seen. It should, therefore, be understood as an act of *becoming conscious*.

(Jung, 1948d, p. 158, n. 9)

Jung (1942b, pp. 117–18) attributed reflection to the operation of an instinct, many of whose manifestations are conscious.

Reflection re-enacts the process of excitation and carries the stimulus over into a series of images which, if the impetus is strong enough, are reproduced in some form of expression. This may take place directly, for instance in speech, or may appear in the form of abstract thought, dramatic representation, or ethical conduct; or again, in the scientific achievements or a work of art.

(Jung, 1942b, p. 117)

Jung's distinction between reflection or reflective knowledge, on the one hand, and the reflective instinct, on the other, permitted him to assert that consciousness is not innate, but acquired developmentally. "Judging by all we do know, it is certain that the original psyche possesses no consciousness of itself. This only comes in the course of development" (Jung, 1954e, p. 289).

Jung discussed the alternative to consciousness in various ways. In all formulations, unconsciousness was a momentary quality and never a psychic system or structure as it was for Freud.

> Freud is seeing the mental processes as static, while I speak in terms of dynamics and relationship. To me all is relative. There is nothing definitely unconscious; it is only not present to the conscious mind under a certain light.
>
> (Jung, 1936a, p. 62)

The unconscious was uninvolved with the ego. "The unconscious ... is a mental condition of which no ego is aware" (Jung, 1954d, p. 484). "The unconscious process itself hardly ever reaches consciousness without technical aid" (p. 488). Jung allocated differentiation to consciousness and non-differentiation to the unconscious.

> Differentiation is the essence, the *sine qua non* of consciousness. Everything unconscious is undifferentiated, and everything that happens unconsciously proceeds on the basis of non-differentiation— that is to say, there is no determining whether it belongs or does not belong to oneself. It cannot be established a priori whether it concerns me, or another, or both. Nor does feeling give us any sure clues in this respect.
>
> (Jung, 1938c, p. 206)

Jung credited the amorphousness of the unconscious not only with uncertainty about the differences among its constituent archetypes, but also with experiences of unity.

The unconscious, in sharpest contrast to consciousness and its contents, has a tendency to personify itself in a uniform way, just as if it possessed only one shape or one voice. Because of this peculiarity, the unconscious conveys an experience of unity.

(Jung, 1954e, p. 288)

Like Freud, Jung also attributed timelessness to the unconscious. "It constitutes in its totality a sort of timeless and eternal world-image which counterbalances our conscious, momentary picture of the world" (Jung, 1931e, p. 376). He believed that the unconscious was not merely indifferent to time, but transcended time and space in a manner that made possible the paranormal, which Jung called "synchronicity."

The unconscious has no time. There is no trouble about time in the unconscious. Part of our psyche is not in time and not in space. They are only an illusion, time and space, and so in a certain part of our psyche time does not exist at all.

(Jung, 1954g, p. 287)

As previously mentioned, Jung also appropriated and considerably redefined the term *participation mystique*, which the philosopher Lucien Lévy-Bruhl had offered in description of the mentality of so-called "primitive" peoples. Jung was comfortable with Lévy-Bruhl's systemic racism, as most anthropologists were not; but he found the psychological phenomenon to be more widely spread. "Even today we know of primitive tribes whose level of consciousness is not so far removed from the darkness of the primordial psyche, and numerous vestiges of this state can still be found among civilized people" (Jung, 1954e, p. 289). For Jung, *participation mystique* was synonymous with projection, or perhaps more appropriately, projective identification. "Everything that is unconscious in ourselves we discover in our neighbour, and we treat him accordingly" (Jung, 1931b, p. 65). "Projection is always an *unconscious* mechanism, therefore consciousness, or conscious realization, destroys it" (Jung, 1936a, p. 138; see also 1938b, p. 83; 1938d, pp. 89, 92).

Conforming simultaneously to Freud's (1921) account of group psychology, Jung attributed *participation mystique* or immersion within the social group to unconscious identifications.

186 Consciousness and its expansion

There is nothing "mystical" about identity.... Identity derives essentially from the notorious unconsciousness of the small child. Therein lies the connection with the primitive, for the primitive is as unconscious as a child. Unconsciousness means non-differentiation. There is as yet no clearly differentiated ego, only events which may belong to me or to another. It is sufficient that *somebody* should be affected by them. The extraordinary infectiousness of emotional reactions then makes it certain that everybody in the vicinity will involuntarily be affected. The weaker ego-consciousness is, the less it matters who is affected, and the less the individual is able to guard against it. He could only do that if he could say: you are excited or angry, but I am not, for I am not you. The child is in exactly the same position in the family: he is affected to the same degree and in the same way as a whole group.

(Jung, 1931d, p. 41)

Elsewhere, Jung amplifies on this idea:

Civilized man naturally thinks he is miles above these things. Instead of that, he is often identified with his parents throughout his life, or with his affect and prejudices, and shamelessly accuses others of the things he will not see in himself. He too has a remnant of primitive unconsciousness, of non-differentiation between subject and object. Because of this, he is magically affected by all manner of people, things, and circumstances, he is beset by disturbing influences nearly as much as the primitive and therefore needs just as many apotropaic charms. He no longer works magic with medicine bags, amulets, and animal sacrifices, but with tranquilizers, neuroses, rationalism, cult of the will, etc.

(Jung, 1938a, p. 45)

Working with his antitheses of *participation mystique* and consciousness, Jung speculated on still more primitive mentalities in human prehistory.

A group-consciousness in which individuals are interchangeable is still not the lowest level of consciousness, for it already shows traces of differentiation. At the lowest and most primitive level we would find a sort of generalized or cosmic consciousness, with complete unconsciousness of the subject. On this level there are only events, but no acting person.

Our assumption that what pleases me must necessarily please everybody else is therefore an obvious relic from that primordial night of consciousness where there was no perceptible difference between I and You, and where everyone thought, felt, and acted in the same way.... The psychic equality of all men is an unspoken assumption deriving from the individual's original unconsciousness of himself. In that far-off world there was no individual consciousness, but only a collective psyche from which gradually an individual consciousness emerged on the higher levels of development. The indispensable condition for the existence of an individual consciousness is its difference from other consciousnesses.

(Jung, 1934b, pp. 136–7)

The development of consciousness

The achievement of consciousness was not an unqualified good. "The more consciousness a man possesses the more he is separated from his instincts ... and the more prone he is to error" (Jung, 1952a, p. 415). In clinical situations, increased consciousness tends to create discomfort that had the advantage, however, of motivating therapeutic effort.

For one person deeper knowledge of himself is a punishment, for another a blessing. In general, every active conscious realization means a tensing of opposites. It is in order to avoid this tension that people repress their conflicts. But if they become conscious of them, they get into a corresponding state of tension. This supplies in turn the driving power for a solution of the problems they are faced with.

(Jung, 1943a, p. 817)

In other passages, Jung attributed "segregation," "isolation," and "loneliness" as negative consequences of increased self-consciousness. He was presumably generalizing, without acknowledgment to Otto Rank (1932), on the latter's powerful thesis concerning the solitude inherent in creativity.

The words "many are called, but few are chosen" are singularly appropriate here, for the development of personality from the germ-state to full consciousness is at once a charisma and a curse, because its first fruit is the conscious and unavoidable segregation of the single individual from the undifferentiated and unconscious herd. This means isolation, and there is no more comforting word for it.

(Jung, 1934a, p. 173)

And again elsewhere:

As bringers of light, that is, enlargers of consciousness, they overcome darkness, which is to say that they overcome the earlier unconscious state. Higher consciousness, or knowledge going beyond our present-day consciousness, is equivalent to being *all alone in the world*. This loneliness expresses the conflict between the bearer or symbol of higher consciousness and his surroundings.

(Jung, 1940, p. 169)

Jung maintained that children have little if any consciousness and that consciousness is a developmental acquisition that is greatly enhanced through education.

During the first years of life there is hardly any consciousness.... Only when the child begins to say "I" is there any perceptible continuity of consciousness. But in between there are frequent periods of unconsciousness. One can actually see the conscious mind coming into existence through the gradual unification of fragments. This process continues throughout life, but from puberty onwards it becomes slower, and fewer and fewer fragments of the unconscious are added to consciousness.... We reinforce this process in children by education and culture.

(Jung, 1928b, p. 52)

In a seminar that he gave in 1928–30, Jung offered an interpretation of the three-year-old that was consistent both with his theories of childhood *participation mystique* and with Freud's view that both neuroses and the defenses originate in connection with the Oedipus complex, at age four to five-and-a-half.

Children of three have no such psychic problems of their own. They are not dissociated. They can be terribly nice and amiable one minute

Consciousness and its expansion   189

and the next minute horrid, without being split by it. They have no moral values at that age, because they are not conscious enough. While such a child has no psychological conflict, it is not beyond the reach of parental problems. The father as well as the mother is full of vibrations and the child gets the full impact of the atmosphere.

(Jung, 1984, pp. 154–5)

We may discount Jung's naiveté regarding psychopathologies in childhood. What remains is a valid perception that young children's immaturity permits their moods to remain unintegrated and that the integrity necessary for moral values must await the attainment of a higher order of consciousness, which is to say, self-reflection.

Jung suggested that *participation mystique* comes to an end through the onset of moral judgment and repression—phenomena that Freud dated to the resolution of the Oedipus complex and the post-Oedipal development of the superego.

[The primitive] is still more or less identical with the collective psyche, and for that reason shares equally in the collective virtues and vices, without any personal attribution and without inner contradiction. The contradiction arises only when the personal development of the psyche begins, and when reason discovers the irreconcilable nature of the opposite. The consequence of this discovery is the conflict of repression. We want to be good, and therefore must repress evil; and with that the paradise of the collective psyche comes to an end. Repression of the collective psyche was absolutely necessary for the development of personality.

(Jung, 1938c, p. 150)

Inconsistently, Jung suggested that the child's acquisition of consciousness normally occurs only at puberty. "Psychic birth, and with it the conscious differentiation from the parents, normally takes place only at puberty, with the eruption of sexuality" (Jung, 1933, p. 391).

We assume that a boy or girl ten years of age would be conscious, but one could easily prove that it is a very peculiar kind of consciousness, for it might be a consciousness without any consciousness of the *ego*. I know a number of cases of children eleven, twelve, and fourteen years of age, or even older, suddenly realizing "I am." For the first time in their lives they know that they themselves are experiencing, that they are looking back over the past in which they can remember things happening but cannot remember that they were in them.

(Jung, 1936a, p. 8; see also 1988, p. 663)

To the same age, psychoanalysts attribute the onset of intellectuality, the defensive use of intellectuality called intellectualization, and a considerable elaboration of ego ideals (A. Freud, 1966; Blos, 1962, 1974).

Consciousness expansion

Jung introduced the concept of consciousness expansion in connection with its developmental acquisition. He found that therapeutic change often consisted of nothing more than a widening of consciousness.

I have often seen patients simply outgrow a problem that had destroyed others. This "outgrowing," as I formerly called it, proved on further investigation to be a new level of consciousness. Some higher or wider interest appeared on the patient's horizon, and through this broadening of his outlook the insoluble problem lost its urgency.

(Jung, 1938a, pp. 14–15)

Jung's clinical experiences led him to generalize that therapeutic change always involves the attainment of a "higher level" of consciousness.

I ... asked myself whether this outgrowing, this possibility of further psychic development, was not the normal thing, and whether getting stuck in a conflict was pathological. Everyone must possess that higher level, at least in embryonic form, and must under favourable circumstances be able to develop this potentiality.

(Jung, 1938a, p. 15)

Jung's formulation was easily reconciled with Freud's clinical ambition to make the unconscious conscious. "By understanding the unconscious we free ourselves from its domination" (Jung, 1938a, p. 44). Elsewhere,

Activated unconscious contents always appear at first as projections upon the outside world, but in the course of mental development they are gradually assimilated by consciousness and reshaped into conscious ideas that then forfeit their originally autonomous and personal character.

(p. 35)

And finally, "Consciousness is no longer preoccupied with compulsive plans but dissolves in contemplative vision" (p. 44). Here we could say that one becomes conscious of a very different unconscious.

Because consciousness was acquired developmentally in ways that were powerfully affected by education, consciousness might variously be neglected or pursued in different cultures. Jung associated supreme consciousness with the perfection that he considered to be the goal of Eastern philosophy.

Supreme consciousness is linked up with the idea of perfection or of completion.... As long as one is in *participation mystique* with things, one cannot be conscious of them. Any increase in consciousness brings about an increase of detachment, and the tendency of Eastern philosophy is always to reach that supreme consciousness and with it the supreme detachment. This condition is called Nirvana, that being non-being, for if one is completely conscious and completely detached, it is as if one were not.

(Jung, 1997, p. 182)

Jung also attributed supreme consciousness to "modern man," an individual who was to be found only in the Western world, and only rarely.

The modern man—or, let us say again, the man of the immediate present—is rarely met with, for he must be conscious to a superlative degree. Since to be wholly of the present means to be fully conscious of one's existence as a man, it requires the most intensive and extensive consciousness, with a minimum of unconsciousness.... He alone is modern who is fully conscious of the present.

The man who has attained consciousness of the present is solitary. The "modern" man has at all times been so, for every step towards fuller consciousness removes him further from his original, purely animal *participation mystique* with the herd, from submersion in a common unconsciousness. Every step forward means tearing oneself loose from the maternal womb of unconsciousness in which the mass of men dwells.

(Jung, 1931f, p. 75)

In Jung's view, "modern man" has surpassed both the herd and its history. "He has become 'unhistorical' in the deepest sense and has estranged himself from the mass of men who live entirely within the bounds of tradition" (Jung, 1931f, p. 75). The disconnection of modern man from both other people and history has social consequences. "The 'modern' man is questionable and suspect, and has been so at all times, beginning with Socrates and Jesus" (p. 76). Modern man has distinctive obligations. "Only the man who has outgrown the stages of consciousness belonging to the past, and has amply fulfilled the duties appointed for him by his world, can achieve full consciousness of the present" (p. 76). And he has distinct moral obligations: "Unless he can atone by creative ability for his break with tradition, he is merely disloyal to the past. To deny the past for the sake of being conscious only of the present would be sheer futility" (p. 76).

Within human reach were "levels" of consciousness that reflected stages simultaneously of enlightenment and therapeutic change. For Jung, there was direct continuity from unconsciousness and projection, to grades of consciousness.

Since at the present level of consciousness we cannot suppose that tree daemons exist, we are forced to assert that the primitive suffers from hallucinations, that he hears his own unconscious which has projected itself into a tree. If this theory is correct—and I do not know how we could formulate it otherwise today—then the second level of consciousness has effected a differentiation between the object "tree" and the unconscious content projected into it, thereby achieving an act of enlightenment. The third level rises still higher and attributes "evil" to the psychic content which has been separated from the object. Finally a fourth level, the level reached by our consciousness today, carries the enlightenment a stage further by denying the objective existence of the "spirit" and declaring that the primitive hazard nothing. Consequently the whole phenomenon vanishes into thin air—with the great advantage that the evil spirit becomes obviously non-existent and sinks into ridiculous insignificance. A fifth level, however, which is bound to take a quintessential view of the matter, wonders about this conjuring trick that turns what began as a miracle into a senseless self-deception—only to come full circle. Like the boy who told his father a made-up story about sixty stags in the forest, it asks: "But what, then, was all the rustling in the woods?" The fifth level is of the opinion that something did happen after all: even though the psychic content was not the tree, nor a spirit in the tree, nor indeed any spirit at all, it was nevertheless a phenomenon thrusting up from the unconscious, the existence of which cannot be denied if one is minded to grant the psyche any kind of reality. If one did not do that, one would have to extend God's *creatio ex nihilo*—which seems so obnoxious to the modern intellect—very much further.

(Jung, 1943b, pp. 200–1)

The third level was moralistic, the fourth materialistic. The fifth level, largely to be achieved only in the future, is obliged to account also for paranormal phenomena, by postulating either some sort of universal psyche, or else an extended concept of divine creation through the psychoid.

Jung (1952c) was of the opinion that "there are relatively few who have reached the level of consciousness which is possible in our time" (p. 308).

Since we cannot imagine—unless we have lost our critical faculties altogether—that mankind today has attained the highest possible degree of consciousness, there must be some potential unconscious psyche left over whose development would result in a further extension and a higher differentiation of consciousness. No one can say how great or small this "remnant" might be, but we have no means of measuring the possible range of conscious development, let alone the extent of the unconscious.

(Jung, 1946b, p. 191)

Echoing Freud's claim that psychoanalysis made the unconscious conscious, Jung asserted that increased, higher, or widened consciousness

194 Consciousness and its expansion

was the goal of psychotherapy. "The supreme aim of the *opus psycho-logicum* is conscious realization, and the first step is to make oneself conscious of contents that have hitherto been projected" (Jung, 1946b, p. 263).

> Therapy aims at strengthening the conscious mind, and whenever possible I try to rouse the patient to mental activity and get him to subdue the *massa confusa* of his mind with his own understanding, so that he can reach a vantage-point *au-dessus de la mêlée*.
>
> (Jung, 1946b, pp. 270–1)

In private correspondence with Jolande Jacobi in 1945, Jung maintained a consistent attitude to the therapeutic value of increasing consciousness even in cases of schizophrenia.

> It is a fact that psychological preparation in schizophrenia results in a better prognosis. I therefore make it a rule to let those threatened with schizophrenia, or mild schizophrenics or latent schizophrenics, have as much psychological knowledge as possible, because I know from experience that there is then a greater chance of their getting out of the psychotic interval again. Equally, psychological enlightenment after a psychotic attack is in certain conditions extraordinarily helpful ... I would always recommend psychological education as a prophylactic, measure with schizoids. Like neurosis, psychosis too in its intercourse is a process of individuation, but one that is not associated with consciousness and runs on like an *ouroboros* in the unconscious. Psychological preparation links the process with consciousness, or rather, there is the possibility of such a connection and hence of a curative effect.
>
> (Jacobi, 1965, p. 149)

The long-term impact of therapeutic self-knowledge was not, however, a transcendent disengagement or non-attachment, consistent with the monastic life. Jung often used language that evoked religious concepts, but he was concerned with striking a balance between introvertive withdrawal and extravertive engagement with society and the world.

> The increased self-knowledge which depth psychology necessitates also creates greater possibilities of communication: you can interpret

yourself in the analytic dialogue and learn through self-knowledge to understand others. In that way you become more just and more tolerant. Above all, you can remedy your own mistakes, and this is probably the best chance of making a proper adaptation to society.

(Jung, 1943a, p. 818)

Philosophical assumptions about consciousness

An important aspect of Jung's valuation of consciousness expansion was the pessimism that he shared with much of the medical profession in his era (Luprecht, 1991). In the late nineteenth century, doctors in Central Europe were educated to believe that their primary responsibility was to do research, because scientific medicine was incapable of doing very much toward effecting cures. Freud, in his discovery that psychoanalytic methods were able to effect profound changes in neurotics—that is, in hysterics and obsessive-compulsives—gave rise to an optimism among later generations of psychotherapists that neither he nor Jung shared. Where Freud's practice of what came to be called symptom-analysis aimed at decisive remissions of symptoms, Jung explicitly denied the very possibility of conflict solution. "All the greatest and most important problems of life are fundamentally insoluble.... They can never be solved, but only outgrown" (Jung, 1938a, p. 15).

Because making the unconscious conscious was not, in Jung's view, capable of solving mental conflicts, but only of bringing them to consciousness, he came to regard consciousness and its expansion as ends in themselves. Jung (1997, p. 323) maintained that consciousness was the purpose of human existence and argued the assertion through an appeal to history.

As far as one can make out, the purpose of the development of the human mind is to widen out, to increase, to intensify consciousness. When you look back into the ages, you see that what has happened since is an intensification, a widening out of consciousness. We call that culture and—always assuming that there is a purpose in human development or in the history of the mind—that is obviously the thing people were after. What is increase of knowledge, what is science, what is exploration, research? One aspect is the widening out of consciousness. Another aspect is of course values but that is also a matter of consciousness, for how can you perceive values, how can you attribute and apply values, without consciousness? It needs a particular consciousness to have a realization of values and to apply them at all; without consciousness there are no values there are only natural facts. So in either case, whether you look at the development of man from a merely mental side, or from an ethical side, it always means an intensification of consciousness—it is always the question of the great light, more light, illumination, clarification.

(Jung, 1997, pp. 1360–1)

Jung frequently cited the biblical narrative in connection with the expansion of consciousness.

The widening of consciousness ... has always, it seems, followed the pattern laid down in Genesis 3:4f.: "Ye shall not surely die, for God doth know that in the day ye eat thereof, then your eyes shall be opened, and ye shall be as gods, knowing good and evil."

(Jung, 1970, p. 169; see also 1933, pp. 388–9; 1934b, pp. 139–40; 1988, p. 965)

Jung discussed the inevitability of knowledge or gnosis as both tragic and desirable.

Primitive conditions are all right as long as the conditions *are* primitive, but the unfortunate thing is that man is not only an animal—in a way he is an animal and in a way he is not—because he has the faculty of developing consciousness. His consciousness *wants* to develop; he must give names even to his virtues, and so he is meant for conflict. He cannot escape it, cannot remain at one with himself. He will get into hot water in the end if he develops at all; and if he has once given a name he must continue to give names.

(Jung, 1988, p. 447)

Whether consciousness expansion was desirable, and was to be facilitated through analytical psychology, varied significantly from person to person.

Which is better—what should be? Well, obviously there are two opinions. The God of the Old Testament says: "Don't be an 'I,' don't eat of that tree, or you will see how unconscious and pitiful you are, how pitiful is the thing I have made." And the other point of view is: "Be as conscious as you can, be responsible to your self, for you will thereby spare much evil not only to yourself but also to your surroundings." Now, we don't know which is right. The decision is always the particular task of the time—whether we are forced this way or that, to be a collective people or a more individual people. I cannot decide it in many cases. I have said to quite a number of people that they had better go another way.... I am quite convinced that there are numbers of people who are not meant to be "I."

(Jung, 1988, p. 676)

Although Jung discussed "supreme" or "complete" consciousness in reflection of Eastern philosophical claims, he asserted the impossibility of the accomplishment. "Psychic wholeness will never be attained empirically, as consciousness is too narrow and too one-sided to comprehend the full inventory of the psyche" (Jung, 1970, p. 533). Jung associated complete consciousness with divine omniscience.

Suppose somebody reached ... the state of complete consciousness, not only self-consciousness. That would be an exceedingly extended consciousness which includes everything—energy itself—a consciousness which knows not only "That is Thou" but more than that—every tree, every stone, every breath of air, every rat's tail—all that is yourself; there is nothing that is not yourself. In such an extended consciousness all the cakras would be simultaneously experienced, because it is a higher state of consciousness, and it would not be the highest if it did not include all the former experiences.

(Jung, 1996, p. 59)

By "self-consciousness," Jung was referring to the union of the ego and the self, the conscious and the unconscious, which he identified with the traditional religious experience of *unio mystica* (Jung, 1946b, p. 314). In contrasting complete consciousness with self-consciousness, he excluded the possibility that he was discussing *unio mystica*. Mystical experiences are always necessarily experienced consciously, through the limited aperture of the ego in its perception of its union with the self. Complete consciousness would instead involve the perspective of the self, in its realization of all existence. Because "the self ... is a God-image, or at least cannot be distinguished from one" (Jung, 1969a, p. 22), Jung's concept of complete consciousness referred to divine omniscience. It was humanly unattainable.

Consideration of complete consciousness nevertheless formed part of Jung's system of psychology by providing its ultimate *telos*. "Consciousness," he wrote, "is ... absolutely indispensable to the self because it is the organ of awareness of the self" (Jung, 1988, p. 408). Because the self is indistinguishable from the God-image, Jung's formulation implied what he elsewhere stated explicitly, that self-consciousness—reflection or recursive thinking—is God's means of becoming aware of himself and his works.

> "But why on earth," you may ask, "should it be necessary for man to achieve, by hook or by crook, a higher level of consciousness?" This is truly the crucial question, and I do not find the answer easy. Instead of a real answer I can only make a confession of faith: I believe that, after thousands and millions of years, someone had to realize that this wonderful world of mountains and oceans, sounds and moons, galaxies and nebulae, plants and animals, *exists*. From a low hill in the Athi plains of East Africa I once watched the vast herds of wild animals grazing in soundless stillness, as they had done from time immemorial, touched only by the breath of a primeval world. I felt then as if I were the first man, the first creature, to know that all this *is*. The entire world round me was still in its primeval state; it did not know that it *was*. And then, in that one moment in which I came to know, the world sprang into being. Without that moment it would never have been. All Nature seeks this goal and finds it fulfilled in man, but only in the most highly developed and most fully conscious man. Every advance, even the smallest, along this path of conscious realization adds that much to the world.
>
> There is no consciousness without discrimination of opposites. This is the paternal principle, the Logos, which eternally struggles to extricate itself from the primal warmth and primal darkness of the maternal womb; in a word, from unconsciousness. Divine curiosity yearns to be born and does not shrink from conflict, suffering, or sin. Unconsciousness is the primal sin, evil itself, for the Logos.

Therefore its first creative act of liberation is matricide, and the spirit that dared all heights and all depths must, as Synesius says, suffer the divine punishment, entrainment on the rocks of the Caucasus.

(Jung, 1954c, pp. 95–6)

Jung asserted that God's desire to know translates into an imperative that all people desire to know, because God's subdivision into knower and known, which is to say, God's emergence from unconsciousness into consciousness, is accomplished, in tiny part, by every human act of increased consciousness. Because Jung was speaking not metaphysically about God, but psychologically about the God-image or self within the psyche, his assertion amounts to the claim that the desire to know is intrinsic in our species.

Concluding reflections

Freud's (1900, 1911) topographic hypothesis divided the psyche into two systems, the Unconscious (Ucs.) and Perception-Consciousness (Pcpt.-Cs.); and Jung (1913b) introduced a tripartite model by subdividing the unconscious into personal and collective divisions. After Freud (1923) developed his own tripartite model, the structural hypothesis of the id, ego, and superego, Jung (1934d, p. 3 n. 2; 1951b, p. 120; 1958a, p. 348; 1958b, pp. 39–40; 1970, p. 473) equated the collective unconscious with aspects of the superego that Freud had inadequately appreciated. Jung was guilty of the complementary oversight. He considered the superego only in so far as it was unconscious and failed to consider its conscious operations. Freud's formulation, which instead had the superego both conscious and unconscious, permitted him to assign the term *consciousness*, together with the function of internal and external perception, to the ego, while deploying the term *self-observation* in reference to the reflective or recursive function that he attributed to the superego.

In a classical article, "The Fate of the Ego in Analytic Therapy" (1934), Richard Sterba maintained that clinical psychoanalysis has the inevitable by-product of increasing the ego's involvement in self-observation. The ego is obliged to observe the process and products of free association, to reflect on the analyst's interpretations and, above all, to become self-conscious of the transference. Jung (1954c) may have had a comparable psychological phenomenon in mind when he listed "becoming conscious" as one of the two experiential goals of analytical psychology, the other being "the coming-to-be of the self (individuation)" (p. 226). Jung nowhere stated, that I can find, how his patients attained heightened or widened consciousness, but I should think the achievement is a by-product and necessary condition of becoming responsible for one's shadow.

Jung's concepts of widening and heightening consciousness were metaphors whose meanings remain obscure. They have entered the language, in reference both to consciousness-expanding drugs and to "raising consciousness" concerning particular topics. The popular usages retained Jung's appreciation that an increase of consciousness is both informative and transformative. It is informative in a manner that is not only empowering, as is all knowledge, but also altering of character or personality. Jung did not offer any remark, much less a developed theory, to account for the transformative character of increased consciousness.

In order to address the question, I find it useful first to close the gap between Freud's and Jung's uses of the term consciousness. What was in dispute between Freud and Jung had already been discussed in the Aristotelian terms of medieval psychology, where the *active intellect* was regarded as a divine or angelic mind that informs the universe and is a source of inspiration to the rational faculty of the human soul. When the active intellect imparts an Aristotelian universal, or form, to the soul, the soul receives it as an impression, much as wax receives the form of a ring, and the form that comes to exist within the rational faculty was said to be part of the *acquired intellect*. From al-Farabi onward, the active intellect's ordinary inspiration of every rational faculty, to attain all of the basic universal categories that every child knows, was regarded as the same process that was responsible for the extraordinary inspirations of the philosopher, the ruler, and the prophet (Rahman, 1958). Maimonides championed the medieval Aristotelian theory of prophecy within Judaism (Bakan *et al.*, 2009); and Aquinas' epistemology, which treats our every act of understanding as a gift of grace (Lonergan, 1992), expressed the Aristotelian perspective in Christian discourse. Medieval Aristotelians debated how the imaginative faculty related to the two intellects, but the distinction between active and acquired intellects, and the revelation by the one to the other, were held in common.

Jung's distinction among the unconscious archetypes, their productions of symbols that manifest consciously, and the ego-consciousness that is expanded by the acquisition of the symbols, corresponds at the phenomenological or experiential level to the active intellect, the forms, and the rational faculty of medieval Aristotelian psychology. Jung's ego-consciousness is limited, however, to the moment-by-moment activity of the rational faculty; Jung did not allow for the memory system that the rational faculty builds up. Freud's views were partial, but in a different manner. Freud retained the idea of the inspirative nature of understanding in his clinical concept of "insight." What an analyst interprets must not only be heard by the patient; if it is to be efficacious, it must be internalized in such a manner that the patient acquires it as an insight. Because the analyst serves as an auxiliary superego, whom the patient introjects within the patient's superego, Freud's clinical theory had the patient's unconscious superego (where Jung had the patient's unconscious archetypes) manifest insights, which the patient's ego was subsequently able to acquire for itself.

Freud's views were partial, in that he did not explain why an analyst's interpretations must be taken in by the patient's superego before they could be transmitted to the patient's ego in an efficacious way. In Freud's (1914, 1921, 1933) view, the superego had three basic functions: self-observation, ego-ideals, and conscience. Because the term *self* has become problematic in recent years, a variety of other terms have come into use in reference to the same activity. Jung's preference for *consciousness* is, like the Buddhist term *mindfulness*, sufficiently vague to require clarification. Less misunderstanding arises from the terms *reflective, reflexive,* and *recursive thinking*. These terms fail, however, because they invoke the concept of thinking, when the phenomenon of reflection or recursion consists of brief intellectual acts of understanding, insights, intuitions, and inspirations. When the "aha!" moment of reflection or recursion is developed into thinking, an activity that is willful and can be sustained in time, the superego function is collaborating intimately with the type of thinking that the ego performs, which cognitive scientists call *propositional thinking*.

Jung's concepts of widening and heightening consciousness are confusing. He employed the term *consciousness* to refer in part to consciousness as opposed to sleep and coma, but mostly to consciousness in the reflexive or recursive sense. Projection and behavioral enactments, the hallmarks of primitive and crowd psychologies, are owed to failures not of wakefulness, but of psychological mindedness, which is to say, of reflexive or recursive thinking about the interior life of the mind. Reflective or recursive consciousness, which Freud termed self-observation, is a superego function; but what alone is transformative is the further process, of ego–superego collaboration, in producing reflective or recursive thinking. Insights alone have no transformative power. They must not only occur, but additionally must be worked through.

References

Abraham, Karl. (1909). Dreams and myths: A study in folk-psychology. In *Clinical papers and essays on psycho-analysis*. 1955; reprinted New York: Brunner/Mazel, Publishers, 1979.

Adler, Alfred. (1912). Dreams and dream-interpretation. In *The practice and theory of individual psychology*. Trans. P. Radin (pp. 214–26). London: Kegan Paul, Trench, Trubner & Co., Ltd. 1925. Reprint.

Adler, Alfred. (1917). *The neurotic constitution: Outlines of a comparative individualistic psychology and psychotherapy*. Trans. Bernard Glueck and John E. Lind. New York: Moffat, Yard and Company. (Originally published in German in 1912.)

Alexander, Franz. (1929). *The psychoanalysis of the total personality: The application of Freud's theory of the ego to the neuroses*. Trans. Bernard Glueck and Bertram D. Lewin. New York: Nervous and Mental Disease Publishing Co.

Alexander, Franz. (1952). Development of the fundamental concepts of psychoanalysis. In *Dynamic psychiatry*. Eds. Franz Alexander and Helen Ross (pp. 3–34). Chicago: University of Chicago Press, 1952.

Apfelbaum, Bernard. (1965). Ego psychology, psychic energy, and the hazards of quantitative explanation in psycho-analytic theory. *International Journal of Psycho-Analysis, 46*, 168–82.

Bair, Deirdre. (2003). *Jung: A biography*. New York and Boston: Little, Brown and Company.

Bakan, David, Merkur, Dan, and Weiss, David S. (2009). *Maimonides' cure of souls: Medieval precursor of psychoanalysis*. Albany, NY: State University of New York Press.

Benjamin, Jessica. (1998). *Shadow of the other: Intersubjectivity and gender in psychoanalysis*. Routledge: New York and London.

Benjamin, Jessica. (2004). Beyond doer and done to: An intersubjective view of thirdness. *Psychoanalytic Quarterly, 73*, 5–46.

Bibring, Edward. (1953). The mechanisms of depression. In *Affective disorders*. Ed. Phyllis Greenacre (pp. 13–48). New York: International Universities Press.

204 References

Blos, Peter. (1962). *On adolescence: A psychoanalytic interpretation.* New York: Free Press of Glencoe.

Blos, Peter. (1974). The genealogy of the ego ideal. *Psychoanalytic Study of the Child, 29,* 43–88.

Blum, Harold. (1985). Superego formation, adolescent transformation, and the adult neurosis. *Journal of the American Psychoanalytic Association, 33,* 887–90.

Brenner, Charles. (1976). *Psychoanalytic technique and psychic conflict.* New York: International Universities Press.

Breuer, Joseph and Freud, Sigmund. (1895). *Studies on hysteria. Standard Edition, 2.* London: Hogarth Press, 1955.

Burrow, Trigant. (1914). Character and the neuroses. *Psychoanalytic Review, 1*(2), 121–8.

Campbell, Joseph. (1959). *The masks of God: Primitive mythology.* New York: Viking Press.

Coward, Harold G. (1978). Jung's encounter with yoga. *Journal of Analytical Psychology, 23,* 339–57.

Coward, Harold G. (1985). *Jung and Eastern thought.* Albany: State University of New York Press.

Creuzer, Friedrich. (1810–12). *Symbolik und Mythologie der alten Völker, besoders der Griechen [Symbolism and Mythology of Ancient People]* 4 Vols. Leipzig: Darmstadt.

D'Andrade, Roy. (1986). Three scientific world views and the covering law model. In *Metatheory in social science: Pluralisms and subjectivities.* Eds. Donald W. Fiske and Richard A. Shweder (pp. 19–41). Chicago and London: University of Chicago Press, 1986.

Danesi, Marcel. (2007). *The quest for meaning: A guide to semiotic theory and practice.* Toronto: University of Toronto Press.

Ehrenzweig, Anton. (1957). The creative surrender: A comment on "Joanna Field's book *An experiment in leisure.*" *American Imago, 14,* 193–210.

Ehrenzweig, Anton. (1967). *The hidden order of art: A study in the psychology of artistic imagination.* Berkeley and Los Angeles: University of California Press.

Eliade, Mircea. (1961). *Images and symbols: Studies in religious symbolism.* Trans. Philip Mairet. New York: Sheed & Ward, 1969. Reprint.

Feldman, Burton and Richardson, Robert D. (1972). *The rise of modern mythology, 1680–1860.* Indianapolis: Indiana University Press.

Fenichel, Otto. (1928). The clinical aspect of the need for punishment. *International Journal of Psycho-Analysis, 9,* 47–70.

Fenichel, Otto. (1945). *The psychoanalytic theory of neurosis.* New York: W. W. Norton.

Ferenczi, Sandor. (1932). Confusion of tongues between adults and the child. Reprinted in *Final contributions to the problems and methods of psychoanalysis.* Ed. Michael Balint. Trans. Eric Mosbacher and others (pp. 156–67). London: Hogarth Press, 1955; reprinted New York: Brunner/Mazel, 1980.

References 205

Ferenczi, Sandor. (1988). *The clinical diary of Sándor Ferenczi.* Ed. Judith Dupont. Trans. Michael Balint and Nicola Zarday Jackson. Cambridge, MA and London, UK: Harvard University Press.

Field, Joanna (Marion Milner). (1934). *A life of one's own.* London: Chatto & Windus; reprinted London: Virago Press, 1986.

Field, Joanna (Marion Milner). (1937). *An experiment in leisure.* London: Chatto & Windus; reprinted London: Virago Press, 1986.

Field, Joanna (Marion Milner). (1957). *On not being able to paint.* Los Angeles: J. P. Tarcher.

Flugel, J. C. (1945). *Man, morals and society: A psycho-analytical study.* Reprinted New York: International Universities Press, 1970.

Freud, Anna. (1966). *The ego and the mechanisms of defense,* 2nd edn. New York: International Universities Press.

Freud, Sigmund. (1900). The interpretation of dreams. *Standard edition, 4–5* (pp. 1–625). London: Hogarth Press, 1958.

Freud, Sigmund. (1901). The psychopathology of everyday life. *Standard edition, 6* (pp. 1–279). London: Hogarth Press, 1960.

Freud, Sigmund. (1905). Jokes and their relation to the unconscious. *Standard edition, 8.* London: Hogarth Press, 1960.

Freud, Sigmund. (1907). Delusions and dreams in Jensen's *Gradiva. Standard edition, 9* (pp. 7–95). London: Hogarth Press, 1959.

Freud, Sigmund. (1908a). "Civilized" sexual morality and modern nervous illness. *Standard edition, 9* (pp. 181–204). London: Hogarth Press, 1959.

Freud, Sigmund. (1908b). Creative writers and day-dreaming. *Standard edition, 9* (pp. 143–53). London: Hogarth Press, 1959.

Freud, Sigmund. (1911). Formulations on the two principles of mental functioning. *Standard edition, 12* (pp. 218–26). London: Hogarth Press, 1958.

Freud, Sigmund. (1913a). An evidential dream. *Standard edition, 12* (pp. 269–77). London: Hogarth Press, 1958.

Freud, Sigmund. (1913b). Totem and taboo: Some points of agreement between the mental lives of savages and neurotics. *Standard edition, 13* (pp. xiii–162). London: Hogarth Press, 1958.

Freud, Sigmund. (1914a). On narcissism: An introduction. *Standard edition, 14* (pp. 78–102). London: Hogarth Press, 1957.

Freud, Sigmund. (1914b). On the history of the psychoanalytic movement. *Standard edition, 14* (pp. 7–66). London: Hogarth Press, 1957.

Freud, Sigmund. (1915). The unconscious. *Standard edition, 14* (pp. 166–204). London: Hogarth Press, 1957.

Freud, Sigmund. (1916). Some character-types met with in psycho-analytic work. *Standard edition, 14* (pp. 311–33). London: Hogarth Press, 1957.

Freud, Sigmund. (1916–17). Introductory lectures on psycho-analysis. *Standard edition, 15–16* (pp. 9–463). London: Hogarth Press, 1961–63.

Freud, Sigmund. (1919). Lines of advance in psycho-analytic therapy. *Standard edition, 17* (pp. 159–68). London: Hogarth Press, 1955.

206 References

Freud, Sigmund. (1920). Beyond the pleasure principle. *Standard edition, 18* (pp. 7–64). London: Hogarth Press, 1955.

Freud, Sigmund. (1921). Group psychology and the analysis of the ego. *Standard edition, 18* (pp. 69–143). London: Hogarth Press, 1955.

Freud, Sigmund. (1922). Dreams and telepathy. *Standard edition, 18* (pp. 197–220). London: Hogarth Press, 1955.

Freud, Sigmund. (1923a). The ego and the id. *Standard edition, 19* (pp. 12–59). London: Hogarth Press, 1961.

Freud, Sigmund. (1923b). Joseph Popper-Lynkeus and the theory of dreams. *Standard edition, 19* (pp. 261–3). London: Hogarth Press, 1961.

Freud, Sigmund. (1923c). Remarks on the theory and practice of dream interpretation. *Standard edition, 19* (pp. 109–21). London: Hogarth Press, 1961.

Freud, Sigmund. (1925). Some additional notes on dream-interpretation as a whole. *Standard edition, 19* (pp. 127–38). London: Hogarth Press, 1961.

Freud, Sigmund. (1926). Inhibitions, symptoms, and anxiety. *Standard edition, 20* (pp. 87–172). London: Hogarth Press, 1959.

Freud, Sigmund. (1927). The future of an illusion. *Standard edition, 21* (pp. 5–56). London: Hogarth Press, 1961.

Freud, Sigmund. (1930). Civilization and its discontents. *Standard edition, 21* (pp. 64–145). London: Hogarth Press, 1961.

Freud, Sigmund. (1933). New introductory lectures on psycho-analysis. *Standard edition, 22* (pp. 5–182). London: Hogarth Press, 1964.

Freud, Sigmund. (1939). Moses and monotheism: Three essays. *Standard edition, 23* (pp. 6–137). London: Hogarth Press, 1964.

Freud, Sigmund. (1966). *The standard edition of the complete psychological works of Sigmund Freud*, 24 vols. Eds. James Strachey, with Anna Freud, Alix Strachey, and Alan Tyson. London: Hogarth Press. (Cited elsewhere as *Standard edition*.)

Freud, Sigmund and Binswanger, Ludwig. (2003). *The Sigmund Freud–Ludwig Binswanger correspondence 1908–1938*. New York: Other Press.

Freud, Sigmund and Jung, Carl Gustav. (1974). *The Freud/Jung letters: The correspondence between Sigmund Freud and C. G. Jung*. Ed. William McGuire. Trans. Ralph Manheim and R. F. C. Hull. Bollingen Series XCIV. Princeton: Princeton University Press.

Fuechtner, Veronika. (2011). *Berlin psychoanalytic: Psychoanalysis and culture in Weimar republic Germany and beyond*. Berkeley: University of California Press.

Gill, Merton M. (1983). The point of view of psychoanalysis: Energy discharge or person? *Psychoanalysis and Contemporary Thought, 6*(4), 523–51.

Glover, Edward. (1960). *The roots of crime*. New York: International Universities Press.

Greenberg, Jay R. and Mitchell, Stephen A. (1983). *Object relations in psychoanalytic theory*. Cambridge, MA: Harvard University Press.

Grinberg, Leon. (1964). Two kinds of guilt: Their relations with normal and pathological aspects of mourning. *International Journal of Psycho-Analysis, 45*, 366–71.

Grotstein, James S. (1979). Who is the dreamer who dreams the dream and who is the dreamer who understands it? A psychoanalytic inquiry into the ultimate nature of being. *Contemporary Psychoanalysis*, *15*, 110–69.

Grotstein, James S. (1993). Towards the concept of the transcendent position: Reflections on some of "the unborns" in Bion's "Cogitations." *Journal of Melanie Klein and Object Relations*, *11*(2), 55–73.

Grotstein, James S. (1996). Bion's "transformation in 'O'," the "thing-in-itself," and the "real": Toward the concept of the "transcendent position." *Journal of Melanie Klein and Object Relations*, *14*(2), 109–41.

Grotstein, James S. (1998). The numinous and immanent nature of the psychoanalytic subject. *Journal of Analytical Psychology*, *43*, 41–68.

Grotstein, James S. (2000). *Who is the dreamer who dreams the dream? A study of psychic presences*. Hillsdale, NJ and London: The Analytic Press.

Haartman, Keith. (2004). *Watching and praying: Personality transformation in eighteenth century British methodism*. Amsterdam and New York: Rodopi.

Hannah, Barbara. (1976). *Jung: His life and work. A biographical memoir*. New York: G. P. Putnam's Sons.

Hartmann, Franz. (1885). *Magic white and black: Or, the science of finite and infinite life containing practical hints for students of occultism*, 5th edn. Boston and Madras; Van Nuys, CA: Newcastle Publishing Company, Inc., 1971. Reprint.

Hartmann, Heinz. (1958). *Ego psychology and the problem of adaptation.* New York: International Universities Press, 1958. (Originally published in German in 1939.)

Hartmann, Heinz. (1960). *Psychoanalysis and moral values.* New York: International Universities Press.

Hartmann, Heinz and Loewenstein, Rudolph M. (1962). Notes on the superego. *Psychoanalytic Study of the Child*, *17*, 42–81; reprinted in Heinz Hartmann, Ernst Kris, and Rudolph M. Loewenstein, *Papers on Psychoanalytic Psychology* (pp. 144–81). New York: International Universities Press, 1964.

Holt, Robert R. (1962). A critical examination of Freud's concept of bound vs. free cathexis. *Journal of the American Psychoanalytic Association*, *10*, 475–525.

Holt, Robert R. (1967). Beyond vitalism and mechanism: Freud's concept of psychic energy. In *Science and psychoanalysis, volume XI: The ego*. Ed. Jules H. Masserman (pp. 1–41). New York and London: Grune & Stratton, 1967.

Jacobi, Jolande. (1965). *The way of individuation*. Trans. R. F. C. Hull. London: Hodder & Stoughton.

Jacques, Elliott. (1965). Death and the mid-life crisis. *International Journal of Psycho-Analysis*, *46*, 502–14.

Jung, Carl Gustav. (1911). A criticism of Bleuler's theory of schizophrenic negativism. In *The psychogenesis of mental disease*. Trans. R. F. C. Hull (pp. 197–202). Collected Works of C. G. Jung, Vol. 3. Princeton: Princeton University Press, 1976.

208   References

Jung, Carl Gustav. (1913a). General aspects of psychoanalysis. In *Freud and psychoanalysis*. Trans. R. F. C. Hull (pp. 229–42). Collected Works of C. G. Jung, Vol. 4. New York: Bollingen Foundation/Pantheon Books, 1961.

Jung, Carl Gustav. (1913b). The theory of psychoanalysis. In *Freud and psychoanalysis.* Trans. R. F. C. Hull (pp. 84–226). Collected Works of C. G. Jung, Vol. 4. New York: Bollingen Foundation/Pantheon Books, 1961.

Jung, Carl Gustav. (1913c). A comment on Tausk's criticism of Nelken. *The symbolic life: Miscellaneous writings*, 2nd edn. Trans. R. F. C. Hull (pp. 433–7). Collected Works of C. G. Jung, Vol. 18. Princeton: Princeton University Press, 1980.

Jung, Carl Gustav. (1914). Some crucial points in psychoanalysis: A correspondence between Dr. Jung and Dr. Loy. In *Freud and psychoanalysis.* Trans. R. F. C. Hull (pp. 252–89). Collected Works of C. G. Jung, Vol. 4. New York: Bollingen Foundation/Pantheon Books, 1961.

Jung, Carl Gustav. (1916a). Preface to "Collected papers on analytical psychology." In *Freud and psychoanalysis.* Trans. R. F. C. Hull (pp. 290–7). Collected Works of C. G. Jung, Vol. 4. New York: Bollingen Foundation/ Pantheon Books, 1961.

Jung, Carl Gustav. (1916b). *Psychology of the unconscious: A study of the transformations and symbolisms of the libido. A contribution to the history of the evolution of thought.* Trans. Beatrice M. Hinkle. New York: Dodd, Mead and Company, 1947. Reprint.

Jung, Carl Gustav. (1918). The role of the unconscious. In *Civilization in transition.* Trans. R. F. C. Hull (pp. 3–28). Collected Works of C. G. Jung, Vol. 10. Princeton: Princeton University Press, 1970.

Jung, Carl Gustav. (1921). *Psychological types.* Trans. R. F. C. Hull and H. G. Baynes. Collected Works of C. G. Jung, Vol. 6. Princeton: Princeton University Press, 1971.

Jung, Carl Gustav. (1922). On the relation of analytical psychology to poetry. In *The spirit in man, art, and literature.* Trans. R. F. C. Hull (pp. 65–83). Collected Works of C. G. Jung, Vol. 15. Princeton: Princeton University Press, 1966.

Jung, Carl Gustav. (1923). Psychological types. In *Psychological types.* Trans. R. F. C. Hull and H. G. Baynes (pp. 510–23). Collected Works of C. G. Jung, Vol. 6. Princeton: Princeton University Press, 1971.

Jung, Carl Gustav. (1926a). Analytical psychology and education. In *The development of personality.* Trans. R. F. C. Hull (pp. 63–132). Collected Works of C. G. Jung, Vol. 17. Princeton: Princeton University Press, 1970.

Jung, Carl Gustav. (1926b). Spirit and life. In *The structure and dynamics of the psyche*, 2nd edn. Trans. R. F. C. Hull (pp. 319–37). Collected Works of C. G. Jung, Vol. 8. Princeton: Princeton University Press, 1969.

Jung, Carl Gustav. (1928a). The significance of the unconscious in individual education. In *The development of personality.* Trans. R. F. C. Hull (pp. 149–64). Collected Works of C. G. Jung, Vol. 17. Princeton: Princeton University Press, 1970.

Jung, Carl Gustav. (1928b). On psychic energy. In *The structure and dynamics of the psyche*, 2nd edn. Trans. R. F. C. Hull (pp. 3–66). Collected Works of C. G. Jung, Vol. 8. Princeton: Princeton University Press, 1969.

Jung, Carl Gustav. (1928c). Psychoanalysis and the cure of souls. In *Psychology and religion: West and east*. Trans. R. F. C. Hull (pp. 348–54). Collected Works of C. G. Jung, Vol. 11. Princeton: Princeton University Press, 1970.

Jung, Carl Gustav. (1929a). The aims of psychotherapy. In *The practice of psychotherapy: Essays on the psychology of the transference and other subjects*, 2nd edn. Trans. R. F. C. Hull (pp. 36–52). Collected Works of C. G. Jung, Vol. 16. Princeton: Princeton University Press, 1966.

Jung, Carl Gustav. (1929b). Freud and Jung: Contrasts. In *Freud and psychoanalysis*. Trans. R. F. C. Hull (pp. 333–40). Collected Works of C. G. Jung, Vol. 4. New York: Bollingen Foundation/Pantheon Books, 1961.

Jung, Carl Gustav. (1930a). Some aspects of modern psychotherapy. In *The practice of psychotherapy: Essays on the psychology of the transference and other subjects*, 2nd edn. Trans. R. F. C. Hull (pp. 29–35). Collected Works of C. G. Jung, Vol. 16. Princeton: Princeton University Press, 1966.

Jung, Carl Gustav. (1930b). Introduction to Kranefeldt's "Secret ways of the mind." In *Freud and psychoanalysis*. Trans. R. F. C. Hull (pp. 324–32). Collected Works of C. G. Jung, Vol. 4. New York: Bollingen Foundation/Pantheon Books, 1961.

Jung, Carl Gustav. (1931a). The practical use of dream-analysis. In *The practice of psychotherapy*. Trans. R. F. C. Hull (pp. 139–61). Collected Works of C. G. Jung, Vol. 16. Princeton: Princeton University Press, 1966.

Jung, Carl Gustav. (1931b). Archaic man. In *Civilization in transition*. Trans. R. F. C. Hull (pp. 50–73). Collected Works of C. G. Jung, Vol. 10. Princeton: Princeton University Press, 1970.

Jung, Carl Gustav. (1931c). Problems of modern psychotherapy. In *The practice of psychotherapy*. Trans. R. F. C. Hull (pp. 53–75). Collected Works of C. G. Jung, Vol. 16. Princeton: Princeton University Press, 1966.

Jung, Carl Gustav. (1931d). Introduction to Wickes's "Analyse der Kinderseele." In *The development of personality*. Trans. R. F. C. Hull (pp. 39–46). Collected Works of C. G. Jung, Vol. 17. Princeton: Princeton University Press, 1970.

Jung, Carl Gustav. (1931e). Analytical psychology and "Weltanschauung." In *The structure and dynamics of the psyche*, 2nd edn. Trans. R. F. C. Hull (pp. 358–381). Collected Works of C. G. Jung, Vol. 8. Princeton: Princeton University Press, 1969.

Jung, Carl Gustav. (1931f). The spiritual problem of modern man. In *Civilization in transition*. Trans. R. F. C. Hull (pp. 74–94). Collected Works of C. G. Jung, Vol. 8. Princeton: Princeton University Press, 1969.

Jung, Carl Gustav. (1931g). Basic postulates of analytical psychology. In *The structure and dynamics of the psyche*, 2nd edn. Trans. R. F. C. Hull (pp. 338–57). Collected Works of C. G. Jung, Vol. 8. Princeton: Princeton University Press, 1969.

210 References

Jung, Carl Gustav. (1932). Sigmund Freud in his historical setting. In *The spirit in man, art, and literature*. Trans. R. F. C. Hull (pp. 33–40). Collected Works of C. G. Jung, Vol. 15. Princeton: Princeton University Press, 1966.

Jung, Carl Gustav. (1933). The stages of life. In *The structure and dynamics of the psyche*, 2nd edn. Trans. R. F. C. Hull (pp. 387–403). Collected Works of C. G. Jung, Vol. 8. Princeton: Princeton University Press, 1969.

Jung, Carl Gustav. (1934a). The development of personality. In *The development of personality*. Trans. R. F. C. Hull (pp. 167–86). Collected Works of C. G. Jung, Vol. 17. Princeton: Princeton University Press, 1970.

Jung, Carl Gustav. (1934b). The meaning of psychology for modern man. In *Civilization in transition*. Trans. R. F. C. Hull (pp. 134–56). Collected Works of C. G. Jung, Vol. 10. Princeton: Princeton University Press, 1970.

Jung, Carl Gustav. (1934c). The soul and death. In *The structure and dynamics of the psyche*, 2nd edn. Trans. R. F. C. Hull (pp. 404–15). Collected Works of C. G. Jung, Vol. 8. Princeton: Princeton University Press, 1969.

Jung, Carl Gustav. (1934d). The state of psychotherapy today. In *Civilization in transition*. Trans. R. F. C. Hull (pp. 157–73). Collected Works of C. G. Jung, Vol. 10. Princeton: Princeton University Press, 1970.

Jung, Carl Gustav. (1935a). Foreword to von Koenig-Fachsenfeld: "Wandlungen des Traumproblems von der Romantik bis zur Gegenwart." In *The symbolic life: Miscellaneous writings*, 2nd edn. Trans. R. F. C. Hull (pp. 773–5). Collected Works of C. G. Jung, Vol. 18. Princeton: Princeton University Press, 1980.

Jung, Carl Gustav. (1935b). Principles of practical psychotherapy. In *The practice of psychotherapy*. Trans. R. F. C. Hull (pp. 3–20). Collected Works of C. G. Jung, Vol. 16. Princeton: Princeton University Press, 1966.

Jung, Carl Gustav. (1936a). The Tavistock lectures: On the theory and practice of analytical psychology. In *The symbolic life*. Trans. R. F. C. Hull (pp. 1–182). Collected Works of C. G. Jung, Vol. 18. Princeton: Princeton University Press, 1980.

Jung, Carl Gustav. (1936b). Yoga and the West. In *Psychology and religion*. Trans. R. F. C. Hull (pp. 529–37). Collected Works of C. G. Jung, Vol. 11. Princeton: Princeton University Press, 1970.

Jung, Carl Gustav. (1936–37). The concept of the collective unconscious. In *The archetypes and the collective unconscious*, 2nd edn. Trans. R. F. C. Hull (pp. 42–53). Collected Works of C. G. Jung, Vol. 9, Part I. Princeton: Princeton University Press, 1968.

Jung, Carl Gustav. (1938a). Commentary on "The secret of the golden flower." In *Alchemical studies*. Trans. R. F. C. Hull (pp. 1–56). Collected Works of C. G. Jung, Vol. 13. Princeton: Princeton University Press, 1967.

Jung, Carl Gustav. (1938b). Psychology and religion. In *Psychology and religion*. Trans. R. F. C. Hull (pp. 3–105). Collected Works of C. G. Jung, Vol. 11. Princeton: Princeton University Press, 1970.

Jung, Carl Gustav. (1938c). *The relations between the ego and the unconscious*, 3rd edn. In *Two essays on analytical psychology*, 2nd edn. Trans. R. F. C. Hull (pp. 121–241). Collected Works of C. G. Jung, Vol. 7. Princeton: Princeton University Press, 1966.

Jung, Carl Gustav. (1938d). The visions of Zosimos. In *Alchemical studies.* Trans. R. F. C. Hull (pp. 58–108). Collected Works of C. G. Jung, Vol. 13. Princeton: Princeton University Press, 1967.

Jung, Carl Gustav. (1939a). Conscious, unconscious, and individuation. In *The archetypes and the collective unconscious*, 2nd edn. Trans. R. F. C. Hull (pp. 275–89). Collected Works of C. G. Jung, Vol. 9, Part I. Princeton: Princeton University Press, 1969.

Jung, Carl Gustav. (1939b). In memory of Sigmund Freud. In *The spirit in man, art, and literature.* Trans. R. F. C. Hull (pp. 41–9). Collected Works of C. G. Jung, Vol. 15. Princeton: Princeton University Press, 1966.

Jung, Carl Gustav. (1941). The psychological aspects of the Kore. In *The archetypes and the collective unconscious*, 2nd edn. Trans. R. F. C. Hull (pp. 182–203). Collected Works of C. G. Jung, Vol. 9, Part I. Princeton: Princeton University Press, 1968.

Jung, Carl Gustav. (1942a). Paracelsus as a spiritual phenomenon. In *Alchemical studies.* Trans. R. F. C. Hull (pp. 109–89). Collected Works of C. G. Jung, Vol. 13. Princeton: Princeton University Press, 1967.

Jung, Carl Gustav. (1942b). Psychological factors determining human behaviour. In *The structure and dynamics of the psyche*, 2nd edn. Trans. R. F. C. Hull (pp. 114–25). Collected Works of C. G. Jung, Vol. 8. Princeton: Princeton University Press, 1969.

Jung, Carl Gustav. (1943a). Depth psychology and self-knowledge. In *The symbolic life.* Trans. R. F. C. Hull (pp. 811–19). Collected Works of C. G. Jung, Vol. 18. Princeton: Princeton University Press, 1980.

Jung, Carl Gustav. (1943b). The spirit Mercurius. In *Alchemical studies.* Trans. R. F. C. Hull (pp. 191–250). Collected Works of C. G. Jung, Vol. 13. Princeton: Princeton University Press, 1967.

Jung, Carl Gustav. (1943c). On the psychology of the unconscious, 5th edn. In *Two essays on analytical psychology.* Trans. R. F. C. Hull (pp. 1–119). Collected Works of C. G. Jung, Vol. 7. Princeton: Princeton University Press, 1966.

Jung, Carl Gustav. (1945a). The philosophical tree. In *Alchemical studies.* Trans. R. F. C. Hull (pp. 251–349). Collected Works of C. G. Jung, Vol. 13. Princeton: Princeton University Press, 1967.

Jung, Carl Gustav. (1945b). Psychotherapy today. In *The practice of psychotherapy.* Trans. R. F. C. Hull (pp. 94–110). Collected Works of C. G. Jung, Vol. 16. Princeton: Princeton University Press, 1966.

Jung, Carl Gustav. (1945c). After the catastrophe. In *Civilization in transition.* Trans. R. F. C. Hull (pp. 194–217). Collected Works of C. G. Jung, Vol. 10. Princeton: Princeton University Press, 1970.

Jung, Carl Gustav. (1946a). Psychic conflicts in a child. In *The development of personality.* Trans. R. F. C. Hull (pp. 1–35). Collected Works of C. G. Jung, Vol. 17. Princeton: Princeton University Press, 1970.

212 References

Jung, Carl Gustav. (1946b). The psychology of the transference. In *The practice of psychotherapy*. Trans. R. F. C. Hull (pp. 163–323). Collected Works of C. G. Jung, Vol. 16. Princeton: Princeton University Press, 1966.

Jung, Carl Gustav. (1948a). Address on the occasion of the founding of the C. G. Jung Institute, Zurich, April 24, 1948. *The symbolic life*. Trans. R. F. C. Hull (pp. 471–6). Collected Works of C. G. Jung, Vol. 18. Princeton: Princeton University Press, 1980.

Jung, Carl Gustav. (1948b). General aspects of dream psychology. In *The structure and dynamics of the psyche*, 2nd edn. Trans. R. F. C. Hull (pp. 237–80). Collected Works of C. G. Jung, Vol. 8. Princeton: Princeton University Press, 1969.

Jung, Carl Gustav. (1948c). The phenomenology of the spirit in fairytales. In *The archetypes and the collective unconscious*, 2nd edn. Trans. R. F. C. Hull (pp. 207–54). Collected Works of C. G. Jung, Vol. 9, Part I. Princeton: Princeton University Press, 1969.

Jung, Carl Gustav. (1948d). A psychological approach to the dogma of the trinity. In *Psychology and religion*. Trans. R. F. C. Hull (pp. 107–200). Collected Works of C. G. Jung, Vol. 11. Princeton: Princeton University Press, 1970.

Jung, Carl Gustav. (1948e). The psychological foundations of belief in spirits. In *The structure and dynamics of the psyche*, 2nd edn. Trans. R. F. C. Hull (pp. 301–18). Collected Works of C. G. Jung, Vol. 8. Princeton: Princeton University Press, 1969.

Jung, Carl Gustav. (1948f). A review of the complex theory. In *The structure and dynamics of the psyche*, 2nd edn. Trans. R. F. C. Hull (pp. 92–104). Collected Works of C. G. Jung, Vol. 8. Princeton: Princeton University Press, 1969.

Jung, Carl Gustav. (1948g). General aspects of dream psychology. In *The structure and dynamics of the psyche*, 2nd edn. Trans. R. F. C. Hull (pp. 237–80). Collected Works of C. G. Jung, Vol. 8. Princeton: Princeton University Press, 1969.

Jung, Carl Gustav. (1948h). On the nature of dreams. In *The structure and dynamics of the psyche*, 2nd edn. Trans. R. F. C. Hull (pp. 281–97). Collected Works of C. G. Jung, Vol. 8. Princeton: Princeton University Press, 1969.

Jung, Carl Gustav. (1948i). The structure of the psyche. In *The structure and dynamics of the psyche*, 2nd edn. Trans. R. F. C. Hull (pp. 139–58). Collected Works of C. G. Jung, Vol. 8. Princeton: Princeton University Press, 1969.

Jung, Carl Gustav. (1948j). Instinct and the unconscious. In *The structure and dynamics of the psyche*, 2nd edn. Trans. R. F. C. Hull (pp. 129–38). Collected Works of C. G. Jung, Vol. 8. Princeton: Princeton University Press, 1969.

Jung, Carl Gustav. (1949). Foreword to Harding: "Woman's mysteries." *The symbolic life*. Trans. R. F. C. Hull (pp. 518–20). Collected Works of C. G. Jung, Vol. 18. Princeton: Princeton University Press, 1980.

Jung, Carl Gustav. (1950a). A study in the process of individuation. In *The archetypes and the collective unconscious*, 2nd edn. Trans. R. F. C. Hull (pp. 290–354). Collected Works of C. G. Jung, Vol. 9, Part I. Princeton: Princeton University Press, 1968.

References 213

Jung, Carl Gustav. (1950b). Concerning rebirth. In *The archetypes and the collective unconscious*, 2nd edn. Trans. R. F. C. Hull (pp. 111–47). Collected Works of C. G. Jung, Vol. 9, Part I. Princeton: Princeton University Press, 1968.

Jung, Carl Gustav. (1950c). Concerning mandala symbolism. In *The archetypes and the collective unconscious*, 2nd edn. Trans. R. F. C. Hull. Collected Works of C. G. Jung, Vol. 9, Part I. Princeton: Princeton University Press, 1968.

Jung, Carl Gustav. (1951a). Depth psychology. *The symbolic life.* Trans. R. F. C. Hull (pp. 477–86). Collected Works of C. G. Jung, Vol. 18. Princeton: Princeton University Press, 1980.

Jung, Carl Gustav. (1951b). Fundamental questions of psychotherapy. In *The practice of psychotherapy.* Trans. R. F. C. Hull (pp. 111–25). Collected Works of C. G. Jung, Vol. 16. Princeton: Princeton University Press, 1966.

Jung, Carl Gustav. (1951c). On synchronicity. In *The structure and dynamics of the psyche*, 2nd edn. Trans. R. F. C. Hull (pp. 520–31). Collected Works of C. G. Jung, Vol. 8. Princeton: Princeton University Press, 1969.

Jung, Carl Gustav. (1952a). Answer to Job. In *Psychology and religion.* Trans. R. F. C. Hull (pp. 355–470). Collected Works of C. G. Jung, Vol. 11. Princeton: Princeton University Press, 1970.

Jung, Carl Gustav. (1952b). Forward to Custance: "Wisdom, madness and folly." *The symbolic life.* Trans. R. F. C. Hull (pp. 349–52). Collected Works of C. G. Jung, Vol. 18. Princeton: Princeton University Press, 1980.

Jung, Carl Gustav. (1952c). Foreword to White's "God and the unconscious." In *Psychology and religion.* Trans. R. F. C. Hull (pp. 299–310). Collected Works of C. G. Jung, Vol. 11. Princeton: Princeton University Press, 1970.

Jung, Carl Gustav. (1952d). *Psychology and alchemy*, 2nd edn. Trans. R. F. C. Hull. Collected Works of C. G. Jung, Vol. 12. Princeton, NJ: Princeton University Press, 1968.

Jung, Carl Gustav. (1954a). Archetypes of the collective unconscious. In *The archetypes and the collective unconscious*, 2nd edn. Trans. R. F. C. Hull (pp. 3–41). Collected Works of C. G. Jung, Vol. 9, Part I. Princeton: Princeton University Press, 1968.

Jung, Carl Gustav. (1954b). On the nature of the psyche. In *The structure and dynamics of the psyche*, 2nd edn. Trans. R. F. C. Hull (pp. 159–234). Collected Works of C. G. Jung, Vol. 8. Princeton: Princeton University Press, 1969.

Jung, Carl Gustav. (1954c). Psychological aspects of the mother archetype. In *The archetypes and the collective unconscious*, 2nd edn. Trans. R. F. C. Hull (pp. 73–110). Collected Works of C. G. Jung, Vol. 9, Part I. Princeton: Princeton University Press, 1968.

Jung, Carl Gustav. (1954d). Psychological commentary on "The Tibetan book of the great liberation." In *Psychology and religion.* Trans. R. F. C. Hull (pp. 475–508). Collected Works of C. G. Jung, Vol. 11. Princeton: Princeton University Press, 1970.

214 References

Jung, Carl Gustav. (1954e). Transformation symbolism in the mass. In *Psychology and religion.* Trans. R. F. C. Hull (pp. 201–96). Collected Works of C. G. Jung, Vol. 11. Princeton: Princeton University Press, 1970.

Jung, Carl Gustav. (1954f). On the psychology of the trickster-figure. In *The archetypes and the collective unconscious*, 2nd edn. Trans. R. F. C. Hull (pp. 255–72). Collected Works of C. G. Jung, Vol. 9, Part I. Princeton: Princeton University Press, 1968.

Jung, Carl Gustav. (1954g). The symbolic life. In *The symbolic life.* Trans. R. F. C. Hull (pp. 265–90). Collected Works of C. G. Jung, Vol. 18. Princeton: Princeton University Press, 1980.

Jung, Carl Gustav. (1957a). Foreword to Jacobi: "Complex/archetype/symbol." *The symbolic life.* Trans. R. F. C. Hull (pp. 532–3). Collected Works of C. G. Jung, Vol. 18. Princeton: Princeton University Press, 1980.

Jung, Carl Gustav. (1957b). The undiscovered self (present and future). In *Civilization in transition.* Trans. R. F. C. Hull (pp. 245–305). Collected Works of C. G. Jung, Vol. 10. Princeton: Princeton University Press, 1970.

Jung, Carl Gustav. (1958a). Flying saucers: A modern myth of things seen in the skies. In *Civilization in transition.* Trans. R. F. C. Hull (pp. 307–433). Collected Works of C. G. Jung, Vol. 10. Princeton: Princeton University Press, 1970.

Jung, Carl Gustav. (1958b). A psychological view of conscience. In *Civilization in transition.* Trans. R. F. C. Hull (pp. 437–55). Collected Works of C. G. Jung, Vol. 10. Princeton: Princeton University Press, 1970.

Jung, Carl Gustav. (1958c). The transcendent function. In *The structure and dynamics of the psyche*, 2nd edn. Trans. R. F. C. Hull (pp. 67–91). Collected Works of C. G. Jung, Vol. 8. Princeton: Princeton University Press, 1969.

Jung, Carl Gustav. (1958d). *Civilization in transition.* Trans. R. F. C. Hull. Collected Works of C. G. Jung, Vol. 10. Princeton: Princeton University Press, 1970.

Jung, Carl Gustav. (1959). Good and evil in analytical psychology. In *Civilization in transition.* Trans. R. F. C. Hull (pp. 456–68). Collected Works of C. G. Jung, Vol. 10. Princeton: Princeton University Press, 1970.

Jung, Carl Gustav. (1964). Symbols and the interpretation of dreams. In *The symbolic life.* Trans. R. F. C. Hull (pp. 183–264). Collected Works of C. G. Jung, Vol. 18. Princeton: Princeton University Press, 1980.

Jung, Carl Gustav. (1966a). New paths in psychology. In *Two essays on analytical psychology.* Trans. R. F. C. Hull (pp. 245–68). Collected Works of C. G. Jung, Vol. 7. Princeton: Princeton University Press, 1966.

Jung, Carl Gustav. (1966b). The structure of the unconscious. In *Two essays on analytical psychology.* Trans. R. F. C. Hull (pp. 269–304). Collected Works of C. G. Jung, Vol. 7. Princeton: Princeton University Press, 1966.

Jung, Carl Gustav. (1969a). *Aion: Researches into the phenomenology of the self*, 2nd edn. Trans. R. F. C. Hull. Collected Works of C. G. Jung, Vol. 9, Part 2. Princeton: Princeton University Press.

References 215

Jung, Carl Gustav. (1969b). Synchronicity: An acausal connecting principle. In *The structure and dynamics of the psyche*, 2nd edn. Trans. R. F. C. Hull (pp. 417–519). Collected Works of C. G. Jung, Vol. 8. Princeton: Princeton University Press, 1969.

Jung, Carl Gustav. (1969c). Foreword to Neumann: "Depth psychology and a new ethic." In *The symbolic life*. Trans. R. F. C. Hull (pp. 616–22). Collected Works of C. G. Jung, Vol. 18. Princeton: Princeton University Press, 1980.

Jung, Carl Gustav. (1970). *Mysterium coniunctionis: An inquiry into the separation and synthesis of psychic opposites in alchemy*, 2nd edn. Collected Works of C. G. Jung, Vol. 14. Princeton: Princeton University Press.

Jung, Carl Gustav. (1973a). *Letters, volume 1: 1906–1950*. Eds. Gerhard Adler and Aniela Jaffé. Trans. R. F. C. Hull. Princeton, NJ: Princeton University Press.

Jung, Carl Gustav. (1973b). *Memories, dreams, reflections*. Ed. Aniela Jaffe. Trans. Richard and Clara Winston, 2nd edn. New York: Pantheon Books/ Random House.

Jung, Carl Gustav. (1976). *Letters, volume 2: 1951–1961*. Eds. Gerhard Adler and Aniela Jaffé. Trans. R. F. C. Hull. Princeton, NJ: Princeton University Press.

Jung, Carl Gustav. (1977). *C. G. Jung speaking: Interviews and encounters*. Eds. William McGuire and R. F. C. Hull. Princeton: Princeton University Press.

Jung, Carl Gustav. (1980). Foreword to Allenby: "A psychological study of the origins of monotheism." In *The symbolic life*. Trans. R. F. C. Hull (pp. 656–9). Collected Works of C. G. Jung, Vol. 18. Princeton: Princeton University Press, 1980.

Jung, Carl Gustav. (1984). *Dream analysis: Notes of the seminar given in 1928–1930*. Ed. William McGuire. Princeton: Princeton University Press.

Jung, Carl Gustav. (1988). *Nietzsche's Zarathustra: Notes of the seminar given in 1934–1939*. Ed. James L. Jarrett, 2 vols. Princeton, NJ: Princeton University Press. London: Routledge, 2005. Reprint.

Jung, Carl Gustav. (1989). *Analytical psychology: Notes of the seminar given in 1925*. Ed. William McGuire. Princeton: Princeton University Press.

Jung, Carl Gustav. (1996). *The psychology of kundalini yoga: Notes of the seminar given in 1932*. Ed. Sonu Shamdasani. Princeton: Princeton University Press.

Jung, Carl Gustav. (1997). *Visions: Notes of the seminar given in 1930–1934*, 2 vols. Ed. Claire Douglas. Princeton, NJ: Princeton University Press.

Jung, Carl Gustav. (2008). *Children's dreams: Notes from the seminar given in 1936–1940*. Eds. Lorenz Jung and Maria Meyer-Glass. Trans. Ernst Falzeder with Tony Wolfson. Princeton and Oxford: Princeton University Press.

Kris, Ernst. (1934). The psychology of caricature. Reprinted in *Psychoanalytic explorations in art* (pp. 173–203). New York: International Universities Press, 1952.

Landau, Rom. (1935). *God is my adventure: A book on modern mystics, masters and teachers*. London: Ivor Nicholson and Watson.

216   References

Lévy-Bruhl, Lucien. (1923). *Primitive mentality*. Trans. Lilian A. Clare. New York and London: Macmillan Company and George Allen & Unwin Ltd.

Lonergan, Bernard. (1992). *Insight: A study of human understanding*, 5th edn. Eds. Frederick E. Crowe and Robert M. Doran. Toronto: University of Toronto Press.

Luprecht, Mark. (1991). *"What people call pessimism": Sigmund Freud, Arthur Schnitzler, and nineteenth-century controversy at the University of Vienna medical school*. Riverside, CA: Ariadne Press.

Maeder, A. E. (1916). *The dream problem*. Trans. Frank Mead Hallock and Smith Ely Jelliffe. New York: Nervous and Mental Disease Publishing Company.

May, Rollo. (1975). *The courage to create*. New York: W. W. Norton & Company.

Merkur, Dan. (1993). *Gnosis: An esoteric tradition of mystical visions and unions*. Albany: State University of New York Press.

Merkur, Dan. (1998). *The ecstatic imagination: Psychedelic experiences and the psychoanalysis of self-actualization*. Albany, NY: State University of New York Press.

Merkur, Dan. (1999). *Mystical moments and unitive thinking*. Albany, NY: State University of New York Press.

Merkur, Dan. (2001). *Unconscious wisdom: A superego function in dreams, conscience, and inspiration*. Albany, NY: State University of New York Press.

Merkur, Dan. (2005). *Psychoanalytic approaches to myth: Freud and the Freudians*. New York and London: Routledge.

Merkur, Dan. (2009). Interpreting the sense of badness. *Psychoanalytic Review*, *96*(6), 943–82.

Merkur, Dan. (2010). *Explorations of the psychoanalytic mystics*. Amsterdam: Editions Rodopi.

Merkur, Dan. (2011a). The deletion of will from Freud's theorizing. In *Explaining evil, volume 2: History, global views, and events.* Ed. J. Harold Ellens (pp. 292–318). Santa Barbara, CA: ABC-CLIO.

Merkur, Dan. (2011b). The doubling of conscience in groups. In *Explaining evil, volume 3: Approaches, responses, solutions.* Ed. J. Harold Ellens (pp. 16–40). Santa Barbara, CA: ABC-CLIO.

Merkur, Dan. (2013). The soma function in Jung's analytical psychology. In *God on call*. Ed. John Rush. New York: North Atlantic Books/Random House.

Mills, Jon. (2002). *The unconscious abyss: Hegel's anticipation of psychoanalysis*. Albany, NY: SUNY Press.

Mills, Jon. (2013). Jung's metaphysics. *International Journal for Jungian Studies*, *5*(1), 19–43.

Noll, Richard. (1994). *The Jung cult: Origins of a charismatic movement*. Princeton, NJ: Princeton University Press.

Nunberg, Herman. (1931). The synthetic function of the ego. *International Journal of Psycho-Analysis*, *12*(2), 123–40.

Pink, Thomas. (2004). *Free will: A very short introduction.* Oxford: Oxford University Press.

Radin, Paul, Kerenyi, Karl, and Jung, C. G. (1956). *The trickster: A study in American Indian mythology.* New York: Schocken Books, 1972. Reprint.

Rahman, Fazlur. (1958). *Prophecy in Islam: Philosophy and orthodoxy.* London: George Allen & Unwin.

Rand, Nicholas and Torok, Maria. (1997). *Questions for Freud: The secret history of psychoanalysis.* Cambridge, MA and London, UK: Harvard University Press.

Rangell, Leo. (1974). A psychoanalytic perspective leading currently to the syndrome of the compromise of integrity. *International Journal of Psycho-Analysis, 55,* 3–12.

Rangell, Leo. (1976). Lessons from Watergate: A derivative for psychoanalysis. *Psychoanalytic Quarterly, 45,* 37–61.

Rangell, Leo. (1980). *The mind of Watergate: An exploration of the compromise of integrity.* New York: W. W. Norton & Company.

Rank, Otto. (1932). *Art and the artist: Creative urge and personality development.* New York: Alfred A. Knopf; reprinted New York: Tudor Publishing Company, n.d.

Roazen, Paul. (2002). *The trauma of Freud: Controversies in psychoanalysis.* New Brunswick, NJ and London: Transaction Publishers.

Sandler, Joseph, with Anna Freud. (1985). *The analysis of defense: The ego and the mechanisms of defense revisited.* New York: International Universities Press.

Serrano, Miguel. (1966). *C. G. Jung and Hermann Hesse: A record of two friendships.* Trans. Frank MacShane. London: Routledge & Kegan Paul.

Shamdasani, Sonu. (2003). *Jung and the making of modern psychology: The dream of a science.* Cambridge: Cambridge University Press.

Silberer, Herbert. (1909). Report on a method of eliciting and observing certain symbolic hallucination-phenomena. In *Organization and pathology of thought: Selected sources.* Ed. David Rapaport (pp. 195–207). New York: Columbia University Press.

Silberer, Herbert. (1910). Phantasie und Mythos. *Jahrbuch der Psycho-analytische und Psychopathologische Forschungen, 1,* 541–622.

Silberer, Herbert. (1912). On symbol-formation. In *Organization and pathology of thought: Selected sources.* Ed. David Rapaport (pp. 208–33). New York: Columbia University Press.

Silberer, Herbert. (1917). *Problems of mysticism and its symbolism.* Trans. Smith Ely Jelliffe. New York: Moffat, Yard and Company. (Originally published in German in 1914.)

Silberer, Herbert. (1955). The dream: Introduction to the psychology of dreams. Trans. Jacob Blauner. *Psychoanalytic Review, 42,* 361–87. (Originally published in German in 1918.)

Skrbina, David. (2005). *Panpsychism in the west.* Cambridge, MA and London, UK: MIT Press.

218 References

Stekel, Wilhelm. (1922). *Sex and dreams: The language of dreams*. Trans. James S. Van Teslaar. Reprinted Honolulu, Hawaii: University Press of the Pacific, 2003. (Originally published in German as *Die Sprache des Traumes* in 1911.)

Stekel, Wilhelm. (1950). *Technique of analytical psychotherapy*. Trans. Eden and Cedar Paul. New York: Liveright Publishing Corporation. (Originally published in German in 1938.)

Sterba, Richard. (1934). The fate of the ego in analytic therapy. *International Journal of Psycho-Analysis*, *15*(2–3), 117–26.

Stone, Leo. (1954). The widening scope of indications for psychoanalysis. *Journal of the American Psychoanalytic Association*, *2*, 567–94.

Wälder, Robert. (1936). The problem of freedom in psycho-analysis and the problem of reality-testing. *International Journal of Psycho-Analysis*, *17*, 89–108.

Winnicott, D. W. (1935). The manic defence. In *Through paediatrics to psycho-analysis: Collected papers* (pp. 129–44). 1958; reprinted New York: Brunner/Mazel, 1992.

Winnicott, D. W. (1958). Psychoanalysis and the sense of guilt. In *Psycho-analysis and contemporary thought*. Ed. J. D. Sutherland. London: Hogarth Press; reprinted in *The maturational processes and the facilitating environment: Studies in the theory of emotional development* (pp. 15–28). New York: International Universities Press, 1965.

Winnicott, D. W. (1963). Morals and education. Reprinted in *The maturational processes and the facilitating environment* (pp. 93–105).

Index

Abraham, Karl 98, 115
abstract thought 183
acquired intellect 200
active imaginary states 147–8
active imagination 46, 48, 53, 94; and the depersonification of archetypes 161–2; inhibitions to 152; and the unconscious 146–55, 158
Active Intellect 82n1
addictions: recovery from 29; treatment for 43–4
Adler, Alfred 52; and dream interpretation 102, 111–14
alchemy 114–15
Alexander, Franz 3
alpha-function 181
ambitendency 5
ambivalence 5, 14, 181
amorality, scientific 19
amplification 46, 97, 144–5
analogues 126
analytic listening 26
analytical psychology 16, 26, 51; client populations 84–7; as complement to psychoanalysis 83; goals of 200; Jung's criticisms of 91; and the numinous experience 96; numinous images in 43–51; for patients lacking meaning 86; and phenomena of the unconscious 140; for religious patients 85
Angulo, Jaime de 53
anima and animus 25, 52, 54, 56, 57, 157, 158, 165–6, 173; depersonification of 162–3

anthropology 52, 53, 185
Anthroposophy 139
Apolline drive 45
archetypal content 147
archetypes 46, 47–8, 87, 92, 97, 200–1; depersonification of 55–6, 161–3, 173; God as 169–70, 171; and individuation 52–61; Jung's theory of 123; personification of 55; racial 53; in the religious context 70, 71; and synchronicity 77–8; wholeness 170–3, 197
Aristotelian Intellect 82
Aristotelian reasoning 79
Aristotle 174, 200
association test 40
atman 59, 164
autosuggestion 115, 147, 174

backsliding 29
Bakan, David 3
"becoming conscious" 46, 50–1, 183, 200
behavioral enactments 201
Benjamin, Jessica 33
Binswanger, Ludwig 99–100
Bion, Wilfred 180–1
Bleuler, Eugen 5
Breuer, Joseph 120
British Middle School 17
Buddhism 79, 201
Burrow, Trigant 3

capacity for concern 34
catharsis 64, 158

220 Index

character analysis 40
children: development of 188–9; education of 188
clairvoyance 74; *see also* synchronicity
collective psyche 8, 147, 187, 189
collective representations 52, 53
collective unconscious 1, 6, 87, 93, 139, 158, 160, 161, 179, 199; and the superego 160; *see also* unconscious
"coming-to-be of the self" 46, 200
compensation 132–4, 157
complexes 4, 7, 10, 54–7, 70, 72, 90, 108, 127, 130, 160–3, 165; *see also* Oedipus complex
compromise-formations 95–6
concrete imagery 183
condensation 60, 104–5, 113, 171–2
conscience 51; and individuation 176–8
consciousness: alternative to 184; autonomy of 11; consolidation of 66; destabilization of 136, 142; development of 187–90; ego- 11–12, 36, 57, 165, 183, 200–1; expansion of 190–5, 200; Freud's concept of 199; functions of 183; Jung's concept of 51, 182–7; levels of 192–3; in the modern man 191–2; philosophical assumptions about 195–9; as purpose of human existence 195–6
conversion 170, 172–3
creative surrender 61, 169
creativity 60, 113, 122, 175, 176, 187; in dreams 106, 112, 113, 122, 131–2, 138; pathologizing 142; unconscious 131
Creuzer, Friedrich 128, 129
crowd psychologies 201
cure of souls 98, 99; Catholic 61–2, 64, 93; pastoral 41–2, 61–2; Protestant 61–2, 96; scientific 61

Das Heilige (Otto) 45
daydreaming 123, 147
defense analysis 27, 36, 110–11

depression, risk of 35–6
depressive position 34, 181
depressive reaction 35
depth psychology 8, 37, 42, 61, 73, 194
dialectical discussion 31, 87, 93
didacticism 97
differentiation 161, 184; *see also* non-differentiation
Dionysian drive 45
directedness 9
divine omniscience 198
dream analysis 38, 41, 74–5, 78; *see also* dream interpretation
Dream Analysis (Jung seminar) 102, 119
dream censorship 171–2
dream interpretation 26, 38, 46–7, 66, 92, 102–3, 111–12, 116; Freud's approach to 124–5; mystical 130–1; synthetic 163; *see also* dream analysis
Dream Problem, The (Maeder) 114
dream psychology 39
dream theory: Adler's approach to 111–14; crisis precipitated by 102–6; Freud's approach to 102, 104–6, 112–13; Jung's approach to 119, 120–3; Maeder's approach to 114–17, 119; Stekel's approach to 106–9, 115, 122
dream-work 104, 105, 108, 112, 114–18, 120, 124, 125, 132; unconscious 104–5, 118
dreams 53, 59, 147; autosymbolic 133; compensatory function of 132–4; day's residues in 117–18; manifest 103–5, 114, 171; as numinous experiences 46; primary function of 132–3; as primitive art 116; problem solving in 112–13, 123; as subliminal process 123; two types of symbols in 115; as wish-fulfillment 104, 118–19
Durkheim, Emile 52

Eastern philosophy 191, 197
ego 6–7, 173; awareness of 58, 165; de-centering of 60–1; and persona

147; preconscious 115; repression of 3; surrender to the self 165–9; synthetic function of 173–4; and the unconscious 184; union with self 197; *see also* self

ego autonomy 10, 36

ego ideal 51

Ego and the Mechanisms of Defense, The (A. Freud) 6–7

ego psychology 37, 40, 92, 111, 160, 180

ego-consciousness 11–12, 36, 57, 165, 183, 200–1

Eliade, Mircea 129

elucidation 26–8

epistemology 200

Eros 5, 59–60, 99

ethical constructivism 20n1

ethical decision 17–18; *see also* moral judgment

ethics, medical 18–19

ethnography 54

"Evidential Dream, An" (Freud) 117–20

evil: renunciation of 34; repression of 8; unconscious 22–3

faith 29, 32, 41, 44, 88, 98, 145, 177, 198

fantasy 3, 47, 48, 71, 113, 131, 135, 147–8, 152–4, 156, 158, 159; archetypal 161; religious 72; *see also* active imagination

fantasy elaboration 147

al-Farabi 200

father-transference 64, 104

Fenichel, Otto 3

Ferenczi, Sandor 31, 33, 37

fixation 26, 52, 87, 97, 161

Fourth International Psychoanalytic Congress 102

free association 26, 106, 107, 121–2, 150

Freud, Anna 6, 36

Freud, Sigmund 1, 2, 36, 60, 164, 171; clinical procedure of 26, 87; on consciousness 51, 200–1; on differences between his method and Jung's 96–7; on dream analysis 47, 107; on dream censorship 172; on dreams 102, 104–6, 112–13, 123; on evil spirits 70; interdisciplinary limitations of 99; letter to Binswanger 99–100; making the unconscious conscious 158–9, 161, 193, 195; misunderstanding of Jung's views on dreams 118–20; moral theory of 17, 19–21; and morbid psychology 39; on neutralized energies 10; on paranormal events 74; on the personal unconscious 52; on psychoanalysis 38; on religion 68, 71, 73, 77; sexual theories of 90; on symbol formation 141; on symptom formation 7; theory of neurosis 6, 26; theory of reaction-formation 23; theory of repression 2–5, 21, 23; on thought-transference 74, 82; topographic hypothesis 199; on transference 61, 63, 65; trauma theory 4; treatment of neurosis 31–3, 38; on the will 9–10; *see also* Oedipus complex

Freud writings: "An Evidential Dream" 117–20; *Future of an Illusion* 41; *The Interpretation of Dreams* 108, 115, 117; *Introductory Lectures on Psycho-Analysis* 172; *New Introductory Lectures on Psycho-Analysis* 3, 4; *Studies on Hysteria* 2; *Totem and Taboo* 108

Frobenius, Leo 53

Fromm, Erich 99

Future of an Illusion (Freud) 41

gnosis 145, 196

Gnosticism 140

God: as archetype 169–70, 171; as a circle 178; existence of 81–2

God within 51

God-image 83, 97, 199

Grotstein, James S. 180–1

group psychology 185

guilt 14; consciousness of 34; neurotic denial of 22–6; unconscious 24–5

222 Index

hagiography 140
Hartmann, Heinz 10, 36, 160
Hegel, Georg 138
Hegelian dialectic 138, 140
heirosgamos 160
hero myth 160
Hinduism 164; concept of self 59, 164
Hobbes, Thomas 10
honesty, as goal of analysis 13
hypnagogic hallucinations 115

I Ching 98
Ibn Sina (Avicenna) 183
identity 186
imagery: concrete 183; mental 48–9, 140
incest (brother–sister) 160
individual psychology 94
individuality 59
individuation 46, 50–1, 65, 87, 92, 93, 157; and archetypes 52–61; and conscience 176–8; and the depersonification of archetypes 161–3; and the discovery of the self 163–5; and the ego's surrender to the self 165–9; and integration 173–4; Jung's process of 160–1; and numinosity 169–70; and revelation 174–5, 178; symbols of 178–80; and vocation 175–6, 178; and the wholeness archetype 170–3
inferiority 109–10
inflation, risk of 35–6
inhibition 5, 9, 11, 71, 148, 152
inner dialogues 155–9
inner voices 136–7, 174
integration, and individuation 173–4
intellectualization 190
Interpretation of Dreams, The (Freud) 108, 115, 117
Introductory Lectures on Psycho-Analysis (Freud) 172
irrational therapy 95
irrationalism, apologies for 88–91

Jacobi, Jolande 194
Jung, Carl Gustav: on acausal orderedness 77–8; conception of conciousness 51; disagreement with Freud 41, 92, 102–3, 124, 184; on dreams 46–7, 119, 120–3, 134; on the existence of God 81–3; interdisciplinary limitations of 99; letter to Freud 119; limited therapeutic ambitions of 91–8; on moral integrity 13–16; on morality 16–22; and normal psychology 39–40; on numinous states 66–8; on the psychoid factor 79–80; racial theories 51; on religion 68–73, 88–9; sexual theories 90–1; on the "shadow" 1–2, 8, 29, 37, 52; on signs and symbols 123–34; on spiritual experiences 43–51; on synchronicity 73–83; on the teleology of dreams 102–3; theory of archetypes 123; theory of compensation 5–6; theory of neurosis 23; on transcendent function 135–41; on transference 61–6; and the treatment of psychotics 38; use of dialectical discussion 31; use of elucidation 26–9; on the will 9–13, 36; *see also* consciousness; individuation
Jung lectures: Tavistock Lectures 48; Terry Lectures (Yale University) 46
Jung seminars: Dream Analysis 119; *Dream Analysis* 102; *Visions* 86, 102, 103
Jung writings: *Mysterium Coniunctionis* 64–5; *On Synchronicity* 73–4; *Psychological Types* 126, 141; *Psychology of Dementia Praecox* 38; *Psychology of the Unconscious* 120, 128; Red Book 152; "The Transcendent Function" 135

Klein, Melanie 34, 35, 37
Kleinian theory 181
knowledge: absolute 78; inevitability of 196
Kris, Ernst 173
Kulturkreislehre 53

Language of Dreams, The (Stekel) 107
Lévy-Bruhl, Lucien 52, 54, 185
libido 71, 116, 128, 141, 142, 143
Logos 77–9, 81n1, 198

Maeder, Alphonse 102, 114–17, 119, 126, 133, 163
Maimonides, Moses 3, 200
manic defense 35–6
materialism 94
May, Rollo 176
medical ethics 18–19
meditative practices 140
mental imagery 48–9, 140
metapsychology 115, 124
mid-life crises 84–5
Milner, Marion 61, 165
mindfulness 201
miracles 75
modern man 191–2
moral codes 19
moral conflicts 19
moral decisions 40
moral inferiority 15
moral integrity, subjective 13–16
moral judgment 17–18; *see also* ethical decision
moral law 16–17
moral reaction-formations 20
moral realism 20n1
moral theory 21
moral transformations 35, 36
moral underachievement 14–15
morality: vs. amorality 21; biological basis of 21–2, 25; as imposition of culture 16; inborn capacity for 37; psychological complexity of 16–22; repression of 37; as unwholesome standard 3–4
mutual analysis 31
Mysterium Coniunctionis (Jung) 64–5
mystical experiences 197–8
mystical states 130–1
mysticism 50, 130–1, 181
mystics, psychoanalytic 99, 100–1
mythology 87, 96, 97, 114–15, 178; comparative 178; construction of 53; imagery of 180; and religion 38–9

narcissism 61, 130
negative values 8, 13–14
neurosis/neuroses 15; as moral reaction 3; and projection 32; as splitting of personality 8; treatment of 83–4, 86–7, 91–2, 195
Neurotic Constitution, The (Adler) 109
neuroticism, unconscious 32
New Introductory Lectures on Psycho-Analysis (Freud) 3, 4
Nietzsche, Friedrich 19, 45
non-differentiation 186; *see also* differentiation
numinosity, and individuation 169–70
numinous experiences: in analytical psychology 96; and religion 66–8; religious 82; sexual theories of 90–1; *see also* synchronicity
numinous states: archetypes 47–8; "becoming conscious" 46, 50–1, 53, 183, 200; dreams 46–7, 53, 59; individuation 50–1, 60–1; mental imagery (active imagination) 48–50; *see also* active imagination; archetypes; dreams; individuation

object cathexis 130
object relations theory 108, 180
Oedipus complex 8, 92, 108, 109, 160, 161, 188, 189
On Synchronicity (Jung) 73–4
Otto, Rudolf 45
Oxford Movement 117

panpsychism 80
paranoia 59–60
paranormal phenomena 73–4, 79–80, 178, 193
parapsychology 75, 178
participation mystique 54
Perception-Consciousness system 182, 199
persona, dissolution of 147
personal development 50–1
personal unconscious 1, 13, 36, 52, 87, 139, 158; *see also* unconscious
personality development 40

224 Index

personification: consolidation of 55; of shadow and archetypes 55
Pfister, Oskar 61, 65–6; interdisciplinary limitations of 99
phenomenology 73
Platonic Ideas 65
pragmatism 90
precognition 75
problem solving, in dreams 112–13, 123
projections 185, 201; evil spirits as 70; owning 29–35
prophecy 75, 82, 200
propositional thinking 201
psyche: collective 8, 147, 187, 189; consciousness of 165
psychic conflict 6
psychic energy 10, 36, 71, 120, 139–40
psychic equilibrium 134
psychoanalysis 16, 94, 163, 165, 178, 193, 199; and the cure of souls 41–2, 99; Freud's view of 7; genetic orientation of 126; as humanistic religion 100; Jung's view of 7–8, 90; potential benefits of 28; relational 31; spirituality inherent in 38, 99–100
Psychoanalysis and Yoga (Schmitz) 97
psychoanalyst, as surrogate parent 62–4
psychoid 79–80, 177–8
Psychological Types (Jung) 126, 141
psychology *see* analytical psychology; depth psychology; dream psychology; ego psychology; individual psychology; metapsychology; parapsychology; psychology of religion; superego psychology
Psychology of Dementia Praecox (Jung) 38
psychology of religion 47
Psychology of the Unconscious (Jung) 120, 128
psychopathology 37, 96, 168; in children 189; and immorality 3; role of trauma in 4

psychosexuality 41
psychosis: management of 68; and the numinous experience 67; psychoanalysis of 38; renegade 150
psychosomatic illness 12
psychotherapeutic intervention 43–4
psychotherapy: as cure of souls 41–3; goal of 194; reasons for seeking 15; as semiotic science 78; *see also* psychoanalysis; psychology

Radin, Paul 53
Rand, Nicholas 106
Rank, Otto 176, 187
rational therapy 94
reality principle 9
reality testing 153
recursive function 199
recursive thinking 164, 201–2
Red Book (Jung) 152
reflection, as becoming conscious 183–4
reflective function 199
reflective thinking 164, 201
reflexive thinking 201
regression in the service of the ego 165, 169, 173
Reich, Wilhelm 36
Reik, Theodor 101
religion: comparative 178; compensatory function of 71–2; Jung's view of 68–73, 88–9; and mythology 38–9; nature of 68–73; and the numinous experience 66–8; psychology of 47
religious conversion 170, 172–3
religious experiences 45; as numinous 82; *see also* spiritual experiences
représentations collectives 145
repression: of the ego 3; of evil 8; of morality 37; of sexuality 3, 26, 37; theory of 1–7, 8, 9, 11–12, 21, 23
revelation 174–5, 178
Roazen, Paul 160

schizophrenia 38, 150, 194
Schmitz, Oscar A. H. 97
"Secret of the Golden Flower, The" 98

seduction theory 4

self: as *atman* 59, 164; attainment of 57–8; coming-to-be of 46, 200; discovery of 163–5; as divine macroanthropos 180; ego's surrender to 165–9; as God-image 42–3, 198, 199; as "God within us" 59; laws of 40, 175–6, 180; metaphor of the center 178–9; union with ego 197; *see also* ego

self-analysis 64, 151

self-consciousness 187, 197–8; *see also* consciousness

self-esteem 111

self-knowledge 15, 28, 117, 164; therapeutic 194–5

self-observation 51, 92, 104, 111, 164, 199, 201, 202; *see also* consciousness

self-realization 58, 60, 133, 164, 167

self-reflection 51, 180, 189

semiotic sciences 78, 100

semiotics 79, 125–7

sexual abuse 4

sexuality 60, 189; evaluation of 4; repression of 3, 37

"shadow" 1–2, 8, 29, 37, 52; assimilation of 12–13; awareness of 35, 36; becoming conscious 146–7; becoming responsible for 200; negative values of 13–14; and neurosis 15; personification of 55; projections of 29–35

shame 14, 35

Silberer, Herbert 114–15, 116, 120, 122, 126, 129, 133, 143

sin 3, 23–4, 29, 33–4, 72, 198

spiritual experiences 43–4; *see also* religious experiences

spiritual rebirth 170

spiritual therapy 73; *see also* cure of souls

spirituality: natural 100; and psychoanalysis 99–100; in therapy 39–40

Steiner, Rudolf 97

Stekel, Wilhelm 23, 37, 106–9, 115, 122

Sterba, Richard 199

Studies on Hysteria (Freud) 2

sublimations 41, 52, 60, 97

suffering 16

superego 1, 3, 8, 51, 105, 115, 164, 172–3, 174, 175, 189, 199, 201; collaboration with ego 202; and the collective unconscious 160; repression of 37; unconscious 23

superego psychology 160

superego theory 180

symbol formation 5, 49, 88, 96, 97, 108, 141–4, 157, 200–1; in dreams 96; and transcendent function 141–4

symbol production, amplification of 145

symbol-creating function 5

symbolic equations 107

symbolic meaning 122

symbolism: comparative 145; conscious 115; in dreams 82, 146; manifest 102, 108, 117, 171; of mythology 8, 87; secondary elaboration of 143; vs. symbols 125; *see also* symbols

symbols: from alchemy 50, 127, 128; as analogies 126; archetypal 48, 165, 170, 174, 200–1; autosymbolic 116, 122, 133; choice of 67; compromise-formations as 95; cultural 53–4; of divinity 42–3, 129, 171, 175; in dreams 102–8, 114, 115, 116–17, 119, 120–2, 123–5, 133; healthy 161; as hierophany 128–9, 129; of higher consciousness 188; of individuation 50, 178–80; manifest 54, 122; of mythology 47, 115, 129, 145; production of 143–4; religious 67–8, 88, 95, 145; selection of 94; of the self 42–3, 175; vs. signs 125–9; vs. symbolism 125; of the transcendent function 144–6, 157; unconscious 119; of unity 50, 127, 171; of wholeness 170, 172; *see also* symbolism

symptom analysis 39, 195

symptom formation 7

226 Index

synchronicity 73–83, 185; defined 73–4; *see also* numinous experiences

Tausk, Victor 120
teleology 102, 109, 115, 116; in Adler's dream theory 110; theology 34, 178
theory of compensation 6, 23, 71–2
theory of economics 5n1
theory of morality 17, 19
theory of neurosis 23, 26
theory of reaction-formation 23
theory of repression 9, 11–12, 21, 23
Theosophy 139–40
therapeutic interpretation 34
thing-presentations 123–5, 127–9
Thomas Aquinas 200
thought-transference 74, 82
Tibetan Buddhists 79
Tillich, Paul 46
timelessness, and the unconscious 185
Torok, Maria 106
Totem and Taboo (Freud) 108
transcendent function 92, 135–41; and active imagination 152; and inner dialogues 157; spontaneous 146; and symbol-formation 141–4
"Transcendent Function, The" (Jung) 135
transcendent position 181
transcendental causes 77, 79
transference 96, 97, 199; onto God 65; resolution of 61–6
transference cure 63–4
trauma 2, 3, 4
trauma theory 4
treatment 26–9
Trickster, The (Radin *et al.*) 53
Trinity, as symbolic of stages of personal development 50

unconscious 2, 6, 105, 199; and active imagination 146–55, 158; and

amplification 144–5; analysis of 40; bridge to 56; and dreams 133–4; and the ego 184; as evil 8; Freud's concept of 123–4; function of 131–2; and inner dialogues 155–9; knowledge of 164; making conscious 158–9, 161, 193, 195; manifestations of 135–9; and symbol-formation 141–4; and transcendent function 141–4; verbal inspirations from 174–5; *see also* collective unconscious; personal unconscious
unconscious existence 59–60
Unconscious Wisdom (Merkur) 105
unification 157, 188
unitive experiences 59–60
unity 59; and the unconscious 184–5
Universal Mind 79

Vergote, Antoine 98–9
Viennese School 125
virtues 19
visionary experiences 50, 59
Visions (seminar) 86, 102, 103
visualizations 157; occult 140
vocation 178; and individuation 175–6
von Hattingberg, Hans 98
von Keyserling, Herman (Count) 97–8
vox Dei 177; *see also* conscience

waking consciousness 137, 147
waking dream states 48
wholeness archetype 170–3, 197
Wilhelm, Richard 98
will: and consciousness 9–13; freedom of 9–12; medieval concept of 10; as moral action 11
Winnicott, D. W. 17, 25, 34, 37

yoga 140, 164

Zurich school 121, 122, 125